Tips and Traps When Mortgage Hunting

Other McGraw-Hill Books by Robert Irwin

Pocket Guide for Home Buyers

Tips and Traps When Buying a Home

Tips and Traps When Selling a Home

Tips and Traps for Making Money in Real Estate

Buy, Rent, & Hold: How to Make Money in a "Cold" Real Estate Market

How to Find Hidden Real Estate Bargains

The McGraw-Hill Real Estate Handbook

Tips and Traps When Negotiating Real Estate

Tips and Traps When Mortgage Hunting

Robert Irwin

Second Edition

McGraw-Hill

New York   San Francisco   Washington, D.C.   Auckland   Bogotá
Caracas   Lisbon   London   Madrid   Mexico City   Milan
Montreal   New Delhi   San Juan   Singapore
Sydney   Tokyo   Toronto

Library of Congress Cataloging-in-Publication Data

Irwin, Robert.
    Tips and traps when mortgage hunting / Robert Irwin—2nd ed.
        p.   cm.
    Includes index.
    ISBN 0-07-032968-0
    1. Mortgage loans. I. Title.
HG2040.15.I78 1999
332.7'.22—dc21   98-44547
                                                 CIP

McGraw-Hill

A Division of The McGraw-Hill Companies

    4 5 6 7 8 9 0 AGM/AGM   0 3 2

ISBN 0-07-032968-0

The editing supervisor for this book was Caroline Levine and the production supervisor was Clare Stanley. It was set in Palatino by Terry Leaden of McGraw-Hill's Professional Book Group composition unit.

Printed and bound by Quebecor Martinsburg.

This book is printed on recycled, acid-free paper containing a minimum of 50% recycled, de-inked fiber.

Contents

Preface

Although this book is the second edition, this is actually the fourth in a series of books going back nearly 20 years in time. The first, *The New Mortgage Game*, was written in 1981 and was one of the first books to fully describe the benefits and pitfalls of "adjustable rate" mortgages.

The market eventually absorbed the adjustable rate mortgages and made changes in fixed-rate, government-insured and guaranteed mortgages. Thus in 1986 I wrote, *Making Mortgages Work for You*, to explain those differences.

With the real estate recession of the early 1990s came an explosion of mortgage varieties as well as new methods for handling properties in cases where the seller owed more than the property was worth. Thus in 1992 I wrote *Tips & Traps When Mortgage Hunting* to help borrowers wend their way through the mortgage minefield, and it quickly became one of the most widely read books on real estate finance.

Now, once again, it's a new world in real estate borrowing. The old methods of qualifying borrowers (arcane formulas) have given way to sophisticated "profiles" and "scoring." Today, anyone can get a mortgage or a refinance, occasionally for more than the property's value and sometimes at a very low interest rate—if they know how.

Hence, the completely rewritten and updated *Tips and Traps When Mortgage Hunting*, Second Edition.

One thing has remained constant, however. This book is intended for *you*, the home buyer or the refinancing home owner. It will help you get the cheapest, quickest, best real estate mortgage available. Lenders may also find this book a good resource. However, my hope continues to be that the harried and confused home borrower will find it a balm and guiding light.

As with other books in the top selling Tips and Traps series, I've pointed out where the mortage minefields are located (the traps), as well as the hidden advantages (the tips). If you're looking for a real estate loan, this book will help you find just the right one for you. Good mortgage hunting!

Robert Irwin

1

What Are the Mortgage Hunting Traps?

Shopping for a mortgage today is a bit like shopping for a car. The advertisements in newspapers, on radio, even on television promise the sky: "Get low payments"; "your credit worries are over—we don't care even if you've had a bankruptcy or foreclosure!"; "Get a mortgage for 125 percent of your purchase price!"

You would think that you're doing lenders a favor by applying for a mortgage. (Indeed you are, but lenders would prefer you didn't look at it that way.) The truth is that, as with many things in life, there tends to be more sizzle than steak. Actually, in most cases those who borrow are at the mercy of those who lend.

Consider this: mortgage lending is a very sophisticated business. Even many of those who have been in the field for years confess that they don't understand many types of financing. Just the other day I was talking with a mortgage broker, and I asked him if he was offering any of those 125-percent-of-purchase-price mortgages. He said that he wasn't. Further, he admitted that he didn't have a clue how they worked and how anyone else could offer them. And this from someone who has been in the business for more than 25 years! What chance does someone have who gets a mortgage once or twice a decade?

The truth is that most people only buy a home occasionally. How can you know what's accepted practice in the field and what's outlandish and overpriced behavior? How do you know if your lender is treating you right?

The traps when borrowing money to buy a home are many and deep. Here are just a few of the pitfalls:

- You could end up paying a higher interest rate than the market requires.

- You could pay more points than needed or pay points when none are needed.

- You could end up paying unnecessary "garbage" fees when you close.

- You could be dunned for expensive extras to "set up" the financing.

- You could get a mortgage whose payments rise to the point where you can't afford to make them.

- You could pay tens of thousands of dollars of extra interest over the life of the loan.

- You could be denied a mortgage because of a credit problem, even though today virtually *everyone* who wants a mortgage can get one.

You could fall into a dozen more traps as well. In short, for the consumer, borrowing can be a minefield, and if you don't know where to step, you can walk into a disaster.

Where Do You Turn?

Where do you turn for a loan? To your neighborhood banker? In case you haven't noticed, he or she has been gobbled up by a megabank. In many cases the representatives at the local branch can't make any kind of loans at all. Often if you want a loan, you have to call the central office and talk over the phone to a loan officer. And very often that officer only presents the few loans the bank is favoring, none of which may be ideal for your situation.

What about the various mortgage brokers who advertise on TV and radio? Mortgage brokers tend to offer a far broader spectrum of loans than most banks (or S&Ls), but often they are volume brokers and don't want to make the effort to analyze your situation and come up with the best loan for you. Like pharmacists, they often expect you to have a prescription for the loan you want ready to go so they can fill it. They simply may not have the time to educate you on what's out there and diagnose what's best for you.

That leaves your real estate agent. But many agents are hesitant to ask their clients the delicate financial questions that they need to know in order to determine what kind of mortgage would be best for you. Besides, while agents may be excellent at finding a home for you, a great many simply aren't that knowledgeable about financing. Further, many agents feel it could be a conflict of interest for them to both represent you in a purchase and in finding a mortgage.

So, where do you turn?

What Do You Need to Know to Get the Right Mortgage?

In this book I endeavor to give you the information you need to know in order to get the very best mortgage. I try to present it as an extremely quick and easy read. (You've got enough things going on in your life without poring over technical explanations.) Within a few quick chapters, you should get an overview of what's out there. Then you can check out specific types of mortgages that may be of interest. In short, *Tips & Traps When Mortgage Hunting (Second Edition)* is designed to guide you through the minefield of mortgage traps, successfully getting you across to the best loan for you.

Who Should Read This Book?

The answer to that question is easy. You need the information in these chapters if:

- You're a first-time home buyer.
- You're moving up (selling a home in order to buy another).
- You're going from tenant to home owner.
- You want to refinance your home.
- You're an investor in real estate.
- You just want to understand what kinds of mortgages are out there.
- You're thinking about buying any type of real estate.

This second edition has been completely revised and contains information on all of the latest mortgages. In addition, it points out the traps to watch out for and gives you tips along the way to help you get better financing.

Don't pay extra interest, don't waste money on added points, and don't get caught overpaying setup and closing charges. Most important, don't get the wrong loan when a better one is just waiting for you. *Tips & Traps When Mortgage Hunting (Second Edition)* gives you the answers and the knowledge to make powerful financial decisions that can save you money and get you the mortgage you want at minimal cost.

2

The Most Frequently Asked Mortgage Questions

You need a mortgage in order to buy a home. Or perhaps you already own a home and want to refinance to get lower payments. Or you want to get in on the local boom in real estate, so you want to borrow money to buy an investment property. Whatever the reason, more than four million people this year will seek new mortgages. If you've picked up this book, chances are one of them is you.

Yet unless you're in the mortgage finance industry, getting a mortgage without getting taken (paying too high an interest rate, too high a monthly payment, too much in closing costs, or being told you can't qualify) can be a serious concern. Indeed, while mortgage money is gushing out from lenders, finding the right mortgage remains a daunting task. This is especially the case if it's your first home or if you haven't been through the real estate finance process in the past year or two.

So how do you get started? In this chapter we're going to answer the most frequently asked questions about mortgages. Along the way we'll learn the ABCs of real estate finance.

Can I Buy for Nothing Down?

You certainly can buy for nothing down. But do you want to? I was at a conference recently talking with a man who had just bought three investment properties putting no down payment on any of them. He was boasting about his financial acumen.

"So," I asked, "How's it going?"

Not well, he confided. The monthly payments were killing him. Because he had put nothing down and had less than top credit, he was paying a higher-than-normal interest rate on the mortgages, which translated into higher monthly payments. He couldn't rent the properties out for nearly enough to cover his costs. He had an enormous negative cashflow. It was costing thousands a month out of pocket just to keep the properties solvent.

"Why don't you sell?" I asked.

He said he would like to, but in the process of buying for nothing down, he had been forced to pay higher than market price for the properties. And he couldn't afford to sell and pay the transaction costs (commission plus other closing costs). He was waiting for the market to go up far enough so he could dump the properties.

"Doesn't sound like you're doing so well," I said.

No, he responded, he really wasn't.

We'll discuss techniques for buying with nothing down in various places in this book. If you've got sterling credit and lots of money in the bank, it may make sense for you to do it. (But if that's the case, you don't need to buy with nothing down, anyway.) Generally speaking, however, unless the market is skyrocketing in value (or you have platinum credit), it usually costs too much to make it worthwhile.

Don't be taken in by those increasing numbers of gurus who promote nothing-down investing through testimonials on tapes and seminars. Ask yourself, if it were such a panacea, why would anyone bother to sell books, tapes, and seminars on the subject?

Why wouldn't they simply keep it a secret, do it themselves, and make their fortune in real estate instead of the talk circuit?

TRAP

Don't be hoodwinked into thinking that the only consideration when mortgage hunting is the down payment. The monthly payment is just as, if not more, important.

How Do I Determine My Mortgage Payment?

Any loan officer, computer mortgage program, or amortization table can quickly tell you what your mortgage payment will be. (Also see App. A and App. B in this book.) It's simply a mathematical function of the interest rate, the term (how long you're borrowing), and the amount you borrow.

The real question is, how can you get your mortgage payments down? This is the real reason that most people shop around for interest rates. The rate moves up and down daily, usually in small increments. For most people those fluctuations are of little interest. (Do you really care if it's 7.25 or 7.50 percent?) It begins to matter, however, when it gets personal. On a $200,000, 30-year mortgage, a quarter percent difference is about $35 a month ($420 over a year, or $5040 over the full term of the loan). When most people realize that a quarter percent difference in the interest rate can make a $35 a month difference in payments, suddenly getting that interest rate down so the payments will drop becomes critical.

TIP

While there is a "market rate," the actual interest rate charged at any given time will vary slightly from lender to lender depending on their source for funds. Thus, shopping for the lowest interest rate can pay off.

TRAP

 Don't just think interest rates. You can also lower your payments by getting a longer term, putting more money down, or buying a less expensive property.

Should I Put More Money Down, If I Can?

The traditional thinking is to put as little down as possible. That way you maximize your leverage. If you put 5 percent down and your property goes up 5 percent in value, you've made 100 percent on your investment. If you put 50 percent down and the property goes up the same 5 percent in value, you only made 10 percent. Thus, the argument goes, you maximize your profit potential by putting down as little as possible.

On the other hand, most people are buying shelter ahead of investment. The more you put down, the lower your payment, and the lower the payment, the more secure most people feel. A paid-off house can be one of the most secure feelings in the world. This speaks well for putting in a bigger down payment, if you can.

Besides, if you have the money, what are you going to do with it if you don't put it into a house? As of this writing, interest rates are historically low. If you're doing well to get 6 percent invested in bonds or elsewhere on your money, it may make more sense to stick it into the home where it might earn 10 percent or more over time.

What Are Points?

Each point represents 1 percent of a mortgage. For a $100,000 mortgage, therefore, 3 points is $3000. If the mortgage is $150,000 and there are 2 points, it comes to $3,000.

Points are charged by a lender to increase the *yield,* or the true return on money loaned. It is usually possible to reduce the number of points required to get a mortgage by paying a slightly higher interest rate. See Chap. 15 for more details.

Where Do I Get a Mortgage?

You can get a mortgage at lots of places, including mortgage brokers (listed as such in the yellow pages of your phone book), banks, savings and loan institutions, and credit unions. You'll even find direct and indirect lenders online through the Internet (see Chap. 4).

However, while a great many people are eager to lend you money, what you want is someone who is willing to lend at the lowest interest rate and for the fewest costs. That's where shopping around pays off (see the next chapter).

How Long Does It Take to Get a Mortgage?

This is a very good question. The time frame varies enormously. Historically, it has taken around a month to get real estate financing. That includes the time spent filling out the application, including documentation; getting the credit report and the appraisal on the property; and then waiting for the lender to act.

However, that time frame really doesn't make sense in a computerized world. Consider, for instance, when you buy a car. The dealer can usually arrange financing within the hour. Now if you can get a car loan in an hour or less, why should it take a month to get a home loan?

The biggest reason, historically, is inertia. Most of those in mortgage lending have been slow to computerize and to change their old ways of doing business. Many still cling to the old method of filling out forms by hand, sending them through the mail, waiting for a committee to make a decision, and on and on.

On the other hand, some in the field, including the biggest underwriters, Fannie Mae (Federal National Mortgage Association) and Freddie Mac, who ultimately end up putting up the money for most loans in this country, do it much faster. Computers and electronic mail are used to facilitate lending. It is now possible to get approval of a mortgage (though not necessarily the actual money) within about an hour. Funding can be handled within as little as 3 days or less. Check into Chap. 5 for more details.

TIP

 Speed in securing a mortgage, while important, may not be essential to your real estate transaction. Most sellers, in fact, are prepared to wait a month or more for the financing and the deal to close. What can be more important is a lender's letter stating that you qualify for a mortgage. When you're able to give a lender's pre-approval letter to a seller, you're in a much better position to negotiate a good deal for yourself.

What Is Pre-approval and Should I Get It?

A relatively recent phenomenon, *pre-approval* means that a lender is willing to give you a mortgage, up to a certain amount, before you locate a property. But more important, as noted in the preceding tip, the lender *is willing to put it in writing*. A letter of commitment, called a pre-approval, can be worth its weight in gold. Consider a real estate deal from the seller's perspective. You show up and offer to buy the property at a certain price, offering so much down (with a cash deposit). If the seller accepts, then in most cases you want the right to spend the next 30 days shopping for financing, during which, for practical purposes, the seller's home is off the market.

However, the seller usually doesn't know you from any other person on the street. Will you get the financing you need to make the deal? Maybe. But if you're unsuccessful, at the end of a month you can say, "Sorry, things didn't work out; give me back my deposit—the deal's off." This is not amusing to most sellers.

Most sellers will go along with you on the preceding scenario because it's the way things have always been done in the past. In addition, if the market's slow, you might be the only buyer to come along in 6 months. If the market's strong, however, and if there's a competitive bidder with a lender's letter, you stand to lose out—sometimes even if you're offering more money.

That's why the letter of pre-approval from the lender is so important. It allows you to step ahead of other buyers who don't have such letters and to give the seller something tangible that says, "Yes, I can get the loan. You needn't worry."

TRAP

There's an important difference between getting a solid letter of commitment from a lender and simply being qualified. Anyone can qualify you for a mortgage—the real estate agent, the mortgage broker, even the guy at your local gas station. Usually it's nothing more than asking a few questions about your income and expenses to see how big a mortgage you are likely to get. You can do it yourself with the amortization tables in App. B of this book. However, getting qualified really means nothing without the backing of a lender. It's having the lender *commit,* saying that you will get a mortgage for a certain amount at a certain interest rate and term that carries water. (See the next chapter for more details.)

How Do I Lock in the Lowest Interest Rate?

Most lenders will hold, or "lock in," an interest rate for a period of time, typically around 30 days. This means that if interest rates go up, you get to pay the old lower rate in effect when you locked in your loan. But you must ask for the lock-in feature—many lenders won't volunteer it, and some charge extra for it.

The drawback is that in many cases, if you lock in and rates go down, you're committed to the older, higher rate. This is only a minor problem, however, because if the lender refuses to give you the new, lower interest rate, you can always go to another lender.

TIP

It's hard to switch lenders late in the game—you lose time, and time lost can mean a deal lost. Also, if you've paid the lender any money up front, then you could lose that money by switching. Some lenders will now give you the benefit of a lower rate without any hassle. If the rates go up, you're locked in; if they go down, you get the lower rate (or at least a lower rate than the lock-in).

TRAP

Beware of paying extra for a lock-in. During times when the rates are rising and lots of people are refinancing as well as buying, some lenders will charge up front for the lock-in. If it's a minimal fee, say $25, you may want to pay for it. But if it's higher, consider carefully. It may be cheaper to reapply later on when rates go down. (Time, of course, is a consideration, but given the speed with which it is possible to process some loans today, it's not as big a concern as in the past.)

How Much Will My Mortgage Fees Cost?

The actual amount of your mortgage fees are determined by your lender. They will vary, sometimes greatly, depending upon the lender you use. The federal government under RESPA (the Real Estate Settlement Procedures Act) requires the lender to give you a good faith estimate of these charges when you apply. But the government does not regulate which charges are reasonable and which are excessive.

TRAP

Watch out for "garbage fees." These are unwarranted charges that lenders slap on that can sometimes amount to hundreds of dollars. See Chap. 12.

Can I Get a Bigger Mortgage?

You probably can get a bigger mortgage, but you'll need to shop around. The amount you can borrow is determined by your financial profile and includes the following factors:

- You (and your spouse's) income
- Your credit score (based on how much you borrowed, how promptly you repaid it)
- The amount of your down payment
- Your financial resources (net worth)
- How much you already owe to others

and several other factors (see Chaps. 6 and 7 for details). Some lenders are more conservative than others. Some lenders "sell" your mortgage to quasi-government organizations such as Fannie Mae and Freddie Mac (discussed in Chap. 6), and they have very strict guidelines. Other lenders hold your mortgage themselves, and their guidelines may be more liberal or even stricter. Some lenders don't care at all about your financial profile but just lend based on the property's value.

Also, you may be able to arrange a second or even a third mortgage from a lender in addition to the first mortgage. Or the seller may be willing and able to carry back a loan for you. All of these and other strategies are discussed in various chapters in this book.

Is There Any Advantage in Getting a Shorter Term Mortgage?

Yes, there are two big advantages and one big disadvantage. The first advantage is that you can usually get a lower interest rate. Cut the mortgage term from 30 to 15 years, and you can probably save a quarter percent in the annual interest. Take it down to 7 years, and you may be able to save up to an eighth percent more. Take it down to 3 years, and you could save up to another eighth percent. The shorter the length of the loan, the lower the interest rate and, consequently, the lower the monthly payment.

The second advantage is that you save enormously on the total amount of interest borrowed. A 15-year loan saves more than half the interest paid over the course of a 30-year loan. After all, you're paying interest for fewer years.

The big drawback is that very often the shorter-term mortgage carries a bigger payment. For example, if you borrow $100,000 at 8 percent for 30 years, your monthly payment will be $734. Drop that same loan to 15 years and your monthly payment jumps up to $956, an increase of $222, or 23 percent.

TIP

Many modern loans offer a 30-year payment plan but a shorter payoff. For example, a common loan today is the 7/30. It is all due and payable within 7 years, although your payback schedule is based on 30 years. As a result, you get the advantage of a lower interest rate (because it's due in 7) and a lower monthly payment (based on 30 years). The drawback is that at year 7, your mortgage isn't fully paid off, and you owe a substantial amount, called a "balloon" payment (discussed in detail in Chap. 13).

How Is a Mortgage Different from a Car Loan?

When you borrow on a car it's essentially a *chattel* or personal property loan. You can take the car with you (hide it or move it out of state), and that increases the risk to the lender. Hence, car loans generally are for a higher interest rate (unless the manufacturer is helping with the costs). Also, if you fail to make payments, not only can the car be repossessed, but you can still be held liable for repayment of the loan.

When you borrow on a home, it's a real-property loan, which is called a mortgage or, in a different form, a *trust deed*. The property is the primary security, and since you cannot move it (and it is largely protected from destruction by fire and other insurance), the risk and, accordingly, the interest rate tend to be lower.

Also, if you fail to make payments, while the property may be foreclosed (taken back by the lender), in many cases you will not be held responsible if the sale of the property does not yield enough money to pay off the mortgage plus costs.

TIP

 Some states have "purchase money" laws that give you added protection. If part of the purchase price of a home is a mortgage, the lender may not be able to come back at you personally if the house is sold at foreclosure and does not bring enough money to pay back the loan. You can essentially walk away from such a house (although this could have a disastrous effect on your credit).

How Much Information about Myself Must I Tell the Lender?

You will probably need to give more information than you will feel comfortable with. The lender will want to know everything about your finances, including:

- Your income from *all* sources
- Your reserves, including all bank and brokerage accounts
- Any problems you may have had with foreclosures, bankruptcies, repossessions, and late payments
- How long you've been employed (2 years' worth of 1040 tax returns if self-employed)
- How much you currently pay in rent or mortgage payments
- What your credit card debt is and how much you pay monthly
- Whether you pay or receive alimony or child support
- All other expenses, including utilities and even phone

■ If you are in any stage of a divorce

In short, the lender wants to know you as well as you know your-self in order to make a risk determination. We'll see how to dis-close this in the best light in Chap. 8.

TIP

In the past, some lenders used to actually conduct investigations of borrowers, including checking with neighbors to ask about personal habits such as drinking or carousing. This has not been the case for many years. Today, however, a three-part credit report (from the three nationwide credit reporting agencies) is routinely done, and it tends to paint a complete financial picture.

TRAP

Remember, what you don't tell the lender, the lender may find out through credit checks. Better to be up-front and keep an explanation handy than to have an unhappy surprise later on.

What Are the Steps Involved in Getting a Mortgage?

There are seven steps to getting a mortgage. These will be dis-cussed throughout this book but are presented here so you can get a better picture of the process involved:

---

7 Steps in the Mortgage Process

1. Find an appropriate lender—one who offers the type of mortgage you need and want.

2. Get a letter of commitment from a lender.

3. Apply for the mortgage by filling out an application.

4. Supply all necessary documentation (such as bank records, 1099 or W-2 forms, paycheck stubs, and so on).

5. Pay for a credit check and property appraisal.

6. Wait for the underwriter's approval. (If there is an underwriting problem, you may need to increase the amount down or lower the borrowed amount.)

7. Wait until the lender funds the money, then close the deal.

What's the First Thing I Should Do Right Now?

The first thing you should do is to get preapproved. You can make a decision later on the type of mortgage you want. You can even decide later on the house you want to buy. However, in order to be a competitive buyer in today's marketplace, you need to get a letter of commitment from a lender. It will make you more acceptable to a seller and will help you negotiate better price and terms. We'll take a closer look at the pre-approval process in the next chapter.

3
Should I Get "Pre-Approved?"

Pre-approval has become an important negotiating tool in the purchase of property. Today, more buyers than ever use it. What we're talking about is a letter that you obtain from a lender telling the sellers that you're pre-approved to get a loan up to a certain amount at a certain interest rate and term. In a way it's like a blank check—all you have to fill in is the seller's name, and the money gets funded, right?

No, of course it's not that easy. The deal still has to go through the sales process, and if your job or financial situation changes, you still might not get the mortgage. From a seller's perspective, however, it's a whole lot better than a seller who has nothing to back him or her up.

Does It Really Work?

A friend recently sold a property to buyers who presented her with a pre-approval letter. The home was in the San Francisco Bay area at a time when the market was very hot. She was selling "by owner," and she had only placed the home on the market 2 weeks earlier when she received calls from two brokers and an individual who wanted to make offers. She told them to bring their offers in. (Sellers should receive all offers as they are presented, not simply consider them one at a time in turn.)

TIP

When you sell "by owner," it's still possible, even desirable, to work with agents. Typically you agree to pay them half the usual commission for bringing you a buyer. Yes, it costs you money, but you get a quick sale, and the broker is often able to better facilitate the transaction with the buyers.

All the offers were for around the asking price, with $2000 separating the highest from the lowest. Offer A wanted her to carry back a second mortgage to help the buyer make the purchase. Offer B offered 20 percent down to a new mortgage. Offer C likewise offered 20 percent down to a new mortgage but also included a pre-approval letter. Offer C was for $1000 less than offer B. Offer A was for the most amount of money.

Here's a recap:

A   Highest offer, carry back second mortgage

B   Second-highest offer, 20 percent down to new mortgage

C   Third-highest offer, 20 percent down to a new mortgage with a pre-approval letter.

Which would you accept? She didn't want to carry back any paper (which involves a second mortgage), so even though that was the highest priced offer, she rejected it. (Indeed, the reason the offer probably was higher was because it was weaker—not all cash to her.) The choice, therefore, was between B and C. B was $1000 higher, but C had the pre-approval letter. She countered back on C, asking for a higher price. The party involved agreed, and the deal was made.

What made the difference? The pre-approval letter did. It assured her that if she signed the deal with C, those buyers had an excellent chance of getting a mortgage and the deal could be quickly concluded. The pre-approval letter was the determining factor and the critical element.

While the circumstances may be different in homes on which

you make offers, don't think the importance of the pre-approval letter is exaggerated. It makes sellers sit up and pay attention. And it can get you a deal, sometimes a better deal, than a competing buyer who doesn't have such a letter. In a slower market than in our example, it can even save you money on the price. (The seller might accept a lower offer with a prequal letter if it's the only offer.)

What Should Go into the Pre-approval Letter?

It's important to understand that what we're talking about here is an informal document. There is no set government form. In a way it's like a letter of credit that a bank might issue. The banks' letters will look somewhat different from one another, but certain important elements will be common to all.

TRAP

Today in real estate there are a whole bunch of different letters that are called "prequals," or prequalifying letters. These range from a true lender's commitment to a letter from a broker stating an opinion regarding the borrower's ability to get financing. Savvy sellers, and their agents, read the fine print in these documents to determine what they actually do and don't say.

The key to the pre-approval letter is the level of commitment that a lender gives. Is the lender going out on a limb stating that you definitely can get a mortgage? Or is the lender hedging its bets with all sorts of conditions. Here are some statements that might go into a letter and what they mean:

Firm Commitment. The lender commits to offer a mortgage to the buyer (up to a maximum amount and interest rate) subject only to the buyer's financial condition not changing prior to close of escrow (and, of course, the property appraising out). This means that the buyer has fully qualified with the lender who will make the loan. The only thing that could go wrong would be something such as the buyer losing his or her job.

Limited Commitment. The lender commits to offer a mortgage to the buyer (up to a maximum amount and maximum terms) subject to the buyer's completing any or all of the following:

- *Application.* Sometimes a mortgage broker will simply take your application over the phone, will check nothing out, will have you sign nothing, and will then issue a "prequal" letter. This letter will state that you are qualified, but it usually has a clause in it that says your qualification is "subject to verification of credit, bank statements, employment, and completing an application." In other words, it's based on nothing more than your own verbal comments.

- *Credit check.* The buyer has presumably completed an application, and based on the statements made, the lender has offered the letter. However, because the lender has not checked the buyer's credit, the lender is holding back a firm commitment. The lender is saying, essentially, yes, we'll make the loan *if* the buyer's credit proves to be as good as he or she says it is. Again, this isn't much to go on. An old rule in this business is that everyone's credit is perfect, until the credit report comes in.

- *Documentation.* The buyer has presumably completed both an application and a credit check. What's missing are documents such as proof of employment; proof of resources, including the cash for the down payment; proof of other sources of income (such as alimony); and so on.

- If only this documentation is missing, the prequal letter is still fairly sound. With documentation, however, the lender may be willing to give a firm "pre-approval" commitment.

TIP

Note that in all of these letters of commitment, there is also a statement saying that the property must appraise high enough to qualify for the mortgage. If the seller's property doesn't appraise out, obviously there will be no loan.

Who Should Issue the Commitment Letter?

Ideally the commitment letter should come directly from the lender. Therefore, the bank, savings and loan (as may be the case if you're getting a "jumbo" or very large mortgage), or credit union with whom you are working provide it (although, it may be harder to get a firm commitment letter from some of these).

However, these days chances are you may not be working directly with the lender. Instead, you'll be working with a mortgage broker—a middleman who represents a great many lenders. Thus, the mortgage broker may have a lender issue the letter.

TIP

Having the pre-approval letter made out just before you make an offer and for just enough money to make the deal is a good idea. (The lender/mortgage broker can fax it to your agent.) If the seller thinks you can qualify for a bigger mortgage than you offer, the letter may encourage that seller to counter your offer for more money. Keep the sellers guessing about how big a mortgage you can get.

How Much Does the Pre-Approval Letter Cost?

Usually the lender doesn't charge for writing the pre-approval letter. It's done as a service to borrowers in the hope that they will then use that lender when they actually take out the mortgage. However, real estate is an industry where additional fees are the norm. It wouldn't surprise me in the least to see lenders start charging a small amount (probably in the range of $100) for such letters in the near future.

There are, however, other incidental fees that you may be

charged—for instance, a credit check fee to the lender, who can be expected to pass that on to you. If the lender simply uses a local credit agency, the fee is typically around $35 or less. However, if the lender goes all the way and does a three-bureau check (which is what is required for most mortgage lending), it can be higher. Sometimes lenders will hold off charging these fees until you actually get the mortgage.

TIP

A three-bureau credit check goes to the three national credit checking agencies: Experian, Equifax, and Trans Union. The three-bureau check involves looking up your credit history in each and produces a combined report. It is useful to lenders because it reveals credit information anywhere in the country.

In addition, having the lender send your application through underwriting involves a fee to the lender, which will probably be passed on to you. The fee varies but is usually under $100.

TRAP

There's usually a time limit on the pre-approval letter, even if it doesn't say so. Typically such letters are good for around 30 days. After that, it might be necessary to go through the process again to verify that your financial status hasn't changed.

4
Where Do I Get a Mortgage?

When you are buying a home, just as when you are refinancing, you will quickly discover that it's up to you to locate financing. In some cases the real estate agent may direct you to another agent in the office or in another office who handles mortgages. In other cases you may be given a list of lenders and told to contact one or more. Or you can always go to the phone book and look under "mortgages."

In all cases, even when you are led to a person who handles mortgages, it is up to you to get the best mortgage for your needs. Just remember that regardless of who offers you the mortgage, there are only five basic sources of funds, as described in the list that follows. What you are after is the best deal for you, not necessarily the most conveniently located source.

TRAP

Don't be swayed by the fact that your agent recommends one lender over another. What you are after is the least expensive loan you can get. Money is money. You owe it to yourself to investigate several lenders to be sure you're getting the best deal available.

When you apply for a mortgage on a home today, there are essentially five sources. These include the following:

1. Commercial and savings banks
2. Credit unions
3. Mortgage bankers
4. Mortgage brokers
5. Online lenders

These are called "retail sources" because they deal directly with the consumer. If it seems like there's a lot to choose from, there is. However, there are ways to whittle the numbers down. Most communities have a service that prints a referral sheet listing the various retail mortgage-lending sources in the community, as well as the rates they are currently charging and any fees they may have. These are often distributed by real estate agents, who pass them on to you.

Most of the time these listings are free, with title insurance or escrow companies picking up the costs of compiling the information. Sometimes they are offered as part of the computerized printout of a multiple listing service. Other times, however, you may have to pay for them. As long as the fee is nominal, a few dollars at most, it's usually worthwhile.

TRAP

These "shopping lists" are typically compiled by someone, usually a secretary, who calls the various lenders and asks for the information. As a consequence, while they are generally reliable, the rates are not guaranteed. Further, some lenders have gotten quite sophisticated at putting out "teaser" rates to induce you to call or come in. When you do, you find out that there are hidden restrictions on the advertised mortgage and that the one you really want is more expensive.

Another emerging source is to get your mortgage online. This is becoming such an important avenue that we'll discuss it separately in the next chapter.

Should I Try a Bank?

Historically, the largest lenders on residential real estate were savings and loan associations. Today most go by a different name: a savings bank. With the collapse of the Federal Savings and Loan Insurance Corporation (FSLIC) in the late 1980s, many S&Ls converted to banks and joined the Federal Deposit Insurance Corporation (FDIC). Thus, in your town, yesterday's S&L may be today's savings bank. The change is more than in name only. The way the institution handles funds and makes loans may also be slightly different.

Both commercial banks (which tend to specialize in business loans) and savings banks (which specialize in real estate loans) offer a wide variety of mortgages, including both fixed-rate and variable-rate loans. For our purposes we'll consider both as "banks" in this chapter.

TIP

If you are looking for an FHA-insured or VA-guaranteed home mortgage, a bank is still probably your best source. Also, if you're looking for a construction loan, because it is of a short duration, a bank will usually be in a position to offer you better terms than most other lenders.

What Is a Mortgage Banker?

Although well known in the lending industry, mortgage bankers are still not so well known among consumers. A mortgage banker is like a bank that doesn't offer commercial services such as checking or savings accounts. It simply offers mortgages.

The way it works is that the mortgage banker funds your loan with its own money. Then it "sells" your mortgage to a secondary lender such as Fannie Mae or Freddie Mac. This gives the mortgage banker back most of the money it loaned to you. The mortgage banker, however, usually still has a small interest in the mortgage and continues to receive a small percentage of the interest you pay plus (often) a fee for collecting the payments.

What Is a Mortgage Broker?

In lending, as elsewhere, there is wholesale and there is retail. The person you deal with is typically a retailer—he or she is retailing a loan to you. There is a whole class of companies called "mortgage brokers" that do nothing but retail loans. They are the salespeople for banks, savings banks, mortgage bankers, insurance companies, and others who want to offer mortgages, but who don't want to deal with the public.

Mortgage brokers are licensed by the state to deal in mortgages. Sometimes they are individuals who came out of banking. Other times they are former real estate agents whose strong suit was finance.

These brokers arrange with lenders to market their product (mortgages) to the consumer for a fee. (It can be a flat fee, say, $1500, or a percentage of the mortgage, such as 1 or 1.5 percent.) Thus when you deal with a mortgage broker, that person is getting a fee for handling your needs (including taking the application, finding and assembling all the documentation, working out any problems, and so forth).

TIP

Mortgage brokers normally don't get a fee from the lender unless you actually get the mortgage. Therefore, they are definitely on your side and will often stretch to help you get the loan wherever possible.

TRAP

Mortgage brokers sometimes try to charge you fees in addition to those they receive from the lender. This can be in the form of extra points or extra direct costs. I wouldn't pay these. Find out up front what the charges for working with a mortgage broker will be. If he or she is adding on extra costs, find another broker who isn't.

Note: Today, mortgage brokers can be the salespeople for not only an insurance company in a distant state but also for the bank across the street. They often represent as many as 100 different lenders and usually offer you the biggest selection when mortgage hunting.

TIP

There is always the temptation to go to the bank across the street and offer to borrow from them, *if* they will save you the fee they offer the retailer, the mortgage broker (MB). Usually attempts to circumvent the MB's fees are unsuccessful. You want only one loan, the MB brings in hundreds. No lender is going to cut its own throat by undercutting its retailers. (An exception is some online services.) You'll find that the charges are typically the same whether you deal directly with the lender (when you can) or with a mortgage broker.

TRAP

Almost any agent who has a real estate license can also get a mortgage broker's license. That entitles the agent to collect a fee for getting a mortgage for you. However, not all mortgage brokers are able to arrange loans at retail. There are some agents who call themselves mortgage brokers who actually arrange mortgages at *above* retail. In other words, they do for you what you can do for yourself, and then they charge you a fee for it. For example, they may arrange a mortgage for you through a bank and then charge you one point (above what the lender charges) for their services. If you had gone to the lender direct or to a true retailer, it wouldn't have cost you the extra one point. Beware of these self-styled mortgage brokers. You don't need them. Shop around to find out the true costs.

Credit Unions

A credit union is a lender that is not subject to the same kinds of taxes and regulations as a bank and that caters to a special group. Hence, it can afford to offer mortgages at slightly lower costs to you.

In the past, credit unions (there are more than 15,000 of them nationwide) dealt primarily in short-term consumer and auto loans. However, during the 1980s the major auto manufacturers began offering their own financing, and this put a dent into the credit unions' ability to find borrowers. As a result, they turned increasingly to mortgages.

As they expanded their offerings and attracted more people, however, the banks protested, and the courts indicated that credit unions must only make loans to special groups who they represent, not the public in general. This may (or may not) slow their growth in the future. Today, if you are in the group they service, many credit unions can offer you a wide variety of mortgages. The big catch, of course, is that you must be a member of the credit union in order to borrow from it.

TIP

If you belong to a credit union, check out the terms they are offering on mortgages. When compared with other lenders, they may come out looking more favorable. Remember, money is money, and if the credit union gives you a better deal, why not take it?

Can I Get a Mortgage Without Leaving My House?

You don't have to physically go to any lenders to check them out. As noted, there are "shopping lists" available from most real estate agents in your community. In addition, if you want to contact the lenders directly, you can do all your information gathering over the phone. Just go to your phone book and look up "mortgage bankers," "savings and loans," and "banks."

(Presumably you will already know if you belong to a credit union.) Then just call a few. Ask to speak to a "mortgage loan officer."

Of course, you can also check out online resources, which we'll discuss in the next chapter.

What Are Secondary Lenders?

The best answer here is that it's not necessary to know what secondary lenders are in order to get a good consumer mortgage. However, if you do know, it could help you to better understand the process and therefore locate the best lender.

Secondary lenders include the following:

■ Quasi-government organizations such as Fannie Mae and Freddie Mac

■ Insurance companies

■ Out-of-state banks

■ Other large companies involved in loaning mortgage money.

They almost never deal directly with you, the consumer. Rather, they go through retailers such as mortgage bankers or mortgage brokers (banks can act as retailers for them as well).

When you apply for a mortgage through a retailer, the application you fill out is typically forwarded to a secondary lender for underwriting approval. If it's approved, you get your loan. If it isn't, you don't. The secondary lenders, ultimately, are the ones who make most mortgage loans in America.

What Is the Difference between a "Conforming" and a "Portfolio" Loan?

Knowing the difference between a "conforming" and a "portfolio" loan is also helpful. A conforming loan is one that meets the standards of Fannie Mae or Freddie Mac, the two big quasi-government secondary lenders. Generally that means it's within their guidelines to include a maximum amount, currently $227,150. Any loan for more than this amount is called "nonconforming." Any loan not underwritten by Fannie Mae or Freddie Mac is called "nonconforming."

A portfolio loan, on the other hand, is a mortgage that a lender does not sell on the secondary market but instead holds in its own portfolio. A bank may offer you a loan and then fund the money out of its own reserves and collect the interest. Most jumbos (loans over the maximum) are portfolio loans.

TRAP

There is some confusion in the industry regarding conforming versus portfolio loans. For example, if a bank lends $200,000 (under the conforming maximum) but does not sell the loan on the secondary market, is it conforming or not? Technically speaking, only those mortgages actually sold to Freddie Mac and Fannie Mae are conforming. Yet some lenders refer to their own portfolio loans for less than $227,150 (currently the maximum) as conforming. It's just a matter of linguistics.

5
Can I Get a Mortgage Online?

The latest development in mortgage hunting is to look for a mortgage over the Internet. Although, as of this writing, it's only a miniscule part of the total mortgage picture in this country, it appears to be growing by leaps and bounds. Yes, you can get your mortgage online. However, there are some important traps to watch out for, as well as some definite advantages. In this chapter we'll look at how it's done, along with the pros and cons.

How Do You Get Started?

Getting a mortgage online does involve some familiarity with the computer. As those in the computer world know, in order to get online, in addition to a modern computer (not necessarily the latest or fastest), you need a modem, a phone line to connect to, and a service provider such as America Online (AOL), Microsoft Network (MSN), or any of the dozens of other Internet Service Providers (ISPs)

TIP

This chapter is for those who are fairly computer-literate, but even if you're not, you may want to peruse it to see if it's something you'd want to investigate further. Just keep in mind that if you prefer to talk face-to-face with a lender, you're in the vast majority. I recently spoke with a representative of one of the largest independent (not affiliated with a bank) mortgage lenders in the nation with extensive online capabilities and learned that the month before, they had received 55,000 mortgage applications, but only 400 of these were online.

Once you're set up, go online and then check out the various Web sites offering mortgages. I will suggest several of the larger sites at the end of this chapter, but you can use a search engine such as Yahoo or Lycos to locate many more. (Yahoo is at www.yahoo.com; Lycos is at www.lycos.com.) At the time this is written, I located over 50 different sites offering mortgages to consumers.

Who Offers Mortgages?

As you will quickly find out once you begin investigating on the Web, just about everybody offers mortgages. There are Web sites for some of the country's biggest banks. Mortgage bankers, such as Countrywide, have Web sites. And many local mortgage brokers likewise have their own Web site.

At many of these sites you will find a "calculator," which is a built-in program that does all the calculations for you, to help you determine how big a mortgage you can afford. You simply input a few bits of information such as the amount of the mortgage you want, the down payment, your income, and your expenses, and in a few seconds, you are given your maximum mortgage based on then-current interest rates. Some of these are also "wizards" and are even more sophisticated and attempt to select the best type of mortgage for you or provide you with the type of mortgage to give you the lowest payments.

TRAP

I've tried out many of these wizards and find their accuracy varies greatly. It's the old story of the information that you receive is determined in large part by who writes the program. In many cases these programs don't really ask for enough detailed information to get an accurate picture of your finances and as a result cannot give you a highly accurate statement of what you can afford. They merely give you a best guess. On the other hand, many of them come out fairly close.

At these sites you can also find out what the lenders are offering as their current interest rate, the different types of mortgages they have to offer, and other information that's helpful when mortgage hunting.

Can I Actually Get a Mortgage Online?

The answer to this question is yes—and no. You can go through much of the process involved in securing a mortgage. However, at some point you will need to present documentation and to give your signature. Perhaps going through a typical procedure for getting an online mortgage will be helpful.

Online Mortgage Procedure

Step 1. Locate a lender's Web site and check out the information offered. Go through their wizard to find out what they consider the best mortgage for you. Determine what they have to offer, along with the interest rate and points.

TIP

Be sure to check that the lender offers mortgages in your area. Remember, the Internet is international in scope. You don't want to apply for a mortgage in

Tallahassee only to discover that the Web site is run by a local mortgage broker in St. Louis.

Step 2. Fill out an online application. This is different than simply running the wizard. Here you will be asked all sorts of highly confidential information about yourself and your finances. This application usually asks the same questions you'd be asked if you were speaking face-to-face with a lender.

TRAP

 You will be asked some very confidential information. Be aware that you may be at some risk by putting it up over the Internet. See the next topic.

Step 3. Pay a fee up front using your credit card to cover the cost of a credit check and appraisal of the property. The lender will usually order both.

Step 4. Get approval. Many lenders can give you approval online within a matter of hours or certainly within a day or two. Ask for proof of the approval. You can usually get it by e-mail, fax, or letter. I personally like the idea of a signed letter, although a fax will probably do. I don't believe an e-mail confirmation is worth anything.

Step 5. Close the deal. When you're ready to close, you'll meet with an escrow officer (or attorney) who's handling the closing and with an officer of the lender. There you'll be asked to sign the application you filled out over the phone. You'll also be asked to present any documents required such as paycheck stub, W-2 forms, 1040 tax statements, bank statements, and so on. If everything is as you originally represented, you should get your mortgage and be able to complete the purchase or refinance of the property.

TIP

If anything is not exactly as you said it was online, the closing can be held up until you can provide the proper documentation. That's why it's a good idea to double-check to be sure you know exactly what's needed beforehand.

How Secure Is Confidential Information Sent Over the Internet?

This is a good question. Unfortunately, there's not a really good answer. There are a couple of excellent encryption programs that are used to provide secure lines. I regularly buy items over the Internet using secure Web sites and my credit card, and I haven't had a problem—yet. However, as we all know, computers are the playground of some extremely creative hackers, and who's to say that what's secure today will remain secure tomorrow?

A bigger issue, however, may be knowing with whom you are dealing. Just because someone puts up a Web site and says he or she is offering mortgages doesn't necessarily mean that person is doing so. And then if some poor soul gets sucked in and sends his or her most confidential financial information, what's to prevent the online lender from using it in a criminal way?

As far as I know, there is no policing of mortgage sites on the Internet. Therefore, you had best know exactly with whom you are dealing. Obviously, you can feel more secure if you're sending information to a major bank or mortgage banker. But what about sending it to a mortgage broker? (You'll recall this is basically a real estate agent who helps consumers secure financing.) The Web site may be huge and elaborate, but the person may be working out of his or her bedroom and not have all the contacts that are suggested by the Web site advertising.

In short, you can't be too careful. If you're not comfortable giving your most confidential information out over the Internet, don't. It's very little inconvenience to go down and see a lender in person.

Are There Any Advantages of Using the Internet to Mortgage Hunt?

Yes, there can be. You'll recall in earlier discussions that today many lenders use retailers (typically mortgage brokers) to secure borrowers for them. When you use a Web site and apply online, however, you eliminate this salesperson. And some lenders are willing to credit you at least with part of the fee they would otherwise pay for retailing.

TIP

The amount you can save by going online will vary. But it can be as much as one and one-half points, which can be a considerable amount of money. Usually, however, to get this advantage, you must apply entirely online and frequently you must be a prime "A" borrower (see the next chapter). Be sure to query the lender on exactly how much you'll save by applying online and what it takes to qualify.

In an earlier chapter I noted that lenders would not undercut their retailers by offering consumers who went direct a lower price. That's certainly the case with face-to-face borrowing. But the Internet is different. Many lenders consider this a totally different kind of service and are willing to give you a break when you use it.

TIP

Some Internet lenders will also help you out with other costs. For example, they may refund back the cost of your credit check and not charge for the preparation of documents (since, with the information you input, they can do it virtually automatically using computers). This can save an additional couple of hundred dollars.

Keep in mind, however, that lenders are very adept at manipulating the various factors in a mortgage. They may, for example, offer you a 0-points mortgage, but on the other hand raise the interest rate you are being charged. Or they may offer a reduced interest rate, only to jack up other fees and points.

TIP

Your best insurance against getting taken is to become savvy as to what to expect (by reading books such as this) and then by shopping around.

Is Online Mortgage Hunting for Me?

Generally speaking, those who benefit most from hunting for a mortgage online are the more sophisticated borrowers. This does not mean they are necessarily more sophisticated with computers. It doesn't take a whiz kid to be able to get onto the Internet and check out Web sites.

On the other hand, if you're unfamiliar with mortgage finance, it's much more difficult to determine what type of loan is best for you and whether or not you're getting a better deal or a lesser one. When you deal with a person face-to-face, you can ask questions, and more important, the other person can sense where you are and can provide expert information to help you.

That's not the case online. While most sites offer FAQs (frequently asked questions), my experience in checking these out is that they tend to be not that helpful. Frequently the questions asked and answered are either too hard, too easy, or irrelevant to many borrower's needs. In short, if you're mortgage-literate, know what's available, and know what's best for you, then by all means check out the Web sites and what they have to offer. You may very well find that you're able to get the very best mortgage deal there, bar none.

On the other hand, if this is your first home and first mortgage, if it's been awhile since you took out a mortgage and you aren't quite sure what's what in the mortgage lending field, or if you're just not sure what you want, then my suggestion is that you contact a physical lender (in other words, a real person). Nothing can take the place of person-to-person interaction. A good lender will anticipate your needs and answer those questions you need to have answered even before you figure out the questions.

Online Resources

If you want to try mortgage hunting online, check out the following Web sites. I am not personally endorsing any of these, but I found them interesting and, overall, helpful.

Chase Manhattan Mortgage (http://www.chase.com). One of the country's leading banking lenders.

Countrywide (http://www.countrywide.com). This is the largest independent mortgage banking lender in the country.

ELOAN (http://ELOAN.com). One of the most thorough mortgage lending sites I've seen. Definitely check it out.

Fannie Mae (http://fanniemae.com). This is the country's largest secondary lender. You won't find consumer mortgage loans here, but you will find all sorts of information on mortgage. (Much of it, unfortunately, tends to be highly technical.)

Freddie Mac (http://freddiemac.com). This is the second-largest secondary lender. Again, no loans directly to consumers, but this site's filled with lots of useful information (also lots of technical information).

HomeShark (http://homeshark.com). This is an independent lender that claims it will save consumers money on mortgages.

Home Fair (http://www.homefair.com). This is an independent mortgage lender site.

HUD (Federal Government Department of Housing and Urban Development) (http://www.hud.com). HUD does not offer mortgage online, but it has an incredible wealth of mortgage-hunting information that should prove invaluable.

North American Mortgage (http://www.namc.com). This is a large mortgage banker.

QuickenMortgage (http://www.mortgage.quicken.com). These are the people from Intuit who developed the excellent Quicken home financial programs. I found their wizard to be one of the best I tried. As of this writing, their site offers mortgages from six national lenders.

6
Can I Get a Prime "A" Mortgage?

Whenever I think about how big a mortgage a person can qualify for, I'm reminded of that old saw about two speculators in New York City who wanted to buy a $20 million office building. After a meeting with the lender, one turned to the other and said, "There's good news and there's bad news."

"What's the good news?" asked the partner.

"They've agreed to loan us the mortgage money."

"Good," said his friend, "then what could be the bad news?"

"They're requiring that we put $500 down."

The simple truth is that if you want a mortgage, you have to meet the lender's requirements no matter how illogical they may seem. Sometimes the requirements are easy. Other times they are very difficult to meet.

In this chapter we will look at prime "A" loans. These are the most popular mortgages because they offer the lowest interest rates and costs. They are also sometimes called "conforming" loans because they conform to the underwriting standards of Fannie Mae and Freddie Mac, the two large quasi-government secondary lenders that "buy" the mortgages from the lenders who loan the money to you. These loans have a maximum amount that changes as housing prices go up. (Currently the maximum is $227,150.) They also require that you have sterling credit.

If you want to see whether you're likely to qualify for one of these mortgages, check out the short quiz at the end of this chapter.

TIP

Most prime mortgages are available only if you intend to occupy the property.

How Do Lenders Evaluate You?

How do lenders of prime loans discriminate between those who get mortgages and those who don't? How does a lender determine how big a mortgage you can get or how little you must put down?

Mortgage lending separates borrowers between prime and subprime. Prime borrowers have virtually no credit problems, strong income, and lots of cash in the bank. They are also called "A" borrowers. Everyone else is subprime and is rated from A− down to D.

To see how you rate, check out the chart shown below. *Note:* These are unofficial guidelines—each lender has its own yardstick.

What Kind of a Borrower Are You?

Rating Description

A   Most creditworthy. Fit underwriter's profile (described below).

A−   One unpaid bill, under $1000, turned into collection, or no more than one late payment of over 60 days or two late payments of over 30 days in credit cards or installment debt all within the last 2 years. No bankruptcies or foreclosures on record (at least in previous 7 years).

B   Within the past year and a half you have up to four late payments of no more than 30 days in credit cards or installment debt. You may have had a bankruptcy or a foreclosure concluded at least 2 years before applying for loan.

C   Within the past year you have up to six late payments of no more than 30 days in credit cards or installment debt. You may have accounts currently in collection, but mortgage may be granted if they are no more than $5000 and paid in full by the time the mortgage is funded. Mortgage funds may be used to clean up these debts. If you have a bankruptcy, it was resolved at least a year before applying for the mortgage. If you had a foreclosure, it was concluded at least 2 years before applying for loan.

D   You have many current late payments, have several accounts in collection, and have judgments against you. These can be paid off from the proceeds of the new mortgage. If you have a bankruptcy, it was concluded more than 6 months before you applied for the new mortgage. If you had a foreclosure, it was concluded at least 2 years before applying for loan.

Also, check out the quick quiz at the end of this chapter to see whether you're likely to qualify as an A borrower.

How Do You Stack Up?

If you're a prime A candidate, read on. The material in this chapter is designed to show you how lenders evaluate you for the amount of down payment, loan amount, and whether or not you'll actually get the financing. If you're A− or lower, you may want to check into the next chapter, where you will find there are mortgages available for you too.

For prime borrowers, whether or not you actually get the mortgage you want is determined by a very arcane method that makes little sense, even to many of those in field. We are going to cover it very quickly in just a few pages. You will see just how strange and sometimes arbitrary "A" mortgage lending really is. *Note:* For this chapter we are only going to talk about institutional lenders such as large banks and mortgage bankers as well as large secondary underwriters such as Fannie Mae and Freddie Mac. The rules we'll describe here do not apply to individuals such as an individual seller making a home loan to a buyer.

TRAP

There are many vagaries in mortgage lending. You can be an excellent credit risk, yet by doing something as simple as having too many credit cards (even if you don't have any balances on them), you can lower your rating. On the other hand, you may be a terrible credit risk, but by presenting your credit information in just the right light, you can secure excellent financing.

Do You Fit the Profile?

In the old days (read: about 5 years ago, before computerization took hold in the field) you could pretty much tell the size of a mortgage you were getting by using a couple of simple formulas. Add in a good credit report and you were home free. In those days, basically, if you put 20 percent down, your monthly mortgage payment couldn't be much more than a little above a quarter of your income. If you put 10 percent down, it couldn't be more than a little less than a third. Have the right percentages and a clean credit report and you would get your mortgage.

Not so anymore. Today's institutional lender uses a sophisticated "profile." Like the profiles that supposedly identify terrorists at airports to ticket agents, these profiles supposedly separate the good credit risks from the bad for lenders. They are based on hundreds of thousands of mortgage lending case histories. Essentially what the underwriters (those who ultimately determine whether a mortgage is worth the risk) have done is to statistically compile the characteristics of low- to high-risk borrowers. The result is the profile.

If you fit the profile of a low-risk borrower, you get the loan. If you're off a bit, you might have to come up with more cash and get a smaller loan amount. If you don't fit at all, you can't get the mortgage.

TIP

Remember, we're here talking about prime or A loans. In the next chapter we'll discuss subprime or A− and lower mortgages, which those who don't fit the profile for prime may more easily secure.

Thus, in today's world, who gets the top mortgages is a matter of fitting the profile. For the rest of this chapter we'll look at what that profile asks of you.

TRAP

Note that the profile of a low-risk borrower is drawn from statistical case histories. That means that anomalies may be introduced. For example, statistically, a low-risk borrower won't have more than three credit checks in the previous 6 months. (Whether or not the credit checks reflect actual money borrowed isn't relevant.) If you apply for four (or more), you're out of the profile and may be disqualified. Yes, it's arbitrary and almost capricious, since in the real world you might be shopping for a car and stop at half a dozen dealers. Each of them might have run a credit check on you; you may not have bought any car or borrowed any money! Nevertheless, the statistics show that more than three credit checks in 6 months means added risk. Go fight the system!

Basically, when you apply for a mortgage you are asked to fill out a standardized application that identifies a whole series of categories, including, but not limited to the following:

- Your income
- Your expenses
- The amount of cash you're putting down
- Where you're getting that cash from
- Your reserves (money in the bank)

The lender then determines additional information from a credit report:

- Your history of repaying borrowed loans
- Your current outstanding debt
- How long your credit history is

And they glean other information as well. Based on how you score in all of these areas, you will or will not be granted a new mortgage. Or you may be granted the mortgage *if* you put down more cash and get a lower mortgage amount.

Let's consider some of the individual categories.

How Big Is Your Income and Your Expenses?

Your income is obviously how much money you make before taxes. It also includes such things as alimony. In addition, if both spouses have a long history of career work, their entire salaries may be counted. On the other hand, if one spouse works only part-time or has only a short work history, only a portion of his or her income may be counted. Your expenses include PITI (principal, interest, taxes, and insurance) on the property plus living expenses and other debt.

TIP

When filling out a mortgage application, of course, do not lie about anything. However, when explaining income it usually pays to emphasize length and continuity. For example, you're a teacher who has gotten his first job in years just a month ago. The lender is bound to wonder if you will succeed at the work. However, if you note that you were a teacher with 5 years' experience a decade ago before leaving the field to help raise children, it puts your application in a whole new and better light.

The method by which you receive your income is important too. If you work for an employer and receive wages (meaning you will get a W-2 form at the end of the year), you get preference mainly because it is easy to verify your income and because, presumably, you have something called "job security." (The only way a lender can determine this is by asking your employer what your chances for future employment are—a question frequently asked!)

On the other hand, if you're self-employed, you may be turned down prima facie without further consideration. Some prime loans will not be granted to self-employed individuals. In other cases you will be asked to produce the last 2 years of your 1040 federal tax filings. The concern here is actually verifying your income. (You could submit false records, although now many lenders are capable of verifying income directly with the IRS!) And when you are self-employed, unless you can show a long work history, you are presumed to be at risk of job loss. See Chap. 11 for more information on how to better present yourself on a loan application when you're self-employed.

The amount of your income will have to be big enough to allow you to make the mortgage payments plus have sufficient monies left over for all your living expenses and your taxes. Complex formulas for "front end" (the ratio of your house payment including principal, interest, taxes, and insurance to your income, usually around 40 percent) as compared to "back end" (the ratio of your total payments to your gross income, usually 28 percent—for a 90 percent LTV loan—to 31 percent for an 80 percent LTV loan) are used. These formulas aren't helpful to most borrowers who are trying to figure out if they will qualify for a mortgage. Suffice to say, you need as much income as possible.

TIP

If possible, it usually is a good idea to pay off any short-term debt (such as from credit cards) *before* applying for a mortgage. That way you increase your income (less is set aside to pay for the short-term debt), and you may have a better chance of qualifying. On the other hand, the more of your available cash you use to pay off debt, the less you will have available for a down payment and closing costs. Again, it's a trade-off.

How Much Cash Should I Put Down?

The amount you should put down depends on the perspective. For most home buyers/borrower, as little as possible is usually a good idea. That's certainly the case if you want to leverage your investment.

From the lender's perspective, on the other hand, the more the better. The reason is the more of your own money you have invested in the property, the less likely you are to let it go to foreclosure if the market turns down or you lose your job. The more you have in, presumably, the harder you'll fight to keep the home.

Another consideration is where you get the money. Ideally it will be your own money earned over the years and set aside as savings. Borrowing the down payment is a no-no. It suggests to the underwriter that you really can't afford the property. Let the lender know you're borrowing your down payment, and you almost certainly will be scuttling the loan.

TIP

If you borrow money that you intend to use as part of the down payment, do it well in advance of applying for the mortgage (at least 6 months). That way the money will be seen as part of a savings account and the loan will be long established. In other words, you won't be borrowing specifically to make the home purchase.

Gifts from relatives are acceptable. These must, however, be legitimate gifts. They can't be given with strings attached—for instance, an agreement that you'll repay them so much a month, and when you sell the property, you'll repay the balance in full. In that case they are nothing more than a disguised loan.

TRAP

In the past many underwriters insisted that those offering gifts as part of the down payment and closing costs cosign the mortgage and also qualify for it.

This effectively nixed the deal in many cases. That requirement, however, has recently been removed for many federally underwritten mortgages. Today a gift with a simple gift letter may suffice. Check with your lender.

How Much Should I Have in Reserve?

Reserves mean what you have left in the bank after you make the down payment and take care of the closing costs. Ideally lenders would like to see at least 3 months' or more worth of monthly expenses. If you have only a month or two, you could be turned down, or more likely, you may be asked to arrange for a smaller loan.

In the real world, more important than a few meaningless months of reserves is your ability to generate income and to secure additional borrowing (from lines of credit, credit cards, and so on) should something untoward occur (such as illness, job loss, and so on). If you can continue to generate income one way or another to meet your monthly housing expenses, who cares how much you actually have in reserve? The underwriters care because it's part of the low-risk profile.

What Is Your Creditworthiness?

This is the critical question. It's broken down into many categories, including your payment history, the amount of your outstanding debt, how long you've been borrowing, the number of inquiries, and the kind of credit you use. We'll consider each.

TIP

Lenders get all of this information from a credit report. For a mortgage this special report usually covers the three national credit reporting agencies:

- Trans Union
- Experian (formerly TRW)

■ Equifax

A three-bureau credit report is obtained, and it usually reveals everything there is to know about you. If you ever held out any hope of concealing bad credit, forget it. If it's there, the underwriters will find it.

What Is Your Payment History?   The credit companies check the public records to see if you have had any bankruptcies or foreclosures. They also look for any loans you have that are now in collection. The credit agencies also try to determine whether you are delinquent in any of your trade lines (credit cards). Any adverse notation can be cause for not issuing the mortgage.

TIP

If you're behind in payments, catch up *before* applying for the mortgage. Try to stay caught up for at least three months before applying so your delinquencies will show up as old rather than recent. Old delinquencies are much easier to forgive. However, be aware that frequency and severe delinquent payments can also sink you, even if you're caught up now. The best policy is to preserve your good credit by always paying on time. If you can't make the payments, don't borrow the money.

TRAP

A recent bankruptcy can sink you. However, if it's been seven years or more, it may simply be ignored by the lender. A discovered foreclosure, however, is almost never ignored. Lenders don't like to offer mortgages to people who have in the past allowed their homes to sink into foreclosure.

What Is Your Outstanding Debt?   What are the recent balances on all of your trade lines (credit cards), the average balances over the past 6 months, and how close are you to your credit limits? The underwriters are concerned about people who live on their credit. They don't mind if you borrow, as long as you have plenty of credit left. On the other hand, if you have 10 credit cards and are borrowed to the limit on all of them, it suggests a poor money manager . . . and someone who might not be able to make mortgage payments.

TIP

If you are borrowed out, before applying for a mortgage, consider paying down or at least consolidating some of your outstanding debt. Perhaps you can obtain a single loan that will not only pay off all existing debt but leave you a considerable buffer of unused credit. It will certainly look better to your mortgage underwriter, but do it well in advance (at least 6 months) of your mortgage application.

How Long Have You Been a Borrower?   Lenders want to know that you've been successfully borrowing for a long time. That tells them that you're a good money manager. To determine this they look at your oldest trade line. The older the better.

TIP

Hang on to credit card accounts. Keep a credit card that you've had for years, even if a new credit company offers you a somewhat better deal. That old credit card shows that you have a long history and may help you get your mortgage. This is the case even if you just keep the card in a box and almost never use it.

How Many Inquiries Have You Had and New Accounts Opened?   We covered this earlier. More than three credit checks in 6 months is a mark against. Yes, it's irrational, but go argue with a profile. Similarly, if you open too many new credit card or other charge accounts, it looks suspiciously like you may be planning to borrow a lot of money and leave the country. The underwriters check your most recent new account. An account opened in the previous 3 months is not good.

What Types of Credit Do You Have?   A good balance between credit cards, car loans, personal finance companies, and other installment loans is best. You don't want a lot of any of these or even a huge total. But the fact that you've got a car loan, three credit cards (the ideal amount—no more, no less), and perhaps a department store card, and you've maintained reasonable balances all suggests you're a good credit manager. And that's what the underwriters actually want the most.

Who Actually Sizes You Up?

The credit reporting bureaus simply report. The underwriters, in many cases, want an independent analysis of your credit history. Which leaves it up to a couple of companies to take a look at your overall credit picture and see where you fit. The most well-known in the trade, which most people have never heard of, is called "Fair Isacc," or FICO.

FICO, for a fee to lenders and underwriters, will examine your overall credit background and then give you a score based on a rating scale between a low of 400 and a high of 900. The higher your FICO number, the more chance you have of getting a mortgage. The lower your number, the less your chance.

TRAP

I was recently talking with an individual who had been turned down for a mortgage in a most unusual way. He had applied a few months earlier at several different lenders for a mortgage and had been accepted by two of them. He had learned his FICO score was 640. However, at the time he couldn't get the property he wanted for unrelated reasons, so he obviously also did not get the mortgage. More recently, he applied again and was turned down with a lower FICO score. Since he hadn't had any recent bad credit, he inquired as to why his score had dropped. He was told it was because he had too many recent credit inquiries. He protested that the inquiries were all for a mortgage that he applied for but hadn't gotten earlier because the deal for the house fell through. He now wanted the mortgage because he had a new deal. The underwriter said the matter would be looked into.

What about Conditional Approval?

Chances are that if you have reasonably good credit, you won't be turned down for a new mortgage. Rather, you'll be given a conditional approval provided that certain conditions are fulfilled. These conditions may be something as simple as providing missing documentation, such as a W-2 form or an old paycheck stub. Or they might be something more severe. The underwriter may feel that in order for you to meet the profile, you must increase your down payment and, accordingly, reduce the amount you are borrowing.

That's a lot to ask. You may not have any more cash and may need the maximum loan. If that's the case, you might not be able to take the loan.

Should You Get Discouraged?

Remember at the beginning of this chapter I said that we were concentrating on prime A mortgages in this chapter. These go to the very best borrowers, those with sterling credit and lots of cash. In other words, people who probably don't need the money in the first place.

However, if you get turned down, there are a tremendous number of other mortgage alternatives available, including assuming an existing mortgage (see Chap. 20) or getting a subprime loan (see Chap. 7). In other words, if you're given a hard time, don't get upset. Don't get discouraged. You can get a mortgage. You may just have to dig a little deeper.

Quick Quiz—Rate Yourself

Answer the following questions to see how likely you are to be seen as an A borrower by an underwriter. *Note:* The following quiz does not qualify you—only an underwriter can do that. Further, the questions are only approximations. For example, if you put less than 20 percent down but have good reserves, you may still get the mortgage. Other factors also apply, such as your FICO score. To find out if you actually do qualify for an A loan, check with a mortgage broker or other lender.

	YES	NO
1. Are you putting at least 20 percent down?	[ ]	[ ]
2. Will the total loans be no more than 80 percent of the purchase price (in case you have a second mortgage)?	[ ]	[ ]
3. Is your income at least three and a half times your total monthly payment?	[ ]	[ ]
4. Do you have little to no outstanding debt running six months or longer?	[ ]	[ ]
5. Do you have enough cash in reserve so that after paying the down payment and all closing costs you will have at least 3 months' worth of expenses in savings?	[ ]	[ ]
6. Do you work for an employer (not self-employed)?	[ ]	[ ]
7. Have you been caught up in all of your credit card and installment debt payments for at least 2 years?	[ ]	[ ]
8. Do you have no trade lines in collection within the past 5 years?	[ ]	[ ]
9. Have you had no bankruptcy within at least the past 5 years?	[ ]	[ ]
10. Have you had no foreclosure within at least the past 10 years?	[ ]	[ ]
11. Do you have at least, but no more than, three trade lines (credit cards)?	[ ]	[ ]
12. Have you had no more than three credit checks within the past 6 months?	[ ]	[ ]
13. Are your credit card balances no more than half of your total credit line?	[ ]	[ ]

14. Is your oldest trade line (installment or credit card) at least 2 years old?   [ ]   [ ]

15. Are your current housing expenses roughly equivalent to your new housing expenses?   [ ]   [ ]

If you answered yes to *all* of the questions, chances are excellent that you will qualify for the lowest interest rate prime loans. On the other hand, if you answered no to one or more questions, you might still qualify. Remember, only a lender can tell you for sure and only after you've filled out and applied for a mortgage.

7
Can I Get a Subprime Mortgage?

In the last chapter we discussed the difference between prime and subprime. As you'll recall, a prime borrower was basically one who had a lot of cash in the bank, a good income, and virtually no credit problems of any kind. Subprime includes all the rest of humanity.

If you're subprime, don't take it as a criticism. It merely suggests that you're human, that once in a while you forget or can't make a payment on time. That's not a terrible crime or even a moral issue. For many of us, it's simply a fact of life.

And it shouldn't and doesn't mean that you can't get a mortgage. In this chapter we'll discuss subprime borrowing, including the types of mortgages you can get and what they will cost you.

Can You Get an Institutional Mortgage?

In many cases, particularly if you're an A− or B borrower (see the last chapter for a chart explaining the different grading levels), the answer is yes. Indeed, many of the prime lenders now offer mortgages to subprime borrowers. The only difference is that they may charge an extra point or two or the interest rate may be a percent or two higher.

For example, Countrywide, the nation's largest independent lender, has offered subprime mortgages through its Full Spectrum unit. Other national lenders, such as Aames Home Loan, offer mortgages to virtually every category of subprime borrowers. And there are dozens of other lenders who have similar programs.

Your best bet is to check with a good mortgage broker. Most will have several subprime lenders, and as soon as the broker determines you're in this category, the broker can refer you to one of them.

TIP

You'll end up paying more in interest and points for a subprime mortgage. On the other hand, you'll still be able to get a loan. A few years ago, it was almost impossible for subprime borrowers to get real estate financing.

TRAP

There is a tendency for some lenders to "stick it to" subprime borrowers. Don't accept the first terms you are offered, particularly if they seem onerous. Check around. Today there are plenty of subprime lenders available.

How Much Extra Will It Cost for a Subprime Mortgage?

The answer depends on what category you're in. If you're a C borrower, for example, it could cost you as much as 4 or 5 percent more to get the mortgage than it will cost an A borrower. For example, a prime borrower may be paying a 7 percent interest rate. A C borrower might be asked to pay 11 or 12 percent in interest. Of course, that translates into higher monthly payments and, as a result, may mean that in order to qualify you'll have to get a smaller mortgage. But, at least, you can get a loan.

Subprime borrowers also have alternatives other than the institutional lenders we've been discussing thus far. In fact, in some cases, as with a seller, there may be no qualifying and no grading distinction at all. Following are some of these other opportunities.

Can I Assume a Mortgage?

One of the most underused techniques of getting a mortgage when you have some credit problems these days is to assume an existing mortgage. An "assumption" means that you take over the responsibility for making payments and ultimately paying back an existing mortgage. Someone else got the mortgage at some time in the past. It's currently on the home you are buying. You now take it over.

Unfortunately, assuming a mortgage in today's world is often more difficult than it sounds. The reason is that most lenders today prohibit assumptions. The mortgages contain an "alienation" or "due on sale" clause that effectively keeps you from taking them over. The minute the property is sold, the existing mortgage must be paid off in full. Thus, you can't assume it.

However, there are some mortgages that remain assumable. We'll cover three:

VA Loans.   In general, you can assume an existing VA mortgage. However, unless you're a veteran and also qualify for the mortgage, you don't really assume personal responsibility for repayment. That remains with the original borrower. If you don't make the payments and default on the mortgage is declared by the lender, you can walk away virtually free. The original vet who borrowed the money, however, will be held responsible for the VA.

For this reason, many vets won't let others assume their loan. Or if they do, they will require that the new owner sign a notice of assumption that's filed with the VA transferring responsibility for repayment. However, if you're not a qualifying vet, the VA may not go along. (See Chap. 21 for more details on VA loans.)

FHA Loans.   Some early FHA loans are still assumable. More recent loans, however, require that the new owner qualify for the mortgage as if applying for a new loan. The trick is to find one of the older, fully assumable mortgages.

ARMs.   Adjustable-rate mortgages (ARMs) are also often "assumable." However, at the time of the sale, the mortgage frequently jumps up to current interest rates, and the new buyer must qualify as if for a new loan. Hence, the value of the "assumability" is questionable.

TRAP

One of the biggest problems with assuming an existing mortgage is that it is often only a fraction of the purchase price. Typically these loans were put on the property years ago, and prices have gone up (and the mortgage gone down as it's slowly paid off) since then. As a result, the assumable loan may be only for 50 or 60 percent of the sales price.

TIP

A way around this problem is to get the seller to carry back a second mortgage for another 20, 30, or more percent of the sales price. This raises the total mortgage amount to a level where the buyer need only put 10 or 20 percent down. Further, most sellers rarely require the buyer to qualify. Thus, your subprime rating doesn't enter the picture at all!

What about Equity Financing?

This is a totally different approach to getting a mortgage. Here, you don't qualify, the property does. Equity lenders, in fact, don't care what your rating is. They typically don't even order a credit report!

What they do order is a strict appraisal of the property. Then they offer a mortgage that is typically between 60 to 70 percent of the appraised value. The interest rate may also be higher than that of a conforming prime loan, and there may be more points to pay. But if you have D credit, you can get this kind of a mortgage.

TRAP

Some equity lenders are, in reality, simply looking to acquire good real estate. They are actually hoping that you will not make the payments and default so they can foreclose and get the property. That's one of the reasons they make the interest rate high and charge more points, to make it more difficult for you to succeed.

TIP

Before securing an equity loan, do a very careful financial analysis of your situation. Make sure you really do have the wherewithal to make the payments. You don't want to put a lot of your hard-earned cash into the property only to discover later on that you can't hang on to it.

Where Can I Find an Equity Lender?

A mortgage broker may be able to recommend an equity lender, but often brokers don't handle this type of financing. Rather, check in the yellow pages of the phone book under "mortgages." Look for ads that say something like, "We don't care about your credit" or "We'll loan to anyone." That should get you headed in the right direction.

What Is an Asset-Based Mortgage?

An "asset-based" mortgage is like an equity mortgage, only it's for people who have a lot of money in the bank. You want a mortgage, but you have terrible credit or don't want anyone looking at your credit *and* you have a lot of savings. So you approach your banker and explain your situation. You ask for an asset-based mortgage. If the banker is agreeable, you get a mortgage based mainly on your savings (although the lender may also insist on a mortgage covering the property). Typically the interest rate is very low, and there may be no points at all to pay.

TRAP

Be aware that this type of mortgage ties up your savings. The bank probably won't allow you to make significant withdrawals on the asset given as security until the mortgage is either significantly paid down or paid off.

You'll get this type of mortgage primarily from banks. The bank in which you currently have your savings is the first place to look. If it's unwilling, check with other banks, indicating you'll make a substantial deposit into savings *if* they will grant the mortgage. This is an inducement few bankers can overlook.

What about Seller Financing?

Here the seller is your lender. As part of the purchase price, you ask the seller to carry back either a second mortgage (where you get an institutional loan first or do an assumption, as noted previously) or a first mortgage for the full borrowed amount. (Also see Chap. 20 for more details on how to arrange for seller financing.)

TIP

In order for the seller to be agreeable, he or she usually must have either a large equity in the home or have a home that's fully paid off. This allows the seller to carry back the mortgage paper. You probably won't be able to work this deal with sellers who only have a little equity in their property.

8

Can I Improve My Credit Rating?

Whether or not you can get a good mortgage hinges on your credit rating. Have good credit and you'll find mortgage hunting easy. Have bad credit and it becomes much more difficult.

But what if you already have some bad credit? Is there any way you can make it better? That depends on what the trouble is. It's a mistaken belief that you can have all bad credit "fixed." Companies that offer to fix or make any credit problem simply disappear, particularly if they charge you a hefty fee for doing it, could be nothing more than scams. Be wary of credit "fixers."

In this chapter we'll consider some options you may have, however, to legitimately improve your credit.

TIP

Pay your bills on time. Nothing messes up your credit quicker than late payments. Yet these often result from carelessness or forgetfulness. Keep all bills in a special spot and make it a point to pay them at least once a week. This is probably the simplest yet most effective step you can take toward preserving your good credit.

TRAP

If you find that you're unable to pay all of your bills, at least make your mortgage payment. If there's only one bill that you can pay, be sure it's your mortgage. Foreclosure and late mortgage payments are the one thing that mortgage lenders are very reluctant to forgive.

Can I Explain Away a Problem?

Yes, many times you can explain a problem, particularly if it's a good explanation. Lenders are human too, and they realize that sometimes creditworthy people get into trouble. If your explanation shows that you at least tried to solve the problem and, perhaps even more important, that the problem was isolated and isn't likely to happen again, you may very well be able to get the financing you want, even a prime mortgage.

The best way to do this is to be up front with the lender. Don't wait for the problem to surface as part of your credit report. Get it out front, and provide the lender with a clearly written letter of explanation. If you have late payments, explain why they were late. If you defaulted on a loan, give all the details and include verifying information. If you had a foreclosure, explain how it occurred and why circumstances are different now.

TIP

It's a good idea to get a copy of your own credit report in advance of applying for a mortgage. That way you get to see what the lender will see and you can prepare for it. You are allowed to obtain at least one copy of your credit report each year. You probably will want to get it from one of the big credit reporting bureaus. The cost is typically minimal, sometimes as little as $8.

Trans Union	(800) 916-8800
Experian (formerly TRW)	(800) 682-7654
Equifax	(800) 685-1111

Some Explanations a Lender Might Accept

You Were Unemployed or Sick for a Period of Time. This may be acceptable if you have a long history of excellent credit broken by a short period, say, 6 months, of poor credit, followed by another long period (at least 2 years) of good credit. This explanation is particularly helpful in explaining late payments.

You Had a Divorce or Death in the Family. Here again you normally must show that this happened some time ago, and since that time, you've had excellent credit. This is particularly useful when you defaulted on loans. You had a big setback in your life, but now you're back in the saddle, as evidenced by at least 2 years' worth of good credit history.

The Bad Credit Is Someone Else's Fault. Not a great excuse, but a plausible one. Perhaps you cosigned for someone else on a car. They ran off with the car and never made the payments. You were stuck with either making payments for 5 years on a car you didn't have and couldn't sell or simply refusing. You refused.

This shows you had the good sense to not get in debt over your head. However, it also shows that you had the bad sense to cosign for someone else. Further, given tough circumstances, instead of plodding on and making payments, you'll bail out—something that makes good sense to you but that lenders don't particularly like to see.

You Got in over Your Head. You live in California but bought property in Oklahoma just before the oil price bust of the mid 1980s. You couldn't sell or rent the property and weren't there to take care of it. Consequently, you lost it to foreclosure.

But that was years ago, and it was on rental real estate. Here and now you're trying to buy a home in which you plan to live. The circumstances are different. Maybe the lender will agree.

You Were the Victim of a Natural Disaster. A tornado destroyed not only your home but also the factory where you work. You had no place to live and no way to earn income. Naturally you had to let your house go into foreclosure. But since then, the factory's rebuilt and you're back at work. You're ready to start again buying a house.

What If the Credit Reporting Agency Made a Mistake?

I have heard reports that as many as a third of all credit reports contain an error of some kind. Often these errors can cause you to be declined for a mortgage. When that happens, you need to get out and correct that error. (This is another good reason to order your own credit report early on. You can discover if there are errors and take steps to correct them.)

Generally speaking, the best approach to take in correcting errors is to obtain proof that it is indeed an error, then write to the credit reporting agency, offering the proof and demanding the error be corrected. The credit agency must investigate your request and take action within a month or two.

The trick is getting the proof. What's usually accepted is a letter or document from the lender reporting the bad credit saying it was a mistake. Or, in the case of mistaken identity, it's a matter of presenting irrefutable evidence that you're who you are and not the other person the credit company thinks you are. Birth certificates, driver's license, escrow company ID statements, and so forth can help here.

On the other hand, sometimes the problems are just plain weird. Consider this example: I ran into an individual who sold his home and gave the buyer a second mortgage. That buyer eventually defaulted, and the seller was forced to start foreclosure on the second mortgage. To protect his interest in the property, he began making payments on the existing first mortgage. He found, however, that the property had fallen in value to the point where it wasn't worth foreclosing. So he stopped making payments on the first and simply took a complete loss on the second.

However, when the first mortgage went into foreclosure, because he had temporarily made payments on it, he was erroneously listed as a borrower, and the credit reporting agency put a foreclosure against his name. He discovered this when he applied for a new mortgage and was turned down by the lender.

To resolve this, he had to contact the lender of the first mortgage and secure an explanation from the lender. He then had to present that letter of explanation, along with all the documentation from the original second mortgage, to the new lender. Once the new lender understood the situation, his mortgage was approved.

If the borrower had first submitted summaries of all of this to the credit reporting agency, he may never have had problems with the new lender.

TIP

 The basic method of correcting bad credit is two-fold. First, you have to write a letter explaining the problem and why it wasn't your fault. Second, you have to submit documentation proving what you say.

Will the Credit Agency Correct the Mistake?

Whether the credit agency corrects the error depends on your proof. If the original lender who reported the problem now reports an error, the agency will normally remove the offending report.

On the other hand, if your proof tends to be your word against the lender's, who refuses to admit an error, it's a different story. The credit report agency is generally required to insert your letters of explanation along with the bad report and may make your substantiating documentation available to those who ask for reports.

The credit agency, however, doesn't usually take sides. In a disputed case they probably will not remove the offending incident. It will stay on your report usually for around seven years.

For more information on how to correct an error in your credit report contact:

Federal Trade Commission/Division of Credit Practices
Consumer Response Center
Room 130, 6th St. & Pennsylvania Ave., N.W.
Washington, D.C. 20580
(202 382-4357 (FTC–HELP)   http://www.FTC.Gov

TIP

Having no credit is almost as problematic as having bad credit. Check into Chap. 9 for ways to help in this situation.

9

Can I Get a Mortgage If I Don't Have Any Credit?

Having no credit is almost as bad as having terrible credit. In order to give you a mortgage, a lender has to establish your money management patterns. It does that by seeing how successfully you've paid back money that you've previously borrowed. But if you've never borrowed, the lender can't establish a pattern. And in the world of borrower profiles (explained in Chap. 6), that can leave you out in the cold.

That doesn't mean, however, that you can't otherwise establish your credit and get a mortgage. Indeed, having no credit is just an inconvenience. If you make the proper efforts, you can establish a good credit record and be years ahead of the individual who starts off with lots of bad reports.

Where Do I Begin to Establish Credit?

Begin at least 6 months but hopefully a year or more before you plan on applying for a mortgage. It will take time to establish a good credit history. It can't be done overnight.

The first thing you should do is to go to the bank where you do business (not having credit doesn't mean you don't have a checking and savings account) and apply for a debit card. As you probably know, this is like a credit card, only based on your assets in the bank. Today many banks offer these virtually automatically to their customers.

Once you have the debit card, use it frequently, establishing that you can manage such an item. Also, be scrupulous to see that you never bounce your own checks and can always cover any checks from others that you deposit. Ask your bank to establish a small line of credit to cover your checking account, just in case you should be short. This overdraft credit line is also often just an automatic service for good, long-standing customers.

Once you have an overdraft account and a debit account, ask your bank for a credit card. Almost all banks offer them. With your good standing in the bank, it should again be automatic.

Once you get that credit card, you're halfway home. Go out and charge to 75 percent of the limit. Then pay it back promptly. Pay off all your charges each month for 3 months, and you've established a great, but short, credit history.

Very shortly other credit card offers should start appearing in the mail. Apply for two others (no more, no less). Charge a few things on these and make regular monthly payments.

Now go back to your bank and ask for a noncollateral loan—a line of credit. You have your history at the bank, plus your new credit cards, plus the fact that you have no bad credit. Again, it's a slam dunk. Borrow a thousand dollars or so this way, put it in the bank, make regular payments on it, and after a few months, pay it back.

Voilà. With the exception of longevity, you have just established the rudiments of prime credit. Age means how long you've had your trade lines. That first credit card you got? Keep it. It will age, and once it's 2 years old, you've satisfied the age portion.

TRAP

Make all of your payments on time. Remember, you want to establish good credit, not bad.

What If I Need to Establish Credit Instantly?

The above plan is great *if* you've got the time to spend. But what if you want to get a mortgage right now? You don't have time to set up credit cards and installment loans. You want to buy a home, and you have to go with what you've got. Yet you have an empty credit history.

Actually, almost no one's credit history is truly empty. At worst it's usually just a case of not having thought of what to fill it with. Here are some suggestions for creating an instant credit history:

Rent Receipts.   You must have lived somewhere, and if you didn't own, you rented. If you paid rent by check, get those canceled checks. They should show a steady pattern of regular payments. Better still, get a letter from your current and previous landlord stating that you made your rent payments on time. Also have the landlord state the amount, to establish that you can handle a large monthly payment.

Utility Receipts.   You had to have electricity, water, garbage, gas, phone, and probably cable TV. You paid for these. Again, look for canceled checks. Also, call up the companies and ask them for a letter of recommendation. Many utility companies will do this almost automatically if you've had a good payment history for 1 year.

Informal Loans.   People who pay by cash often get loans from friends and family. If you paid these back on time, get your canceled checks or other receipts. Have the person sign a statement showing the amount borrowed, the term, when regular payments were made, and when it was paid back. If the person whom you borrowed it from is able to put a corporate or business name on the statement, even better.

You might need to dig into your memory for some other account that similarly can be used to help establish your credit. Dig as deeply as possible. While none of these individually is as good as a long history of credit cards with prompt repayment, they can go a long way.

Should I Consider a Cosigner?

Yes, you certainly should consider one. If you don't have the credit history, find someone who does and make them a partner. Relatives are usually opportune choices. Good friends, even business associates, are also likely candidates. Remember, you don't need the cosigner to help you with the down payment or the monthly payments. You just need their good, established credit.

TRAP

When someone cosigns with you, his or her credit is on the line. If you default, or worse, if you lose the property to foreclosure, it will reflect badly on the cosigner's credit. It will be as if that person were late on payments or lost the property. For this reason, keep in mind that most savvy people will refuse to cosign for anyone, even close relatives.

To induce another person to cosign for you, you may want to give that person an ownership position in the property. You may want the cosigner's name to appear both on the deed and on the mortgage. That way, should you for some reason stop making payments or go into foreclosure, the cosigner could step in and take over and possibly save the property. This can be a strong inducement to a reluctant cosigner.

TIP

Most lenders will want the cosigner on the mortgage in any event. So it's just a simple additional step to include the cosigner on the deed.

TRAP

Once the cosigner is on the deed, he or she can tie up the property and potentially keep you from selling. To protect your interests, you will want to have an attorney draw up an agreement specifying exactly what interests the cosigner has (none, except in the event you default), what say the cosignee has in managing or selling the property (again, presumably none, unless you have a problem), and what percent of the profit the cosigner will receive in the event the property is sold (again, presumably none). This will help protect your interests.

10

How Do I Get a Mortgage *Fast?*

Sometimes our concern is not so much with getting the mortgage as it is with getting it promptly in order that a deal can go through (or because we need the money from a refinance). Speed is the critical factor.

If you are a prime borrower (as described in the previous chapters), you may indeed be able to get a mortgage fast. In fact, today's computerized mortgage underwriting may allow you to be approved within less than an hour and to have the mortgage funded within 3 days or less! That compares with 30 to 45 days for a typical mortgage.

How Do I Qualify?

The key is that you must be a strong borrower. You must qualify for an A or, at the minimum, A− mortgage (as defined in Chap. 6). These fast mortgages are basically underwritten through the Loan Prospector program of Freddie Mac and the Desktop Underwriter and Originator program of Fannie Mae, who are the two largest underwriters in the country. If you meet their profile requirements, you may be able to get the mortgage almost immediately.

Where Do I Go to Get Started?

Call your nearest mortgage broker. Ask the broker if they handle "automated mortgage underwriting." If they don't know what you're talking about or if they say they handle everything but can't be specific about getting a loan approved by an underwriter within an hour, call elsewhere.

TIP

Also try calling a mortgage banker (look in the yellow pages) that deals directly with consumers. Many are now electronically connected and able to handle automated underwriting.

How Much Documentation Do I Need?

When you find a lender who handles automated underwriting, you'll be asked to come down to his or her office. You'll also be asked to come up with a minimum of documentation. A normal loan often requires that you get a written statement from your employer verifying your employment and telling the lender that you're likely to continue to be employed. You'll also need a statement from your bank verifying that you have the money for the down payment and the closing costs on deposit.

For the fast mortgage, however, all you really need is typically a paycheck stub, savings book showing amounts on deposit, and your last W-2 form. (You may be asked to bring a few other documents down that you're likely to have readily available.) At the office you'll fill out a standardized application with about 60 questions asking everything you can imagine about your financial condition. You will also be asked to come up with around $35 to $50 for a credit report and will have to give permission for the lender to check your credit.

After the application is filled out and you sign it, if you're at a mortgage broker's office, the broker will enter the information into a computer screen. (This is what takes most of the time.)

Once entered, the broker will send the information electronically using a modem over phone lines to a primary lender such as a mortgage banker or a bank. The lender will scan the form and make a quick judgment as to whether you will qualify as a prime borrower. The lender will also look for any questions not answered or information left off and make a call to the mortgage broker and ask for these. The lender takes care here because the next step costs money; usually the lender isn't willing to pop for the cost unless the lender feels you'll survive the scrutiny.

If the lender feels you'll qualify and the form is properly filled out, the lender then sends it via modem to either of the two big underwriters in New York. They receive it in their computers, and the computers automatically scan the application and determine whether you meet the profile they are looking for.

If you meet the profile, the computers then access the big credit reporting companies and draw out your credit report. (Remember, you paid for this up front.) It will then get a FICO number for you from Fair Isaac (see Chap. 6) and will either pass you, pass you conditionally, provided you meet certain criteria, or suggest that perhaps you might not be the appropriate candidate for a conforming loan.

In some cases the computer can also access a data bank that contains appraisals for some properties. This primarily applies to properties in the East and Midwest, which tend to remain stable in price for long periods of time and for which comparable sales are readily available. If this is possible, it can approve the property at roughly the same time it approves you.

TIP

Computerized appraisal is in its infancy. As of this writing, relatively few properties are in the data bank. Chances are you'll have to get a real-life appraiser out there to check out the home you want to buy or refinance.

If you're a "go," the computer can also open escrow, order a title search and title insurance, as well as contact an appraisal company and schedule an appraisal for you. In point of fact, how-ever, usually this is done by the primary lender and the mortgage broker.

Usually within minutes you have your answer. If it's positive, your mortgage is on the way. Most lenders can fund these auto-mated mortgages within 3 days. Some can actually do it within just a few hours.

TRAP

If you're not a prime borrower, you won't be able to take advantage of this automated electronic system. In that case, you'll have to do it the old-fashioned way, waiting for loan approval from a board of direc-tors. This typically takes up to 6 weeks, and a short time is considered around 3 weeks. As of this writ-ing, most subprime lenders simply haven't adopted the electronic automated lending described here for Fannie Mae and Freddie Mac.

What Exactly Is the Role of the Secondary Lenders?

Thus far we've managed to talk about Fannie Mae and Freddie Mac without actually spending any time explaining them. Perhaps now would be a good time to go over their function in the mortgage lending business to see how they affect you.

These are both private corporations with government connec-tions. They receive their money by selling government-backed securities. If you buy a Ginnie Mae (Government National Mortgage Association) security through your stock broker, the money you invest may eventually go to one of these corporations.

Their purpose is to facilitate mortgage loans throughout the country. They do this by "buying" loans from lenders such as banks, savings and loans, mortgage bankers (not brokers), insur-ance companies—indeed, almost anyone, including some indi-viduals. (In order to sell to these giants, you must be able to pool loans in groups of 100 or more; they don't "buy" individual mort-gages.)

The purpose of the underwriting they do is to help lenders get a feeling for which loans are acceptable. A mortgage banker wants to know, for example, that Freddie Mac will actually buy all of the 100 mortgages it is planning to "sell." It gets this assurance by sending the applicant (you) through underwriting first, before actually loaning you the money.

How Are Mortgages Bought and Sold?

When I say Fannie Mae "buys," what I mean is that after the primary lender gives you the money with which to make your purchase or refinance, the primary lender holds a piece of paper— the mortgage loan document—on which you've agreed to repay. It transfers ownership of this paper to Fannie Mae, for example, in exchange for almost all of the money it loaned to you. Now it has most of its money back and can go out and make more loans.

Actually, the primary lender keeps a few percentage points of the mortgage (perhaps as much as 5 percent) in many cases and receives interest on this money. In addition, it usually "services" the loan, meaning it collects the payments from you, for which Fannie Mae pays it a fee. That's how the primary mortgage lender makes its profit.

If you would like more information obtaining a fast mortgage, check out *How to Get an Instant Mortgage* by Robert Irwin and David L. Ganz, (New York: John Wiley and Sons, 1997).

11

How Do I Get a Mortgage If I'm Self-employed?

Self-employed people are automatically suspect by lenders for two reasons. First, it's difficult to get documents that spell out a self-employed person's true income. Second, lenders worry that in their eagerness to get financing, the self-employed may be less than completely honest on those documents that are used (such as 1040 tax returns). Less than forthright answers can be very difficult to detect.

On the other hand, with a salaried individual, a pay stub or a letter from an employer will usually suffice. After all, that employer (presumably a disinterested third party) is usually handling tax withholding and paying social security taxes; hence, the chances of false statements on salary forms are greatly reduced.

All of which means that those who are self-employed have a much more difficult time getting a mortgage.

How Do I Prove My Income
If I'm Self-employed?

The answer has traditionally been to submit 2 years of federal 1040 income tax returns. These returns show on Schedule C the income and expenses of the self-employed person, as well as the bottom-line take-home pay.

TIP

While you may only be asked for 2 years of tax returns, the lender is looking to see that you've been self-employed for many, many years to show that you are successful in your business endeavor. The longer you can show you were successfully self-employed in the same field, the better.

The problem with showing tax returns, however, is that often they don't reflect the true income of the self-employed. For example, there's the matter of SEP-IRAs or Keogh plans. Money placed into these areas is subtracted from the borrower's taxable income. However, most lenders are adept at adding back these amounts, so the problem is largely one of perception rather than reality.

A more real problem, however, is the fact that some self-employed individuals actually take home a great deal more than their tax returns show. This is particularly the case in cash businesses.

But even where all income is declared, it may be reduced significantly by items such as depreciation on equipment or a home office that appears primarily on paper, not in reality. Lenders really can't add back in depreciation and home office expenses, since they are counted as expense items. So what is a self-employed individual to do when he or she can't demonstrate enough income to qualify for a mortgage, even though he or she actually has sufficient income?

Until fairly recently there really wasn't a good answer here. However, in the past few years "no-doc" mortgages have come into existence. They have solved a lot of problems for the self-employed.

TRAP

In desperation to get financing, don't be tempted to submit a false tax return to a lender. While the lender may accept it initially and even issue a mortgage based on it, that tax return stays with your mortgage file forever. If you ever default on the mortgage, the tax return will be dragged up, and you may have to get proof from the IRS that it was authentic. Not being able to do so could be considered fraud in applying for a federally regulated mortgage and could result in severe criminal penalties. Further, today many lenders are connected directly to IRS files and can electronically call up your tax return.

What Are No-Doc and Lo-Doc Mortgages?

No-doc loans simply do not require any documentation at all. There are no verifications from employers or banks. No 2 or 3 years of tax returns. In some cases there aren't even any credit reports!

Instead, there is simply a statement that the borrower signs that says, upon penalty of perjury, he or she made as much money as was claimed. Based on that statement, a mortgage is issued.

Of course, there is a catch...several catches. The three big ones are as follows:

- This mortgage often carries a higher interest rate, often one or two points higher than market.
- The borrower may be required to put more money down (25 percent) instead of the usual 10 or 20 percent.
- There may be more points to pay than for a documented mortgage.

Further, if the borrower later defaults and it turns out that false statements were originally made, the penalties could be severe. It's not something to take lightly.

Nevertheless, especially for the self-employed individual who has trouble showing as much income as he or she actually makes, this type of mortgage can be a godsend. It provides the opportunity to get a mortgage to buy a home simply on a signature.

Unfortunately, while the first wave of no-doc loans were issued with relative abandon a few years ago, a large number of them went into default during the real estate recession of the early 1990s, and the entire process fell into disfavor. If you want a no-doc loan today, you may have to spend quite a bit of time searching for a mortgage broker who handles it. On the other hand, "lo-doc" loans are more plentiful today and require minimal documentation, such as a credit report and bank deposit statement.

TIP

Don't aim for a no-document mortgage. A documented mortgage will usually provide a lower interest rate, lower costs, and a lesser down payment. Even if you are self-employed and cannot show on tax returns as much income as you feel you make, you may still be able to put enough paperwork together to get a good documented mortgage.

Other Alternatives for the Self-employed

If you bank regularly with a particular institution, contact them. For a good depositor, they may be willing to make exceptions. I have a friend who was recently in this situation. He went to his local small bank, where he did over $2 million a year in business, and asked for a $300,000 home loan. When he couldn't come up with the required documentation, the bank turned him down, whereupon he notified the bank president that he was turning the bank down by taking his business elsewhere.

Talk about a turnaround. His mortgage was funded within the week!

12

How Much Should I Pay in Mortgage Costs?

There are almost always costs when obtaining a mortgage. In some cases the lender will absorb some (or even all) of those costs, as in 0-points mortgages, discussed in Chap. 15. But in most cases, you will need to pay these costs out of pocket, and they will be in addition to whatever you put as a down payment.

Unfortunately, over the last few years as interest rates have fallen, some lenders and/or their retailers have added unwarranted charges to the fees for obtaining a mortgage. These costs do not benefit you but instead go toward the lender's or the retailer's bottom line. In this chapter we will examine the various closing costs you may be asked to pay and try to separate the chaff from the wheat.

Is There Any Government Protection for Me?

In 1974 Congress passed the Real Estate Settlement Procedures Act (RESPA). This act grew out of the many abuses that some lenders had perpetrated on home buyers/borrowers. RESPA requires specific disclosures from lenders at different times. It also works to prevent lenders from getting kickbacks from other parties to a transaction.

Your first contact with RESPA will be when you fill out an application for a home mortgage with a lender. The lender is required by RESPA to provide you with a "good faith estimate" of the costs involved in closing the deal, the settlement costs. This estimate must be delivered or mailed to you within 3 working days of receiving your loan application.

What Is a Good Faith Estimate?

A good faith estimate should include all of the costs that can be estimated by the lender. These include points and other fees but do not include prorations for taxes and insurance, which cannot be calculated until the close of escrow. The estimate should include the annual percentage rate (APR), which is the true interest rate you will be paying for the mortgage.

TIP

Be aware that these are only estimates. Your actual costs will not be known until the close of escrow.

TRAP

The APR will usually be different from the quoted rate for the mortgage. Don't be misled by this. The APR takes into account most of the costs, including points, that go into your interest rate. The stated interest rate of the mortgage is just that. The APR is what your effective interest rate will be.

The whole point of the good faith estimate is to allow you some time to shop around. Since it is given so soon after you make the application, you should have time to reject that lender and find another, should you choose to do so. The lender is obligated to attempt to hold to the terms listed in the good faith estimate when the final documents are drawn.

What Other Disclosures Will I Be Given?

Generally speaking, there are two other disclosures. The first indicates whether or not the lender you are dealing with will actually be the one to service your loan (collect the money). Oftentimes lenders will sell the rights to service the loan to other companies. In most cases this won't have much effect on you.

The other disclosure is the "affiliates" disclosure. Pay attention to this. A lender or a broker may refer you to someone else, such as an escrow or title insurance company, to handle the closing of your deal. If this is the case, then you are required to be given an "affiliated business arrangement disclosure." This form lets you know that in most cases you are not required to go with the lender (or broker's recommendation) but may shop around on your own for the best deal.

TIP

In some states the seller may not compel the buyer to use a particular closing agent as a condition of the sale. This enhances your opportunities to search for the best price.

When Will I Know What the Actual Closing Costs Will Be?

You will have to wait awhile to learn the closing cost. RESPA doesn't require that you be given a statement (called a HUD-1 document) until closing. However, on that statement will be listed all the services and fees provided to you. It's your chance to see what you're being charged for.

TRAP

The lender doesn't have to provide you with the statement until closing or in some cases, 1 day before closing. If you do not have a formal closing (where you meet with an escrow officer and sign all the loan documents), then the lender may not have to provide you with the HUD-1 statement until after the loan has closed. Unfortunately, by then it's usually too late to do anything about an error or an overcharge.

TIP

One of the worst feelings is to walk into an escrow company to sign documents only to discover that the mortgage isn't as it should be. You can avoid this problem by demanding that the lender or the person handling the closing show you the HUD-1 settlement statement *1 business day before the closing.* Granted, 1 business day is not a whole lot of time. But if there is something significantly wrong, it does give you time to alert your agent or attorney and, if necessary, to hold up the close of escrow.

What Can I Do If I Find Something Wrong?

By the time you're ready to close escrow, you are going to find it very difficult to hold up the deal for a small problem (such as an unwarranted cost) with the loan. To do so might jeopardize the entire transaction with the seller. In other words, at this point it's probably too late to argue about a cost that you think is unfair. (That should be done when you are given your good faith estimate, which we'll discuss shortly).

What you can argue about, however, is a cost that appears on your settlement statement that did not appear on your good faith estimate (exclusive of prorations). If you think there is an unjustified cost here, let the lender, agents, attorneys, and everyone else know. You can be sure that every attempt will be made to explain the cost to you, and it may turn out to be perfectly justified. Or it may turn out to be a mistake or something else.

When Should I Check Out the Costs?

You should check the costs out when you are given your good faith estimate, within 3 days of filling out a mortgage application. The chances are very good that all of the costs, warranted and not, will be listed here. If you're going to argue about them, now's the time to do it.

But, you may wonder, how can I complain? The lender represents a giant institution. It sets the rules by which the game is played.

Not necessarily. Keep in mind that the lender wants your business. Point out a fee you think is completely unjustified, and if the loan broker or other loan officer you are dealing with can't justify it to your satisfaction, it may be taken off. The lender knows which fees are justified and which aren't. You complain about an unjustified fee, and it might get removed. (Unfortunately, in an active market where borrowers are plentiful, it seldom is removed.)

Or, you can walk away. If you don't like the fees the lender is charging, find a new lender. The power of choice is ultimately your best weapon.

What Are Typical Mortgage Settlement Costs?

Here, then, are your typical mortgage settlement costs.

Appraisal Fee

The lender sends out an appraiser to give a written estimate of the property's value. This estimated value is what the mortgage is based upon. The cost of the appraisal will vary enormously. It might be as inexpensive as $125 and as costly as $350. However, since the lender picks the appraiser and sets the charge, your only two choices are to pay it or get a different lender.

TIP

An appraisal is a necessary part of the mortgage lending process, and you will be told that it is customary for the borrower to pay for it. That's true. However, there is nothing to keep the lender from absorbing this cost, if it wants to. In a tight market with lots of lenders and few borrowers, some lenders will offer free appraisals. It's something to shop for.

Assumption Fee

If you are assuming an existing mortgage, the lender will probably charge a fee for handling the paperwork. This fee is usually around $100 minimum.

Attorney's Fees

If you have an attorney, you can expect to be charged a fee. However, if the lender has an attorney, you may be also charged a separate fee.

There is no reason you should have to pay for the lender's attorney. This should be a cost of doing business for the lender. You may want to challenge this fee.

Commission

Paid to the real estate agent, this shouldn't normally appear on the buyer's estimate-of-cost sheet. It could, however, show up if you used a buyer's agent or agreed to pay part of the seller's agent's fee.

Credit Report Fee

This fee is the lender's charges for a credit report and usually is under $50, often $25 to $35. It is a normal and customary fee. You have to pay it, unless the lender agrees to absorb the cost, which some highly competitive lenders do.

Discount Points

This is a one-time charge. Each point is equal to 1 percent of the loan. Points are used to adjust the yield of the mortgage to correspond to market conditions.

TRAP

Some lenders charge points as a way of confusing you, the borrower, as to the actual interest rate you are paying. You think you are getting a low interest rate mortgage. But, when the points are added in, you may be paying above market! Your best bet is to shop around. Find the lowest rate with the lowest points.

Document Preparation

The escrow company will usually charge a fee, often under $50, for the preparation of documents such as the deed. However, some lenders will also charge an additional document preparation fee for preparing the deed of trust or mortgage. I have seen these fees range from $35 to $300.

This fee makes no sense at all to me. If the lender is giving you a mortgage, it should be a cost of business to prepare the mortgage document. I always challenge this fee.

Escrow Charges

The "escrow" is an independent third party who accepts all the monies, gets the deed prepared, and then actually handles the closing of the transaction. In the Midwest and West there are actual escrow companies (often the same company that issues the title insurance) that handle this. On the East Coast in some states this function is performed by an attorney. There are often many fees associated with this service.

Again, shop around. You normally aren't bound to use any particular escrow company that a lender recommends. You can use the one that gives you the best price.

Fire Insurance

You will be required to provide a fire and hazard insurance policy to protect the lender. Typically you must pay for these policies at least 1 year in advance into escrow. However, the policies are written for 3 years, and some insurers require all 3 years paid in advance. Check with your insurance agent.

Impounds

If your mortgage was for more than 80 percent loan to value ratio, you will probably be required to impound taxes and insurance. Setting up this account requires a "cushion." What this means is that the lender will collect a portion of the money for taxes and insurance from you in advance and then pay them when due. The lender should collect a couple of months of insurance and taxes in order to get this account started.

TRAP

In the past some lenders collected as much as 6 to 12 months' worth of payments in advance, then put the money into their own account and received interest on it. This practice was halted when RESPA required the lenders to collect **no more than 2 months'** worth of insurance and taxes for the impound account.

Also, be aware that some lenders charge a separate fee for setting up the impound account and yet another fee for administering it. These last two, to my way of thinking, are totally unjustified.

TIP

If your mortgage is for 80 percent loan to value ratio or less, you can ask that instead of an impound account, you be allowed to pay your own taxes and insurance. The lender usually will do this, unless there is some sort of problem (such as you have a bad history of managing such monies). If you handle the taxes and insurance yourself, you will have a much lower monthly payment. **But** you will have to come up with lump-sum monies to pay for taxes and insurance at different times during the year. If you opt for this, be aware of your saving and budgeting habits. It only works if you're able to save the money on your own to pay taxes and insurance when they come due.

Interest

You will be obligated to pay the interest from the date of the closing to the first monthly payment.

TIP

Unlike rent, interest on a mortgage is paid in arrears. Thus, if you can arrange to have the escrow close on the last day of the month, the next payment won't be due until the first day of the month after next. This means you won't have to pay any interest into escrow, and you'll have a whole month before your first payment comes due.

Lender's Title Insurance

Most lenders will require a separate, more comprehensive, and more expensive policy of title insurance. This is frequently required because of underwriting. You'll simply have to pay it.

Mortgage Insurance Premium

For an FHA loan, this has to be paid all in advance into escrow. For private mortgage insurance, the amount may be for several months in advance to cover the payment in the event you default on the mortgage.

Origination Fee

This is a charge to cover the lender's administrative costs in processing a loan. It is standard with FHA government-insured loans. With conventional loans it is often expressed as a few hundred dollars plus points. For example, a particular mortgage might be two points plus $350. The $350 is the origination fee. It goes to pay a mortgage banker or a loan officer for processing the loan.

To my way of thinking there is no justification for this fee. The lender is getting the interest—that should be sufficient. If there are other administrative costs, the final lender should advance these, and the interest rate should be adjusted accordingly. However, almost all lenders do squeeze in a few hundred dollars as a way of milking you of additional money when obtaining a mortgage.

TIP

If the fee is under $350 and if it's a good mortgage, you may be just as well off paying it. On the other hand, if it's higher, then you will certainly want to shop elsewhere.

Title Insurance

In most cases you will want title insurance in order to protect your title. I would never buy property without title insurance. The fees for this insurance vary slightly. Remember, in most cases you don't have to go with the title insurance company the lender may recommend. Check around for the best rates.

In addition to the costs listed in this chapter, there could be additional charges that may or may not be reasonable. You'll have to use common sense here or check with your real estate attorney. The time to challenge lender's fee is when you first get your good faith estimate. If you don't like a fee, ask the lender about it. If the explanation isn't adequate, ask that the fee be removed. If the lender refuses, consider finding a different lender.

What about a Prepayment Penalty?

A prepayment penalty is just what it sounds like. It's a penalty for paying off a mortgage earlier than its due date. The payment amount varies, but sometimes it can be substantial, running into the many thousands of dollars. You may want to check the documentation of your mortgage to see if it includes a prepayment.

As a buyer, prepayment comes into play because today most mortgages do not include it. As an enticement to include a prepayment clause, lenders will sometimes offer a cash incentive, typically anywhere between $500 and $2500 when the mortgage is made. Accept the cash and have a penalty for paying off the mortgage early.

TIP

If you're quite sure you're going to live in the property a long time, it may make financial sense to accept a prepayment penalty for which the lender offers a cash payment. After all, you'll be getting the cash for nothing. Just be sure that there's a time limit on the prepayment penalty, typically 5 to 10 years. After that, there should be no penalty. Also, keep in mind that if your plans change, it could cost you money.

TRAP

The money bonus offered by lenders is often much smaller than the penalty. For example, if you're offered $1000, the penalty could be $2500 if you pay off the mortgage anytime in the first 5 years. If your plans change or if you plan to sell the property or refinance, accepting this offer probably would make little sense for you.

Unfortunately, most people don't check until they're ready to close escrow on a sale or refinance. By then it may be too late.

Check out your mortgage documents, if you're not sure, before you put your house up for sale or before you begin the refinancing procedure. A hefty prepayment penalty may lead to a change in your plans.

What If I Want to Complain about a Lender?

At any time, you can complain about lender's actions directly to HUD, which administers RESPA. You should be aware, however, that HUD, rather than look closely at individual complaints, tends to investigate those lenders who have had a whole battery of complaints leveled against them.

If you want to complain, write out a statement of the problem and include copies of all supporting documents. Send them to the following:

U.S. Dept. of Housing and Urban
  Director
Office of Insured Single Family
  Housing
Attention: RESPA
451 Seventh St. S.W.
Washington, D.C. 20410

Also check to see if there are any agencies at the state level that likewise supervise lenders. You may have an even better chance of getting help there.

A Great Booklet to Check Out

HUD also prepares an excellent booklet, "Buying Your Home—Settlement Costs and Other Information." It is available from HUD or may be downloaded (in a variety of formats) from HUD's Web site:

www.hud/gov/fha/res/stcosmsw.bin

It is the best-prepared booklet on settlement costs that I've ever seen.

13

ARMs, 7/30s, Buy-downs, and Convertibles

Getting Lower Payments

You can always reduce your mortgage payment by increasing your down payment. Of course, almost no one wants to do that, and few people can afford it. So, the real question becomes, how do I get the lender to lower the payment?

There are two factors influencing the monthly payment (besides the size of the mortgage): the interest rate and the term. In this chapter we'll look at four methods of reducing the monthly payment by manipulating either the term or the interest rate. Each has advantages and disadvantages, as we'll see. The methods are as follows:

- *Using a balloon payment*
- *Getting a buy-down*
- *Getting an adjustable rate mortgage (ARM)*
- *Using a convertible mortgage*

What Is a Balloon Mortgage?

A "balloon" in real estate finance is nothing more than one payment of a mortgage (usually, but not always, the last) that is bigger than any of the others. The balloon payment has been talked about so much (often erroneously) in the general press that it has achieved legendary proportions. However, there is nothing wrong with a balloon mortgage, as long as you, the borrower, understand it and know when that one payment is coming. In truth, the balloon payment is nothing more than a financial device that can be of benefit to the borrower. It's simply a matter of understanding when and how to use it.

TRAP

Be aware that many mortgages with balloon payments *do not explicitly* **state this fact.** Rather, the mortgage might be written in such a way that it only specifies interest and term. It leaves it up to you to figure out whether or not a balloon is involved. Ask your lender, your agent, and your attorney if you're not sure.

What Are 5/30, 7/30, or 10/30 Mortgages?

Keep in mind that any mortgage can have a balloon payment; it depends simply on the way it's written. One of the most popular mortgages as of this writing is the 7/30. In this mortgage, the payments are amortized (paid out) over 30 years. However, the entire mortgage is due in 7 years. In other words, there is a balloon of all the unpaid balance at payment number 84.

The purpose of this mortgage is to give you a lower monthly payment. This is possible because, from the lender's perspective, this mortgage is actually a 7-year loan (you owe the balance in 7 years). The relatively short term affords the lender less risk over time than a 30-year payback and, thus, you get a lower interest rate and payment.

TIP

Varieties of this mortgage offer payoffs at years 3, 5, 10, and 15. These are known as 3/30, 5/30, 10/30, and 15/30 mortgages. The shorter the payoff term, the lower the interest rate.

For example, on a straight 30-year mortgage for $100,000, the interest rate might be 7.5 percent. However, on a 7-year mortgage, since the exposure for the lender is much shorter, the interest rate might only be 7 percent. (The actual spread will vary depending on market conditions and the lender's goals.) The difference in payments can be significant:

30-year mortgage at 7.5%   = $699
30-year mortgage due in 7 at 7%   = $665

You save $34 a month. Keep in mind that if the entire mortgage were to be amortized (paid off in equal payments) in just 7 years (no 30-year amortization), the monthly payment would jump to $1324.

TRAP

Be sure you're clear about what a 7/30 mortgage really is. It's a 30-year loan with a balloon payment at year 7. That means you need to come up with cash at the end of 7 years either by refinancing or by selling the property.

TIP

Don't assume you can always refinance when the balloon payment comes due. Your financial condition may be far different 7 years from now. There could be a recession, and you may have lost your job. You may not quality for a new mortgage, and if you couldn't refinance the balloon, you could lose the house to foreclosure. Always insist that the 7/30 have a rollover clause. This means that at the end of the 7 years, it automatically rolls over into another mortgage, typically an ugly adjustable-rate mortgage (explained later in this chapter) with a high interest rate. Never mind about the type of mortgage. You just want to be sure that should your financial situation change, you can always get some kind of loan to protect your home.

What Is a Buy-down?

The buy-down is not so much a particular kind of mortgage as it is a tool that can be used with any kind of mortgage (with the lender's cooperation) to lower your *initial* monthly payments.

In a buy-down you end up with a lower interest rate for the first years of the mortgage. A typical buy-down is a 3/2/1 (Table 13-1). Here, the first year your interest rate is 3 percent below market, the second year it is 2 percent below, and the last year it is 1 percent lower. Your monthly payments are correspondingly lower as well.

Who Gets Charged for the Buy-down?

It's important to understand that in a buy-down there is no money that is actually saved. The lender still collects the full interest rate. The only difference is that instead of it being paid monthly, it is paid in advance.

Table 13-1. Buy-down Example

$100,000 @ 11 percent for 30 years: 3/2/1 buy-down

	Interest rate, %	Monthly payment, $
Year 1	8	734
Year 2	9	805
Year 3	10	878
Year 4–30	11	952

In order to get a buy-down, someone must pay a willing lender additional points up front. The more points that are paid up front, the bigger the buy-down. (The actual number of points required to lower the interest rate 1 percent per year will vary with market conditions. Check with your lender.)

The most common example of a buy-down occurs when you are buying a brand-new home from a builder. The builder may advertise, for example, "5 percent interest for the first 5 years." That, of course, is an extremely shocking advertisement in an era when 7 percent mortgages are exceptionally low. It is almost guaranteed to get buyers flocking to the builder trying to buy those properties.

But how does the builder really offer such a low interest rate mortgage? Is that builder somehow tied into an exceptionally altruistic lender? Of course not. Here's what happens: The builder goes to a lender and negotiates a mortgage for the buyers. The builder gives the lender a certain number of points up front, perhaps five or more. In addition, the lender may require an adjustable or higher-than-market fixed-interest rate after the first 5 years. The builder has paid the lender to lower the interest rate. The actual interest rate on the mortgage may be 7 percent. But the builder has "bought down" the rate on the first 5 years to 5 percent.

Of course, the money has to come from some place. Consequently, you, as the buyer of the home, can expect to pay a higher price. (Of course, in a cold market, the builder may be taking a sizable amount of the cost out of its would-be profits.)

TIP

What's important to understand is that the buy-down does not mean that the mortgage costs less. It only means that someone has paid the lender to lower the interest rate so you can get a lower monthly payment.

TRAP

Money is money to the builder. If you would rather have a lower price and a current rate monthly payment, almost any builder will convert the buy-down to a lower sales price. Be sure that you calculate what is best for your own particular situation. You may find that you'd rather have a lower monthly payment than a lower-priced home.

What Are the Types of Buy-downs?

The types of buy-downs are limited only by your imagination. We have already looked at the 3/2/1, as well as where the interest rate is kept artificially low for a period of years. You can tailor-make a buy-down to suit your particular needs. You can have a 1/1/1/1 (1 percent lower for 4 years) or a 2/3/1 (2 percent lower the first year, then 3 percent, then 1 percent). All you need to do is to get a lender to go along.

Lenders are limited only by their ability to resell the mortgage in the secondary market (and their own conservativeness). If you are a truly qualified buyer, a creative lender should be able to calculate out the points needed to buy down any amount for any mortgage.

TIP

Anyone can buy down a mortgage: you, the builder, or a reseller. It just depends on who is willing to pay the points.

What Is an Adjustable-Rate Mortgage?

In the beginning there was the fixed-rate mortgage. This simply meant that the interest rate remained the same for the life of the loan. If your initial interest rate was 8 percent, you paid 8 percent in year 7, in year 15, in year 22, and in year 30. The rate never changed. The fixed-rate mortgage is easy to understand. It makes sense. It's what made residential real estate so widely owned and so popular in this country.

Adjustable-rate mortgages, or ARMs, are different. Here the interest rate charged to the borrower fluctuates roughly in response to the cost of funds for the lender. Your monthly payment could, for example, be low when you get the loan, higher a year later, and much higher a few years after that. The reason the monthly payment would go up (or go down) would be that the interest rate charged on the loan might go up (or down).

Perhaps an example will clarify just how an adjustable-rate mortgage actually works. Let's say we obtain a mortgage of $100,000 at 8 percent interest per year for 30 years. If this is a fixed-rate loan, our interest will remain at 8 percent for the full 30-year term. Also, our monthly payment will remain at a fixed $734.

On the other hand, if this is an ARM, our interest rate may fluctuate up (for example, up to a maximum of 12 percent) or down (for example, down to minimum of 4 percent) over the term of the loan. With an ARM the interest rate charged is adjusted up or down at regular intervals. Similarly, our payments may fluctuate widely—in this case, between $367 and $1023.

What's the Big Advantage?

It's simple. In order to induce borrowers to take out an ARM, lenders offer a lower-than-market initial starting rate (called a "teaser" and discussed in detail in the next chapter). The corresponding payments are lower. Thus, if you can't qualify for a fixed-rate loan, you might very well be able to qualify for the same mortgage if it were adjustable with lower initial payments.

TRAP

The big plus of a fixed-rate mortgage is that we always know where we stand. Our payments don't vary. On the other hand, the big plus of an ARM is that, at least initially, the payments are always lower than for a fixed-rate mortgage.

Besides a low initial teaser rate, ARMS also have the advantage of always being available. In times of volatile interest rates, such as back between 1978 and 1982, lenders such as savings and loan associations and banks were afraid to lend money long term. They didn't want to commit themselves to a 30-year real estate loan when they had no idea where interest rates would be even 6 months into the future.

Thus, while lenders were quoting fixed rates of 17 percent (to protect themselves), they were also quoting ARMs of 12 percent. They felt comfortable with the ARM because they knew that if interest rates in general rose, the rate on the ARM would also rise. Thus, when fixed-rate loans are difficult or impossible to find, ARMs are usually plentiful. For detailed information on ARMs see Chap. 14.

What's a Convertible Mortgage?

A convertible mortgage is something like a convertible car. With a convertible car you have two different models. You can have the top up and, thus, drive a conventional automobile. Or you can lower the roof and have a sporty open-air vehicle.

A convertible mortgage also has two modes. In one mode it is a staid conventional type of loan. In the other it has sporty adjustable rate features.

The convertible mortgage blends adjustable and fixed features. You can get the big advantage of the adjustable-rate mortgage, lower initial interest rate, but you can also achieve increased stability over the life of the mortgage. For the lender, the convertible is a compromise. It doesn't lock the lender into a long-term fixed rate, which could be catastrophic if interest rates rise. On the other hand, it doesn't give the lender quite as much protection against volatility as the straight adjustable-rate mortgage.

TIP

Convertible mortgages are some of the better mortgages available for borrowers. However, you have to shop carefully, since they come in all sizes and shapes, and some can be quite ugly.

How Does a Convertible Mortgage Work?

A convertible mortgage is really like two mortgages packaged together. In one popular form, you start out with an adjustable rate. Then, after a preset number of years, you are given the option of converting to a fixed mortgage (at the current market rates).

For example, you might have an adjustable rate mortgage with a low initial rate. It would be like any other ARM except that at, perhaps, year 3, you could convert it to a fixed mortgage at the then-current market rate, at your option. Of course, you might have to pay a "conversion fee" to do this.

Once again, the big advantage of a convertible is that it's a way to get a lower interest rate and, thus, a lower monthly payment. The lender gives a lower rate because the mortgage is adjustable. Yet you get the opportunity to convert to a fixed-rate mortgage later on. Most lenders offer convertible mortgages of one sort or another.

TRAP

Be sure you understand how and when the conversion operates. In some mortgages you only have a small window of opportunity to convert, say, between years 4 and 5. Further, if interest rates happen to be high during the conversion window, you won't want to convert . . . and you'll lose your opportunity after the window; the loan then usually remains an ARM for the rest of its life.

TIP

The value of a convertible loan comes from your ability to convert it to a fixed rate at some time in the future. If the conversion window happens to be

during a period of lower interest rates, you can get
into a fixed mortgage for very little in costs.

In this chapter we've looked at four different methods of cutting your mortgage payment. Of them, the ARM is probably the
most sophisticated mortgage in the marketplace. We'll examine it
in more detail in the next chapter.

14

Traps in an Adjustable Rate Mortgage

Don't get me wrong . . . when you need an adjustable-rate mortgage, it can be a lifesaver. Perhaps you can't qualify for a fixed-rate mortgage. Or you want lower payments initially. Or interest rates are high, and you literally can't get a fixed-rate loan (as happened in the early 1980s). An ARM may very well be the best choice for you under those circumstances. However, given low interest rates and the ready availability of mortgage money, I'll take a fixed rate over an ARM every time.

TIP

Interest rates fluctuate up and down. The best time to get an ARM is usually when interest rates are high. That way, when they fall in the future, your payments are likely to go down. The worst time to get an ARM is when interest rates are low. You are almost guaranteed of higher payments as interest rates rise in the future.

ARMs can provide many benefits to you, but unless you truly

understand how they work, they can also result in trapping you into terms you might not be able to live with. In this chapter we'll look at the ARM, both pro and con. And we'll try to figure out if it's really for you.

What's the Teaser Rate?

To induce borrowers to go with their ARM, lenders usually offer a "teaser." When a borrower asks how much the ARM's interest rate is, he or she is usually told the teaser rate, which may be as much as 3 points less than the current market rate. For example, the teaser rate may be 5 percent, while the market rate for fixed mortgages is 8 percent. This is usually quite an inducement to borrowers to consider the ARM.

Typical Arm

Current market rate	8%
Teaser	5%

In point of fact, if an ARM offered the same interest rate as a fixed loan, few people would opt for it. The only way to get most people to go for the ARM is to induce them with the teaser.

Of course, lenders don't conceal the truth. If you apply for the ARM, you will be told what the true APR (annual percentage rate) is. This is a combination of the teaser rate and the current market rate. In the preceding loan, it would probably be around 7.5 percent, depending on other factors.

TRAP

Teaser rates do not reflect what you will be paying in monthly payments after only a short while. Typically it lasts only a few months, then the payments swiftly increase. Some borrowers think (regardless of what lenders may say) that if interest rates go down on an ARM, their payments automatically will likewise go down. This may not be the case for your ARM. If you get a low teaser rate, you are already paying substantially below market interest. The market rate would have to go down to below your teaser rate just for your payments to remain constant. If the market rate goes down, but not as far as your teaser, your payments still have to rise. If the market rate stays the same, your payments have to rise even more.

TIP

If you are going to hold the property for only a very short time, an ARM with a good teaser may be the better loan for you. You'll benefit from the low teaser rate, and then you will sell the property before the ARM's interest rate (and payment) rises. Just be sure that your teaser rate lasts at least through your period of ownership.

Keep in mind that the teaser is temporary. It will change in time, often in a very short time.

Beware of Underqualifying because of Teasers

The worst-case scenario comes about when we are underqualified for a mortgage because of the teaser rate. Lenders in the past have qualified borrowers, not on the market interest rate of the mortgage, but rather on the basis of the lower teaser rate. It's much easier to qualify at the lower interest rate and payments. The unfortunate result was that borrowers frequently got into trouble as soon as the mortgage rate and payments went up.

In the ARM market today, however, most lenders are refusing to qualify borrowers at the teaser rate. However, they are not qualifying them at the current market rate either. Many use a complex formula that qualifies them somewhere in between.

Be sure you understand how your lender is qualifying you. And be sure you can truly afford the mortgage before you get it.

TIP

Be sure to ask your lender, "What will my monthly payment be once the teaser rate is gone?" Can you live with it?

What's the Index?

Each ARM is tied to an index that reflects the cost of borrowing money. The interest rate on your mortgage goes up or down, as does the index it's tied to. You often have a choice on which index to use. That's an important decision.

The most commonly used indices are as follows:

A. Cost of funds for the lender

B. 6-month T-bill

C. 1-year treasury yields

D. 3-year treasury yields

E. Prime rate

F. Average cost of fixed-rate mortgages

G. Libor (London Interbranch rate)

TIP

Lenders want their ARMS tied to indices that record volatility in the market. You, on the other hand, usually want your ARM tied to an index that moves slowly, if at all, so your rate and monthly payment stay fairly constant. Finding the right index is often one of the most important decisions when selecting an ARM.

Here's an explanation of what each of these different indices cover.

Cost of Funds Index. Compiled by the Federal Home Loan Bank Board, this index gives the average interest rate that member banks and savings and loan associations paid during the previous period. It is reported monthly and by district. It represents the cost to members (banks and savings and loans) of money if they have to borrow from the government.

10-Year History. Stable, less dramatic movements up and down. Most commonly used is the 11th district cost of funds index.

Treasury Securities Index. Published weekly by the Federal Reserve Board, this index gives the constant maturity interest rate for treasury securities. This is the interest rate that investors pay to buy these government debts.

10-Year History

> *6-month T-bill.* Tends to be the most volatile of indices; most closely reflects current market money conditions. Based on the weekly auction rates.
>
> *1-year T-bill.* Also volatile. Based on the weekly average of daily yields of actively traded 1-year T-bills.
>
> *3- to 5-year T-bills.* Similarly volatile. Based on constant maturities.

Prime Rate Index. This is the best rate that banks charge their best customers for short-term borrowing. The rate often will vary by as much as half a point between lenders; therefore, when used as an index, the composite prime rate as reported in the *Wall Street Journal* is usually given.

10-Year History. Relatively stable; moves up or down in fairly large increments.

Average Mortgage Rate. This index is composed of the average interest rate for newly originated fixed- and adjustable-rate conventional mortgages of previously occupied homes for major lenders. It is published monthly and is probably the most accurate assessment of mortgage interest changes.

10-Year History. Very stable, particularly in the last few years. One of the least volatile measures.

Libor Rate. Almost no one outside of the lending industry has heard of the London Interbranch index. Yet it is one of the oldest. It also tends to be one of the most stable and the lowest. Some lenders give you this option.

10-Year History. Quite stable.

TIP

When a lender offers you an index, the lender is required to show you the history of the index going back several years. Just be sure that the index history covers the most volatile interest rate period of 1978 to 1982. Those years will tell you more than any others what this index is likely to do if and when interest rates skyrocket.

How Do I Decide Which Index to Use?

Some lenders give you a choice. If they don't, you can shop lenders until you find one who uses an index you want. Generally speaking, most borrowers want to pick a lender and an index that shows stability over time.

Be careful, however. An index that is volatile but is down when you apply may give you a better beginning interest rate than an index that is stable but stays up.

TIP

If you plan to keep the mortgage a long time, go for the index that is most stable. If you plan to keep the mortgage a short time, consider an index that is currently the lowest.

What's the Margin?

The interest rate you pay on your mortgage is not simply the index interest rate. Rather, the lender will add a "margin" to the index to determine your actual mortgage interest rate. For example, the lender may specify in your ARM mortgage documents that the margin is 2.5 percent. That means that when the index is 5 percent, for example, the lender adds the margin of 2.5 percent to the 5 percent, and you have an effective mortgage interest rate of 7.5 percent.

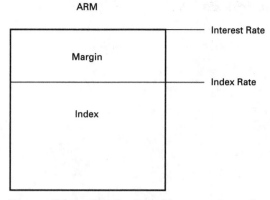

Figure 14-1. The lender adds a margin to the index to determine the actual mortgage interest rate.

The margin is tied directly to the index used (see Figure 14-1). If the index is generally low, the lender will tend to use a higher margin. If the index is generally high, the lender will tend to use a lower margin.

TRAP

Don't trust lenders to look out for you. Ask to see the performance of the margin on its index going back at least 10 years. See how well this index performed with the margin the lender uses. Compare it to fixed interest rates for the same period (something the lender should also supply). Would you end up paying market interest rates most of the time? Or would you be ripped off by higher-than-market rates? It's worth some time investigating.

What Is the Adjustment Period?

After the index, the next critical feature to look at in an ARM is the adjustment period. How frequently can the lender adjust the mortgage rate up or down?

Typical Arm Adjustment Periods

Monthly

Bimonthly

3 months

6 months

Annually

Biannually

Every 3 years

Every 5 years

TIP

Most of the time you will want the longest adjustment periods possible. This gives you the greatest stability. However, most of the time lenders want the shortest adjustment periods. This gives them the greatest protection against interest rate hikes. Therefore, when shopping for a mortgage, it is highly advisable to place the adjustment period as a big priority on the list of terms to look for.

What about Interest/Payment Rate Caps?

Lenders are aware of borrowers' fears of hikes in ARM mortgage payments caused by big jumps in the market interest rate. If the mortgage were allowed to rise without restriction, in a very volatile market we might start out paying 7 percent and end up paying 15 percent or more. As a result our monthly payments could double as well. Few borrowers would go for a mortgage with such a downside risk.

To help reduce borrowers' fears, lenders frequently put "caps" on the ARM interest rate. A cap is a limit on the amount the interest rate, the monthly payment, or both can rise (or fall). For example, if there is a 4 percent cap on the interest rate, it can't rise (or fall) by more than 4 percent. If the market rate rises higher, the ARM would be limited and wouldn't respond.

TIP

The cap puts both a ceiling and a floor on the ARM. The interest rate can't go above a certain amount, but it can't go below a certain amount either. If the cap is 5 percent, for example, the rate can rise above or fall below 5 percent of the current rate. Keep in mind that amounts to a swing of 10 percent.

Are Interest Rate Caps Beneficial?

Nearly all borrowers would agree that interest rate caps are beneficial. Yes, they would say, we want to be protected against runaway interest rates and runaway monthly payments.

However, interest rate caps are deceptive. They don't really give as much protection as they seem to. The reason is that they are set so high. For them to kick in, interest rates would have to reach historical highs, and that's unlikely. Caps are more protection for the long shot than for month-to-month payments.

What about Negative Amortization?

Some ARMs set a maximum limit on the amount the monthly payment can be raised each adjustment period regardless of what happens to the interest rate. Many borrowers like this, since it limits their monthly payment increases regardless of what interest rates do. However, it can also be a trap. The reason is that if the interest rate rises faster than the monthly payment, there's interest that doesn't get paid each month. This is then added to the principal of the mortgage. In other words, the mortgage amount grows.

Without the payment cap, the mortgage payment would rise $151. With it, the maximum rise is $66, and $85 is now added to the principal owed on the mortgage.

Effect of Capping the Mortgage Payment
$100,000 mortgage for 30 years with 7.5% payment cap. Assume
the interest rate rises 2 percent.

Increase in mortgage payment required to handle the interest rate increase	$151
Maximum payment increase allowed	−$66
Shortfall added to mortgage	85

Negative amortization is when the mortgage increases, rather than decreases. As a result, you end up paying interest on interest. Most government mortgages allow up to 25 percent of the mortgage amount to be added interest. In other words, you can end up owing up to 125 percent of what you borrowed because of negative amortization.

Negative amortization today occurs in a substantial number of ARMs. It is something that is often hidden from view, unless you know what to look for in the documents. Although the negative amortization terms are usually explained in those mortgages in which it occurs, many people simply don't understand the implications. Many still fail to see the dangers.

TRAP

Negative amortization means that instead of the mortgage going down, it goes up. Each month instead of paying off some of the loan, you add to it. You end up owing more than originally borrowed.

How Do You Find Out If Your Mortgage Has Negative Amortization?

Look for a payment cap. If your mortgage has one, you can be almost certain that it also has negative amortization. Finally, the ultimate monthly payment with a cap may be higher than without. Consider the example prepared by the Federal Home Loan Bank Board (Table 14-1). In this case various interest rate caps are given, and the monthly payment is shown over a period of 29

Table 14-1. Cap Rate Comparison Chart
($50,000 30-year mortgage)

		Monthly payment			
Year	Interest rate	7% cap	7.5% cap	10% cap	No cap
1	12	514	514	514	514
2	13.5	540	552	565	572
3	15	567	594	622	630
4	16.5	595	638	684	689
5	18	625	686	753	748
6	"	656	738	"	"
10	"	797	800	"	"
15	"	1018	"	"	"
20	"	1112	"	"	"
25	"	"	"	"	"
29	"	"	"	"	"

years. The chart assumes that interest rates start at 12 percent, then rise to 18 percent at year 5 and remain there.

Notice that the lower the monthly payment cap, the lower the monthly payments initially. But over the long run, the lower the monthly payment cap, the higher the monthly payments, as the lender plays catch-up trying to recoup interest not received because of the payment cap.

TIP

Monthly payment caps can mean lower monthly payments now, but higher monthly payments later on.

The preceding example was exaggerated to make a point. (No one expects interest rates to move to 18 percent and stay there.) It also overlooked an important consideration: a mortgage might have *both* a monthly payment cap *and* an interest rate cap.

When a mortgage has both an interest rate cap and a monthly payment cap, you automatically should check to see whether the interest rate cap is set higher than the monthly payment cap. If it is, negative amortization could take place. The reason is simple:

if this weren't the case, if the interest rate cap were set sufficiently low that no negative amortization could take place, then no
monthly payment cap would be necessary.

My suggestion is to avoid monthly payment caps; look instead
for lower interest rate caps, longer adjustment periods, and lower
steps.

What Are the Steps?

Many ARMs also set a maximum limit on the amount the interest
can be raised each adjustment period. For example, many ARMs
have a 1 or 2 percent maximum interest rate adjustment. That
means that regardless of what the real interest rate has moved,
the interest rate on the mortgage can only be adjusted in steps of
1 or 2 percent.

To see how steps work, let's say interest rates on our index have
gone through the roof. Can an ARM mortgage interest rate in
one adjustment period be raised to its maximum cap? If the original rate (as per our example) was 7 percent and the cap was 5
percent, can the interest rate be hiked upward to 12 percent in
one adjustment period?

If the loan did not have steps, then the answer would be yes.
However, nearly all ARMs have steps that limit the hikes in interest rate per each adjustment period. These limits are typically
anywhere from ½ percent to 2½ percent per adjustment period.
Thus, regardless of what the index the mortgage is tied to may
do, the interest rate cannot be hiked more than the step amount
each period.

The smaller the steps, the greater the lag time when there is a
sudden jump in interest rates. (Of course, a sudden decline
would not be felt as quickly, either.) If we assume that interest
rates will tend to move both up and down, the smaller the steps,
therefore, the more stable the mortgage monthly payment. The
steps, in fact, can have a far greater impact on the stability of the
mortgage than can an interest rate cap.

Ideally you would want a mortgage with small steps over one
with larger payment caps.

TRAP

Many ARM lenders are naturally concerned about the lag time in mortgages with small steps. They see that they could lose out on interest during spikes in interest rates. As a consequence, some ARMs are written with catch-up clauses. These clauses provide that even though the step doesn't rise fast enough to keep pace with the index, any interest lost to the lender in this fashion would be carried over to the next adjustment period. With a catch-up clause in a mortgage, the beneficial effects of smaller steps are nullified over a long period of time.

TIP

Shop for a lender who offers both small steps and no catch-up clauses. They are hard to find, but they do exist in many markets. On the other hand, avoid mortgages with catch-up clauses if at all possible.

ARMs have their place. But, generally speaking, they are ugly loans. Lenders like them because they reduce lender's concerns over volatility. Agents like them because they help make sales that otherwise might fall through. Borrowers like them because they mean initially low payments and the ability to get financing that otherwise might not be available.

But don't think of them as a panacea. They are not. They can solve a particular mortgage problem that you might have. But they won't solve all of your problems. And likely as not, after a few years, they will end up causing more difficulty than the problem they originally seemed to cure.

15

Is a 0-Points Mortgage a Good Deal?

Over the last few years some mortgage lenders have been offering to lend money with "no points" to the borrower. Points, as you may recall, are a percentage (1 point equals 1 percent) of the mortgage amount that goes back to the lender. A 0-points mortgage means that the borrower pays no points at all. Should you look for and obtain one of these special mortgages?

First, let's be clear on what we're considering. You want to borrow $100,000 to buy or refinance a home. You go to lender after lender and are told it will cost you around 7 percent in interest plus anywhere from 1½ to 2 points. In other words, there's an additional $1500 to $2000 in loan costs (in addition to settlement fees).

Suddenly another lender pops up and says if you borrow from it, there are no points to pay at all. You save the $1500 to $2000 the loan would otherwise cost you. Should you believe it? Should you jump for it?

Yes...and no. Depending on your situation, it could be beneficial, or it could end up being even more costly.

Do You Believe in the Tooth Fairy?

If you still believe in the tooth fairy, the Easter Bunny, and Santa Claus, then you're ready to accept that one lender will give you a mortgage for $1500 to $2000 less than another. (Maybe you're just such a nice person that the lender can't resist.) On the other hand, if you're an adult who's been burned once or twice, you'll look deeper and ask more.

In truth, the loan without the points can and may be more costly than the loan with the points. To understand how and why, it's important to realize why lenders charge points.

Why Points?

Lenders aren't concerned with interest rates per se. They are concerned with something called "yield." Yield is the true return to the lender on the money that is loaned. It includes not only the interest rate you pay but also all other costs and fees that can be factored in, especially points.

Thus, if you want to borrow $100,000 but pay 2 percent of the loan up front in points, you're actually only borrowing $98,000. Yet your interest rate is based on $100,000. Since the lender loans you less (in this case, $2000 less), it receives a higher yield on the money.

TIP

Figure it out. At 7 percent, the monthly payments for 30 years on $100,000 is $665. However, if you pay 2 points, you're in reality only borrowing $98,000. If you make payments of $665 on $98,000, the true interest rate returned to the lender is actually close to 7¼ percent. Because you borrowed less but made higher monthly payments based on a higher loan amount, the lender gets a better yield.

Does it really work this way? Yes it does. And if you want further proof, consider the APR (annual percentage rate) that must be given to you when you borrow. This is somewhat different from the true yield to a lender because it includes many mortgage costs (some of which are actual expenses to the lender). Nevertheless, you will notice that if you have costs including points, your APR will always be higher than your mortgage interest rate. It is closer to the true yield.

Trading Interest for Points

Now we can get to how a lender can offer a 0-points mortgage. It is done, quite simply, by jacking up the interest rate. You want to borrow $100,000 at 7 percent, and the lender says it will cost you 2 points.

You say you don't want to pay 2 points. You don't want to pay any points. The lender is an agreeable sort and says okay. It's 0 points, only the interest rate is now $7\frac{1}{4}$ percent. Why shouldn't the lender be agreeable? The yield on either loan is the same. (If you're not sure why, reread the tip above.)

Thus, points can be traded for a higher interest rate. Indeed, many modern lenders will offer a sliding scale of points versus interest rate, such as the one shown below.

Sliding Scale—Points vs. Interest Rate

3 points	$6\frac{7}{8}\%$
2 points	7%
1 point	$7\frac{1}{8}\%$
0 points	$7\frac{1}{4}\%$

It's your choice.

TRAP

Don't think that you can automatically trade 1 point for one-eighth of the interest rate. While it often works out close to that amount, as we'll see shortly, there are other considerations that lenders have.

Should You Pay the Points or Pay a Higher Interest Rate?

The answer depends on your financial situation and how long you plan to live in the home. Basically, points are cash to you up front. If you're cash short (as so many buyers are), then a 0-points mortgage can be a good deal. On the other hand, if you've got the cash and plan to keep the property a long time, then perhaps a lower interest rate (and accompanying lower payments) would be advantageous.

There's an additional consideration. Lenders aren't always equitable when they offer 0-points mortgages. By that I mean the trade-off between points and interest rate sometimes can favor the lender. Let's consider an extreme example.

You've got the choice between paying 2 points on a 30-year $100,000 mortgage or an increase of ¼ percent in the interest rate. That's either $2000 in cash up front or $17 a month more. If you're cash short when buying the home, that $2000 can look like a lot of money. On the other hand, that $17 a month can seem a paltry fee. Yet before you leap, consider that the mortgage is for 30 years.

$$\begin{array}{r} \$17 \\ \times\ 360\ \text{payments} \\ \hline \$6,120 \end{array}$$

Over the 30-year life of the mortgage you will pay more than three times the amount you'll save on the points when you buy.

TIP

 Calculate how long you must live in the property before you begin to lose money. In the above example, you'll stay ahead until about year 10. At that point you will have paid roughly an additional $2000. Beyond that, it begins to cost you more money.

TRAP

Our example does not take into account the future cost of money, which means that cash up front is worth more (due in part to inflation) than cash received sometime in the future. Nevertheless, as a rough measure the preceding test works pretty well.

Problems arise when the lender is far less equitable than our example. Let's say, for example, that the choice is between paying 2 points ($2000) up front or a ½ percent higher interest rate. Remember, the lender can charge any rate it wants, as long as it fully discloses that to you. (Some states still do have usury laws against excessively high interest rates, but they usually do not affect institutional lenders such as banks.)

$$\begin{array}{r} \$34 \\ \underline{\times\ 360\ \text{payments}} \\ \$12{,}240 \end{array}$$

Now if you choose the much higher interest rate over the points, you're paying six times as much over 30 years. Your breakeven is in just roughly 5 years.

What's the Bottom Line?

Having said all this, how should you choose? Should you pay the points or pay the higher interest rate? If it were me, I'd try to determine how long I planned to own the property. If I only plan to stay with the property for a few years, then I'd certainly want to take the higher interest rate (and monthly payment) and forgo the points.

On the other hand, if I planned on keeping the property a very long time, then it might be better to pay the points up front and take the lower monthly payment, as it would save me a lot of money over the long haul.

TIP

Sometimes interest rates fluctuate rapidly. For example, when you first look they could be at 7½ percent.
A month later they're at 7¼ percent. When you
finally apply for a mortgage, they're down to 7 percent. Now you're given a choice of points over a
higher interest rate. You might be offered 0 points
at 7½ percent. But if you'd applied for the loan just
a few months earlier, you would have paid 7½ percent even with points! All of which means that sometimes using a sharp pencil doesn't make much
sense. If you can live with the interest rate and don't
have the up-front cash for the points, you may just
want to opt for the 0-points mortgage regardless of
the long-term costs. (Note: the above logic works far
less well when interest rates are rising.)

What about 0-Cost Mortgages?

Sometimes lenders will offer you a mortgage at no initial cost to
you at all. There will be no escrow charges, no title insurance
costs, no settlement fees, and, of course, no points.

Again, this deal is usually too good to be true. All of the other
costs are part of getting a mortgage. If you don't pay them, then
somebody else must. While the lender probably can cut a better
deal with the title insurance and escrow companies than you,
there will nevertheless be some expense. And that expense will
be added to the interest rate. In other words, you'll end up paying an even higher interest rate for a 0-cost mortgage than you
would for a 0-points mortgage. Your monthly payments will be
higher, as will the long-term costs.

Of course, as noted earlier, if you're only planning to live in
the property a relatively short time, or if interest rates have fallen
to where you don't mind paying them, you may want to take it.

16

Can I Get a 125 Percent Mortgage?

Within the past few years a new kind, or at least a new amount, of mortgage money has become popularized. It's the mortgage for *more* than the value of your property. It's frequently called the "125 percent mortgage," and it really is for 25 percent more than your property is worth.

Is it for real? How does it work? Is it worthwhile? We'll try to answer all of these questions in this chapter.

How Did It Get Started?

The 125 percent mortgage was born in the real estate recession of the early 1990s. Property values were dropping to the point where people owed more on their property than it was worth. This situation became known as being "upside down."

When you were upside down it was virtually impossible to sell your home. There was no equity to pay closing costs, including commission, let alone give the seller any cash out. Indeed, the only way to sell in most such cases was either for the seller to come up with more cash or for the lender to take less money (which became known as a "short payoff").

Would-be sellers, and buyers for their properties, faced with such a situation found the market was effectively closed down for them . . . until the 125 percent mortgage came along. Because this mortgage was for more than the value of the property, the sellers could sometimes get enough cash out to pay off their existing mortgage plus closing costs. The loan was a panacea of sorts. For those who borrowed on it, however, there were some serious concerns.

How Can You Borrow More Than the Value of the Property?

As we all know, mortgages are collateralized loans—that means that their security is first the property. That's why traditionally mortgages have always been for a percentage of the property's market value, typically 80 or 90 percent. If the borrower didn't make the payments, the lender could foreclose and resell the property. The 10 to 20 percent margin (the down payment) allowed for costs of foreclosure and resale. How, therefore, can a lender make a loan for 125 percent, far more than the market value of property?

There are two answers here. The first is a little-known federal mortgage lending provision that in some restricted situations allows lenders to increase the value of a mortgage up to 125 percent. For example, if you have an ARM that has negative amortization (interest paid on interest), the lender can keep adding the interest to the principal up to 125 percent of the original mortgage.

A few lenders took advantage of that provision and issued ARMs for near to the full value of the property and immediately moved that up to the 125 percent maximum. My observation is that this type of mortgage is actually seldom used.

In most cases, the 125 percent loan was actually two mortgages: a collateralized mortgage based on a percentage of the property's value, and then a second uncollateralized "loan" based on the good credit of the borrower. This is the typical 125 percent mortgage advertised today.

How Does It Work?

Actually, it's quite simple. Provided that the borrower has excellent credit, a very high mortgage is obtained, between 90 and 100 percent. Then added to the mortgage is, in effect, a personal (noncollateralized) loan for an additional 25 to 35 percent. The combination of the two gives a total loan for 125 percent of market value.

Of course, the loan may specify only one payment to a lender. In that case, the lender may then be separating your payment into two parts, one for the personal loan and the remainder for the mortgage.

TRAP

If you're more than 13 years old, you realize that in this world, you never get something for nothing. There's always the piper to pay. In the case of the 125 percent mortgage, it's typically the interest rate, the points, the closing costs, or all three. They are much higher than for regular mortgages.

The interest rate on the actual mortgage base may be quite competitive, often close to market rates. But the interest rate for the personal loan is often significantly higher. The combined interest rate for both the mortgage and the personal loan, however, may be fairly reasonable.

TIP

You'll see in Chap. 19 that most lenders are very concerned with the CLTV, the combined loan to value ratio. Most won't go much above 90 percent. Therefore, the lender who goes to 125 percent is often one who is trading off higher risk for more profit in terms of interest.

A typical 125 percent combo might look like this:

Mortgage base:	90 percent @ 8 percent interest (close to market)
Personal loan:	35 percent @ 12 percent (close to market for personal loans)
Combined:	125 percent @ 9.15 percent

In the above example, the borrower is paying about a percent and an eighth above market rate to get a loan for 125 percent of market value. If you're a borrower who needs money, this may seem like a good option. After all, the higher interest rate may only make a difference of a few dollars a month on your payments.

TRAP

In our example we've assumed a borrower with excellent credit. If your credit is less than sterling, you may still be offered a 125 percent loan by some lenders, but the combined interest rate could be jacked up very high. It might be 15 or even 20 percent or more!

Should You Go for It?

There are a number of serious reasons why a 125 percent mortgage could be the sort of thing you'd want to avoid:

1. *You have no equity in the property.* If you want to sell (or resell), you'll find it next to impossible. You will owe 25 percent more than the property's worth. You have negative equity. Circumstances such as a job change, a medical problem, or a loss of income could come along suddenly and demand that you sell and move. But your ability to get rid of the property would be crippled by the loans.

2. *You have a personal loan.* In many cases in order to get the 125 percent "mortgage," you must agree to be personally responsible for the payback. In other words, *you* are the security, rather than just the property. If times get bad and you try to walk away from the property, you'll find the lender still coming after you for the money owed plus back interest and penalties.

3. *You're paying a higher-than-market (combined) interest rate.* It may only be a percent or two higher, but on a $200,000 mortgage, an extra 2 percent per year means an extra $2000 in interest. That can be quite a burden.

4. *Some (or all) of the interest may not be deductible.* In most cases the interest on a home mortgage (up to very high maximums) is deductible against federal and state income. The house acts as a tax shelter. However, in the case of a 125 percent mortgage where part of the loan is noncollateralized (personal), part of the interest may not be deductible. Indeed, should the government determine that the loan was primarily personal, all of the interest might be deemed nondeductible.

TIP

If you're seriously considering getting a 125 percent mortgage, take the mortgage documents to a good tax attorney **before** you sign them. Get an expert opinion as to how much, if any, of the interest you pay will be deductible. Remember, interest on a personal loan is, in general, no longer deductible.

What's the Bottom Line?

Everyone's situation is different. You may be desperate for cash for any number of reasons, and if so, the 125 percent mortgage may be the best of several poor alternatives.

On the other hand, sound financial practices suggest that being conservative is usually the best course. If that's your tendency, then I would suggest you stay away from the 125 percent mortgage.

17
How Do I Get a Jumbo Mortgage?

Thus far we have generally been talking about lenders who are issuing conforming loans. This simply means that the mortgages conform to the guidelines generally used by the quasi-government underwriters, Fannie Mae or Freddie Mac. The primary lenders, be they banks, mortgage bankers, insurance companies, or whatever, lend you the money and then "resell" the mortgages on the secondary market. Their biggest consideration is that, in order to be resold, the mortgages must conform to the underwriter's standards. And one of the most inflexible of those standards is the *maximum amount limitation*. While this amount is changed fairly often, the current maximum is $227,150. Thus, no true conforming loan is for more than that dollar amount.

But what if you live in a high-priced area, such as parts of New York or California? What if the average home in your area costs over $300,000 or, in some cases, over $500,000? How do you get financing?

What Is a Jumbo Loan?

If you need a mortgage above the conforming limitation, you are now looking for what the industry calls a "jumbo" loan; currently, that's any loan above $227,150. Suddenly you are in a different ball game.

The good news is that jumbos are readily available in those areas of the country where they are needed. The reason is that they are great loans, from the lenders' perspective.

Jumbos generally cost you about a quarter to a half percent over the conforming market rate. Plus, the lenders often adhere to the conforming underwriting standards (even though the loan won't be resold) just to be sure that the borrowers are good credit risks. Thus, the lenders get more interest for essentially the same risk.

Where Do I Get a Jumbo?

Most mortgage brokers, savings banks, or other lenders offer jumbos or can direct you to a lender who does. The procedure is essentially the same as for a conforming mortgage. You fill out an application, provide the required documentation, get an appraisal, and if everything checks out, get approved and funded.

It's important to understand, however, that jumbo lenders tend to keep these mortgages for themselves, rather than sell them in the secondary market (although there is such a market). Thus, it may take awhile until the lender's own loan committee meets. If the committee meets only once monthly, getting approval could take a fair amount of time.

Why Are They Also Called Portfolio Loans?

If the lender doesn't sell the jumbo on the secondary market, it must keep it in its own portfolio of loans. Therefore, jumbos are frequently referred to as "portfolio mortgages."

Of course, any given lending institution can only fund so many of these mortgages until it runs out of funds. Hence, there tends to be far fewer portfolio loans than conforming loans. On the other hand, there are also far fewer very high-priced properties.

Can I Get the Interest Rate Cut on a Jumbo?

Yes, sometimes you can get an interest rate cut. Some lenders offer a combination mortgage, with one mortgage that conforms up to the maximum amount and then another second mortgage that goes the rest of the way up to the money you need. The interest rate on these loans is a blend of the low conforming rate and the higher jumbo rate, which usually means a slightly lower interest rate and payment for you.

What Is a Piggyback?

A "piggyback" is a blended-rate mortgage, such as is described in the previous paragraph, that for all intents and purposes looks like a single mortgage to you, the borrower. You borrow what seems to be just one mortgage. But you get a slightly lower interest rate than if you had borrowed a straight jumbo.

Here's how it works: You still get two loans, one a conforming at a lower rate and another a jumbo at a higher rate. However, the jumbo loan wraps around the conforming loan. You make only one payment, but the lender takes out enough money from the payment to pay the conforming mortgage and then keeps the balance for itself on its portfolio jumbo loan.

TIP

As far as you, the borrower, is concerned, it couldn't be simpler. You are given one interest rate (which is actually a blend of the two mortgages) and one monthly payment (which the lender then divides between the two loans). From your perspective, it's simply a loan with a slightly lower interest rate than a straight jumbo.

TRAP

Sometimes jumbos are offered at competing lower rates. But be careful. While the interest rate could be lower, the points may be higher. As noted in

Chap. 15, the true yield is a combination of both points and interest rate. Generally speaking, if you pay a higher interest rate, you'll get lower points. A lot will depend on how much cash you want to pay up front and how big a monthly payment you can afford.

Piggybacks are the ideal mortgage for someone who plans to get some money within a year or so that can be applied to the home. For example, I recently purchased a home using a piggyback. However, I had not yet sold another home in a distant area. It took me about 5 months to complete the sale of the second home. When that was done, I took the money I received and, with the lender's permission, paid off the second mortgage part of the piggyback, thus effectively dropping my interest rate to that of the conforming loan. (*Note:* Many lenders will not permit a split payoff such as this. Check with the lender *before* securing the mortgage.) I accomplished the same thing as a refinance, without any refinance costs at all.

As shown in Figure 17-1, combined interest rate of a piggyback mortgage is usually lower than the interest rate of a straight jumbo mortgage.

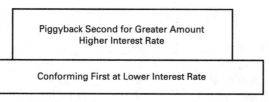

Figure 17-1. Piggyback mortgage.

Can I Combine a Jumbo into Other Types of Mortgages?

You certainly can. A jumbo can be either a fixed-rate or an adjustable-rate mortgage. It can be one of the popular 7/30 mortgages: a 30-year payout period (amortization) with a 7-year balloon.

The big difference between a jumbo and a conforming loan is the amount borrowed. The type of mortgage is a matter of agreement between you and the lender.

TIP

Since lenders directly carry jumbo mortgages in their portfolio, they may have more flexibility than with conforming loans. That means you may be able to make specific offers regarding points, fees, or the structure of the mortgage that they would entertain and, in some cases, accept. In other words, you have greater flexibility in creating just the type of mortgage you want.

18

Should I Opt for a Biweekly or Shorter-Term Mortgage?

The long-term goal for most people is to eventually pay the mortgage off. While that may not make great financial sense (the interest is often deductible, and it gives you greater leverage for making a profit on the property), it's often an overwhelmingly popular psychological motivation. As noted elsewhere in the book, nothing feels more secure than to have a paid-off house.

So, if you decide you want to pay off your mortgage, how do you go about doing it most efficiently? That's what we'll consider in this chapter.

What about a "Biweekly" Mortgage?

One of the most popular mortgages to be "discovered" in the last few years is the biweekly. Here the borrower makes a payment every other week instead of the traditional once-monthly payment. (For example, instead of paying $1000 a month, you pay $500 every 2 weeks.) Since there are 52 weeks in the year, a payment every other week amounts to 26 half payments or 13 full payments (an extra $1000 in our example). With a biweekly mortgage, therefore, each year you make the equivalent of 13 monthly payments instead of 12. That thirteenth payment ($1000 in our example) goes to pay down principal.

The result is that over the life of the loan an amazing amount of interest is saved, and the mortgage can actually be paid off years early. In almost a painless way, you can thus cut virtually a third off the time it takes to pay off a 30-year mortgage.

TRAP

A biweekly mortgage is not for everyone. It works best when you are salaried and getting paid on a weekly or biweekly basis. You can easily budget your money to take care of the payment that way and probably won't feel the extra expense very much. On the other hand, if you're paid monthly or work for yourself, the biweekly setup can be a no-no. Making payments once each month will seem natural. A biweekly schedule will have you making payments more often, probably at times when you don't have money coming in. This schedule can be a nightmare for someone who is self-employed or who is paid monthly.

How Do I Establish a Biweekly Mortgage?

Biweekly mortgages are offered by many mortgage lenders. Just ask your mortgage broker to recommend a lender who uses them. They are set up right from the start with payment coupons that require you to make a payment every 2 weeks.

The mortgage company takes care of the bookkeeping, and as long as you keep making those payments, you are shortening the term of your loan as well as the total interest you will have to pay.

TIP

A biweekly also can be used to reduce the size of your payments instead of shorten your term and cut interest. Say the payments on a 30-year mortgage are $1000 a month and $500 biweekly. On a yearly basis paid monthly, you will have paid in a total of $12,000. However, biweekly that comes to $13,000. The extra thousand dollars can be used to reduce your biweekly payments by $42. Some lenders have encouraged borrowers to try this. Keep in mind, however, that this defeats the entire purpose of the biweekly. You might just as well pay monthly as to pay a reduced amount biweekly. You will not save anything on interest and will not have your mortgage term reduced. The only advantage I can see is for some borrowers who prefer a lower biweekly payments as simpler for their bookkeeping and budgeting.

TRAP

Beware of firms, particularly those that telemarket, that offer to set up a biweekly mortgage for you. They could take your money, never make the mortgage payments, and cause you to lose your home.

I have seen companies that offer to set up a bimonthly mortgage payment schedule with an existing lender when you already have a mortgage. They claim to call the lender and get an agreement to send in money every other week. In reality, some of these firms deposit the extra money in an interest-bearing account, and then, at the end of the year, make an extra payment to principal. For this they often charge a whopping fee, sometimes as much as $1000 or more. Plus, they may require a biweekly charge for the service. They get interest on your money and a fee for doing what you can do yourself.

Can I Set Up a Biweekly Payment Schedule Myself?

You sure can. Ideally, a true biweekly mortgage is arranged between you and the lender at the time you secure financing. The lender agrees to accept payments every 2 weeks, and you agree to make payments on that schedule. If you already have a mortgage in place and a check with the lender reveals that no change in payment schedule is possible, you can still do it. Here's how:

1. First make sure you can make a prepayment without penalty. Most mortgages allow this, but some don't. Check your mortgage documents. If you're not sure, take them to a real estate broker or attorney who can explain them to you.

2. If prepayment is allowed, simply pay half your mortgage payment every 2 weeks into a separate checking account. At the end of each month, make your normal payment to the mortgage company out of that account. As the year progresses you will notice a surplus slowly but surely building in that account.

3. At the end of the year, include that surplus with your December payment. *But be sure to indicate that it is all to go to principal.* If you don't, the mortgage company could simply count it as your next payment and mess up the entire schedule.

Keep in mind that you can accomplish the above on your own and very easily. You do not need anyone to help you do it. You certainly shouldn't pay anyone to set this up for you. To get a true biweekly mortgage, however, you must set it up with the lender.

Why Not Simply Get a 15-Year Mortgage?

One way to pay more money up front is by taking a shorter payback period, 15 years instead of 30, for example. This increases the monthly payment but decreases the interest charged, resulting in a quicker payoff of the mortgage.

Comparison of 30-Year and 15-Year
Mortgages

$100,000 at 8 percent fully amortized

	30 year	15 year
Total interest	$120,000	$51,000
Interest saved		69,000

Note that by making a higher payment, not only does a 15-year mortgage get paid off in half the time, but it also saves a tremendous amount of interest.

Will I Have Higher Payments?

Of course, the problem with a 15-year mortgage is that it has higher payments. In our example of a $100,000 mortgage at 8 percent interest, that's an increase in monthly payment of $222 ($956 rather than $734) on a 30-year mortgage. The payment increases here by about 30 percent. For most of us that's too huge a burden to bear.

TIP

As we've seen elsewhere in this book, lenders like the shorter-term mortgages. If you can afford the higher payments on a 15-year mortgage, a lender will often give you a lower interest rate or fewer points or both. That reduces your payment. It's something worth considering.

Still Don't Get How to Save Money by Paying Off Sooner?

It's all a matter of mathematics. Let's consider a fixed-rate mortgage. While we all understand that monthly payments on a fixed

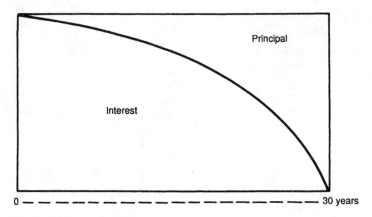

Figure 18-1. A typical 30-year mortgage.

mortgage remain the same, what fewer of us comprehend is the ratio of interest to principal in the payment.

During the early years of a mortgage, virtually all of the monthly payment goes toward interest. It is only in the very last years that the majority of the payment begins going toward principal. Figure 18-1 shows a typical 30-year mortgage.

If the mortgage is for $100,000 at 8 percent interest, the monthly payment is $734. However, of that amount only about $60 initially goes to principal on the first payment. All the rest goes to interest.

As you can imagine, reducing the $100,000 by $60 in the first month isn't going to make much of a difference. However, over time it adds up. Each month the mortgage interest is recalculated, and each month the amount that goes to principal increases while the amount going to interest declines. That's the reason that the curve begins to turn downward.

This steady increase in the amount going to principal continues over the life of the loan, but it actually begins to accelerate by year 20. What's happening is that as the amount of money going to principal increases dramatically, the amount owed decreases significantly, and consequently, the interest charged goes down. This process accelerates precipitously at the end of the loan period. By year 25 of a 30-year loan, you're actually paying more than half of the payment to principal and only half toward interest. By the final payments, virtually all is principal.

What this means is that the vast majority of the interest paid on the mortgage over its life is paid during its first years. If you can reduce the principal in those first years, you significantly reduce the interest paid . . . and in the long run significantly shorten the time it takes to pay off the mortgage.

TIP

Simply making one additional monthly payment in the first year that goes entirely toward principal can reduce the time it takes to pay back the loan by over a year and significantly reduce the interest paid over the term of the mortgage.

Is There a Better Way?

There's a safer way to pay off a mortgage more quickly. A variation of the 15-year mortgage that's been available for a long time is the 30-year mortgage paid back in larger monthly payments. No, it's not exactly a biweekly, but it's like it.

I can remember very savvy borrowers doing this as long as 30 years ago, often over the objections of the lender. Even back then when most mortgages had prepayment penalties, they did allow up to the equivalent of 6 months' interest to be paid in advance, and people took advantage of that clause. Today with most mortgages not having prepayment penalties of any kind, it's even easier to do.

Here's how this plan works: You get a regular 30-year mortgage (with a no-prepayment feature). But you pay it off using a 15-year payment schedule. If you borrowed $100,000 at 8 percent for 30 years, your payments should be $734 a month. However, instead of paying $734 per month, you pay $956 a month—$222 extra.

30-year monthly payment	$734	
Extra principal	222	(prepaid monthly)
Total monthly payment	956	

The advantage is you're not locked into the higher payment ($956 in this case). You are paying it voluntarily. If you get laid off, there's a problem such as sickness and you don't have any extra funds, or anything else untoward happens, you just drop back to the old, lower payments ($734 in this case). The lender doesn't care, since the lower payment is what you contracted for.

Doing it this way, you have the option of making the higher payment or not. You determine which month you'll pay more and which you'll pay less.

The Bottom Line of Early Payoff

Biweekly and 15-year mortgages are becoming increasingly popular, and for good reason. Borrowers are simply tired of paying huge amounts of money for interest over the life of a mortgage when, either by restructuring the frequency of the payment or by adding a small additional amount to principal each payment, they avoid that. Think of it this way . . . paying every other week or paying an extra hundred bucks a month probably isn't going to kill you. But paying tens, sometimes hundreds of thousands of dollars extra in interest over 30 years can be a real backbreaker.

TIP

You don't have to own the property for 15 years or longer to get the benefits of biweekly or 15-year mortgages. Everything that you pay immediately to principal increases your equity as soon as you make the payment. The sooner you pay or the more you pay, the lower the mortgage and the more of the house that you really own.

19
Can I Really Get a No-down Mortgage?

Coming up with the down payment is one of the toughest tasks for many buyers. Many times having enough income is not a problem; it's finding the cash. Even if it's only 10 percent of the purchase price, that's $20,000 on a $200,000 home. For those who have trouble saving, it might as well be a million.

Which brings us to the matter of buying with nothing down. In the past many gurus have touted this as a formula for success in real estate investing. Buy with nothing down, get the property of your dreams, and make a fortune to boot.

Unfortunately, it doesn't always end up that way. A lot depends on how the financing is structured. If you end up with payments that are sky-high, it might be a formula for disaster. You wouldn't be able to make the high payments and could lose the property to foreclosure.

On the other hand, if you can arrange for low-interest, nothing-down financing, it's another matter entirely. After all, if the market rate for a conventional loan with 20 percent down is 7.5

percent, and you can get almost the same interest rate for 0 percent down, why not go for it?

What Is LTV and CLTV?

It's important to remember that virtually all mortgages are based on the market value of the property. They are a certain percentage of that value expressed as "loan to value," or LTV. For example, a mortgage for 80 percent of value is expressed as an 80 percent LTV.

Sometimes in order to get closer to no-down, two mortgages will be combined, a first and a second. For example, the first might be for 90 percent and the second for 10 percent, adding up to 100 percent of the market value. These mortgages are expressed as "combined loan to value," or CLTV. The two mortgages just described would have a 100 percent CLTV. In general most lenders are very hesitant to issue mortgages where either the LTV or the CLTV is more than 90 percent. But it can be done . . . read on.

Are You a Prime Borrower?

True nothing-down financing has become available only within the last year or two. These are mortgages for the entire purchase price from institutional lenders—the same people you go to for the 20 percent down loans.

In the past, any loan that was underwritten (by Fannie Mae or Freddie Mac) had to have at least 10 percent and preferably 20 percent down. This was to assure the lender that the borrower would be dedicated enough about the property to keep up the payments.

However, as we saw in Chap. 6, the big lenders no longer use the old formulas for finding good buyers. Today it's all done on the basis of a computer profile. If you fit the profile of the good borrower who would never let a property go into default, then it shouldn't make any difference if you put 20 percent down or nothing down.

As a result, the major underwriters have begun fielding a variety of trial programs that offer the very best borrower close to

100 percent loans. If you qualify, you don't need to put any money down (or very little). Fannie Mae has, for example, a program called the "97" that requires a borrower to only come up with 3 percent down. Other close to nothing-down programs are currently being offered mainly on a trial basis. To find out about such programs, contact your mortgage broker.

In addition, other lending institutions are jumping on board, such as Bank of America. The Neighborhood Advantage Zero Down program says it will offer such mortgages in more than 20 states to people whose income are generally no higher than 80 percent of the median income of their metropolitan area. In other words, while you still need to fit the profile of a perfect borrower, you don't necessarily have to make a ton of money to qualify. These programs typically involve an insurance company that guarantees your performance on the mortgage. For this you will end up paying an additional fee. (For details see Chap. 24, which is on private mortgage insurance.) Keep in mind, of course, that individual programs from banks or other institutions come and go, and are often changed by the time you apply. Check with the lender for details.

Check with a large bank in your area to see if they are offering similar programs.

What about Government Loans?

In addition, there are the FHA and VA loan programs. These offer low (typically 3 to 5 percent on FHA) or nothing-down (on VA) loans to qualified buyers. Again, you must be a prime borrower, and in the case of the VA loan, you must also be a qualifying veteran. (See Chap. 21 for more details.)

The problem with these government mortgages, however, is that they typically have relatively low maximums. This means that while they are adequate for moderate-price areas, they are irrelevant in high-priced housing markets. As of this writing, however, the government has been toying with the idea of boosting the maximum loan amount on both of these mortgages to the same as for conforming (Fannie Mae or Freddie Mac) loans, which is currently $227,150. Check with a lender, such as a bank, to see what the current maximum is.

What about Closing Costs?

It's important to understand that the down payment is not the only cash you need to come up with in a real estate transaction. There are also the closing costs, which include appraisal, credit check, recording fees, and, of course, points.

With an FHA mortgage, the closing costs, including points, can typically run to more than 5 percent of the mortgage. And the FHA wants these fees paid up front, although in some cases they can be financed as part of the mortgage.

On a Fannie Mae or Freddie Mac underwritten loan, the cost can be similar. Under other programs, it can, however, be much less, as little as 2 percent.

You should check with your lender to see what the actual closing costs are. With these new 0-down mortgages, often the closing costs are the only cash you need to come up with. And sometimes even a part of these can be financed into the mortgage.

What If I'm Not a Prime Borrower?

Not everyone, indeed not most of us, are prime borrowers who can fit the qualifying profile for these 0-down mortgages. Is there any opportunity here for getting such a loan?

Yes, of course there is. There is always seller financing, which used to go by the term "creative financing." In many markets, particularly when sales are slow, it is possible to get the seller to help you finance a portion of the purchase price, sometimes enough so that you don't have to put anything down. We'll cover this in detail in the next chapter.

If you don't want to or can't put anything down, today you may still be able to buy a home. The finance industry has been turned on its heels by the computerized profile system, and it could produce surprising results for you. Just ask your lender about nothing-down mortgages. There may be one just waiting for you out there.

20

What about "Creative" Financing?

"Creative financing" was a term with immense appeal a few years ago. However, because of abuses, it has more recently come into disfavor. Nevertheless, for a buyer it is still worth considering.

Creative financing can be your source of the cheapest, no-qualifying, quickest-to-get mortgage money when you buy a home. With creative financing, the seller carries the mortgage for you. Getting the seller to finance your purchase is one of the best ways to get financing. If the seller is willing to give you a mortgage, either a first or more likely a second, you can get in quickly and without a lot of hassle.

TIP

For practical purposes, creative financing means seller financing.

In the past, creative financing became widely perceived as seller rip-off. The reason was that some unscrupulous buyers and brokers connived to use this tool to cheat sellers out of their equities. So many sellers lost money that for the last few years it has been difficult for an honest buyer to get any seller to go along with it.

In a typical transaction of a few years ago, a buyer might give a seller an inflated price for the home. In exchange, the seller would agree to finance the entire purchase. The seller's anticipation was that the sale was secure and that a monthly payment would be received on the financing.

But, the unscrupulous buyer might only be hoping to quickly resell if the market went up fast. The buyer would rent the home and keep the rents, not making payments to the seller. The frustrated seller's only recourse was to foreclose, which takes time and money. If the market went up, the buyer eventually resold. But, as often happened, if it didn't, the buyer would simply walk away leaving the house a mess, with an angry tenant living there, and all kinds of foreclosure costs for the seller. Is it any surprise that seller financing got a bad name?

TRAP

In some extraordinary cases, particularly with a down market and a desperate seller, buyers would get the seller to agree to help in refinancing the property and then, instead of putting cash in, the buyers would take cash out as part of the purchase! These types of deals too frequently resulted likewise in foreclosures and made sellers wary.

Today, however, most of the rip-offs are gone, and many sellers are once again willing to help buyers purchase their homes. This is particularly true in areas of the country where the market isn't hot and sales aren't plentiful.

How Does Seller Financing Work?

As those familiar with real estate financing know, when a seller "carries back paper," he or she is creating a mortgage with the buyer as the borrower. The buyer, in essence, is loaned a portion of the seller's equity in the home.

TIP

The terms "soft" and "hard" money as applied to real estate have come into vogue. A soft money mortgage is one in which the seller is the lender. A hard money mortgage is where the buyer/borrower goes to a bank or institution for funds.

The most common form of seller financing is the second mortgage. Let's take an example of a seller's second. Helen wanted to purchase a home for $200,000. However, she only had $20,000 to put down (plus money for closing costs.) That meant that she would have to get a 90 percent mortgage.

The problem with this was that Helen couldn't qualify for the 90 percent mortgage. Her borrower profile simply didn't add up. The underwriters said that in order to get a conforming loan, she would have to come up with 20 percent or $40,000 down.

Helen was stretching to get into the property, and she simply didn't have the extra cash. No way could she come up with an additional $20,000. So Helen arranged to borrow from the seller.

Helen still ended up financing the same amount, $180,000. However, 10 percent of it came from the seller. This meant the lender of the first mortgage was only making an 80 percent loan as required. She now easily qualified. See Fig. 20-1 on the following page.

TRAP

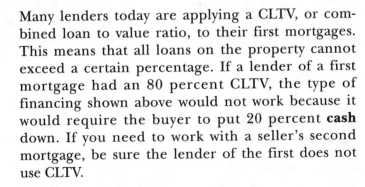

Many lenders today are applying a CLTV, or combined loan to value ratio, to their first mortgages. This means that all loans on the property cannot exceed a certain percentage. If a lender of a first mortgage had an 80 percent CLTV, the type of financing shown above would not work because it would require the buyer to put 20 percent **cash** down. If you need to work with a seller's second mortgage, be sure the lender of the first does not use CLTV.

Seller Financing Second Mortgage

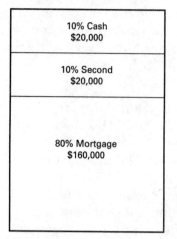

$200,000 Purchase Price

| 10% Cash $20,000 |
| 10% Second $20,000 |
| 80% Mortgage $160,000 |

Figure 20-1. An example of seller financing second mortgage.

TIP

Many lenders of first mortgages have specific rules regarding second mortgages. If they will allow you to use a second mortgage for a portion of the down payment, they may require that the second mortgage must be for a term of at least 5 years, although a few will allow as short a term as 3 years. Their reasoning is that if the second is for any shorter, when it comes due, your house will not have appreciated sufficiently to allow you to refinance. You may need to pay off the second mortgage and not be able to secure cash to do it. As a consequence, the seller/lender of the second mortgage might foreclose, which could threaten the stability of the first mortgage.

What about Putting Nothing Down?

As noted earlier, this got such a bad name from unscrupulous buyers, that today sellers will rarely accept it. Nonetheless, should you want to try such a deal, it works the same as noted above for 10 percent. Only here, you put nothing down and ask the seller to carry the entire difference between the new (or assumed) mortgage and the purchase price. Again, be careful to check with the lender of the new institutional mortgage, who may have specific prohibitions against such a deal.

Will Sellers Cooperate?

Some will cooperate, some won't. You can only ask. In some cases, sellers will agree, but with conditions. Some will not want to give you a long-term second mortgage. They may insist on an 18-month or 2-year second. When you point out that this will preclude you from getting a first mortgage, they may recommend a "trick" second or a "silent" second.

A trick second is where the sales agreement shows a 3- to 5-year second mortgage. But you and the seller agree that you will have a shorter term, and when all the documents are recorded, you record a shorter second mortgage than the agreement calls for. This depends on the lender of the first not seeing all of the documents recorded. These days, however, lenders have wizened up to this trick and often demand to see all documents.

Some buyers, in response, have come up with a silent second. This is where you record the 3- to 5-year second, as agreed. Then, a month or so after the transaction, you and the seller record a new second mortgage for a shorter term or sign a separate agreement to pay off the second earlier. Again, you have subverted the rules of the lender of the first.

TRAP

Beware of either the trick or the silent second. True, you may get away with it because the lender of the first simply won't know what's happened. But if you ever get into trouble and go into foreclosure, particularly during the early years of ownership, everything will come to light, and the holder of the first, besides foreclosing on the property, may charge fraud. Facing fraud means that you could be liable both civilly and criminally and that you could be forced to defend yourself against the federal government. (Most lenders of firsts are protected against fraud by federal law.)

While getting a seller to take back a longer second mortgage may be difficult, it could be a whole lot easier than the trouble you could get into from a trick or silent second.

Can Creative Financing Cut My Monthly Payment?

Another use of creative financing is to help you reduce your monthly payments. This can be an extremely helpful means of financing a home, but only in a soft market. The way it works is simple. As a condition of sale, you get the seller to give you a mortgage with no interest and no monthly payments. (The principal is all due in a single balloon payment a few years down the road.)

Of course, no seller will accept a no interest/no monthly payment second mortgage in a strong market. There's no reason to, unless you sweeten the pot, which usually means offering a higher price. Good buyers will be coming in with cash.

However, this plan may fly without a higher price in a weak market when there simply aren't any buyers around. In order to get any sale at all, a seller may consider it.

TIP

Look for a seller who doesn't need all the cash out of a property in order to move on to another. If the seller needs cash, the deal can't be made no matter how you butter it up. Remember that most sellers are selling only to buy again somewhere else.

I have seen no interest/no monthly payments second mortgages written fairly frequently in a cold market. Often it may be the only way the seller is going to be able to sell the property, and for that reason, it may be acceptable.

Can Creative Financing Cut My Costs and Red Tape?

There is one additional advantage of having the seller carry back the mortgage: the seller will not normally charge any fees for the service. It would be a rare seller indeed who charged points, for example, for a carry-back second mortgage. Or who charged processing or document fees, something that institutional lenders charge all the time. When you have the seller finance the sale, amongst other things, it also means that the financing is a lot cheaper for you.

What Is a Wraparound Mortgage?

Thus far, we've been assuming that the seller would be willing to give you a second mortgage when you offer to buy his or her property. However, some sellers are quite wary. They are concerned about your ability and desire to repay the mortgage. For example, what if the seller gives you a big second mortgage, and then you don't make the payments on the first?

This puts the seller in a difficult position. The seller must learn about the default and foreclose upon you, all the while fending off the institutional lender of the first.

Many sellers who would otherwise be willing to help buyers with financing won't do it because of their fear of the buyer not living up to the obligations on the first mortgage, thereby forcing them into a difficult foreclosure. The wraparound or "all-inclusive second mortgage" is a solution to this problem.

TIP

The wraparound, or wrap, blends two mortgages. Since one of the mortgages is usually of a lower interest rate than the overall wrap rate, it provides the lender with a much higher yield. Because of this, the lender can sometimes offer the borrower a lower interest rate. Thus, a wrap can benefit both borrower and lender.

The wrap has been used for years in commercial financing of real estate. It gained popularity in residential property in the mid-1970s as a way of getting around "due-on-sale" clauses (preventing assumptions), thus allowing buyers to assume sellers' existing low interest rate mortgages.

It fell out of vogue in real estate when the due-on-sale clause in existing mortgages was widely upheld in precedent-setting court cases. However, any time the real estate market dips downward and sellers look for new and creative ways of helping buyers purchase their homes, it comes back into vogue.

How Does a Wrap Work?

In its simplest form, the seller gives you a single mortgage that includes a new second as well as an old, assumable first. However, instead of making two mortgage payments, you make one . . . to the seller. The seller then makes the payment on the existing first and keeps the difference, which is the payment on the second.

Notice the difference here between a wrap and a traditional second mortgage. In the traditional second, you are the borrower of record on both the first and the second and make two payments, one on each mortgage. In the wrap you are the borrower of record on only one mortgage, the wraparound. The seller then forwards your payments to the lender of the first.

In the example shown in Figure 20-2, you put 10 percent down

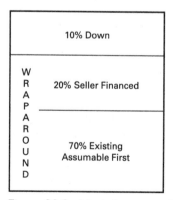

Figure 20-2. A typical wraparound mortgage.

and wrap an existing first of 70 percent of the sales price with the seller advancing 20 percent of the equity.

TRAP

You can get in trouble trying to wrap around an existing **nonassumable** first mortgage. The reason is simple. As soon as the sale is recorded, it gives the lender of the first mortgage constructive notice that the property has changed hands. Foreclosure could result.

If a lender discovers that you've wrapped around a nonassumable first mortgage, it can exert the due-on-sale clause, found in all nonassumable mortgages, and call in the loan. (Remember, *nonassumable* means that as soon as the property is sold, the mortgage must be paid off. Putting the wrap on the property, in effect, results in the first becoming immediately due and payable.)

In actual practice, according to lenders with whom I've talked, most discover the wrap less than 50 percent of the time. And those that do discover it frequently overlook the problem if their loan is current and paid on time. Their philosophy is that they'd rather keep a good, paying borrower than get into the hassle of a foreclosure. Nevertheless, it's not something to risk the price of an entire home on.

What Are the Ideal Conditions for a Wrap?

In order for a wrap to work, the first mortgage must either be new or, if it's existing, must be assumable. (FHA and VA loans are often assumable and may be wrapped in this fashion.) In the case of a new mortgage, often both the seller and the buyer are named in the mortgage. In the event the borrower doesn't make payments, this allows the seller the right to make payments on the first and keep it current while foreclosing on the wrap.

In the case of an assumable mortgage, such as an FHA-insured or VA-guaranteed loan (Note: not all are assumable anymore—

you must verify this first), often no notice of the wrap need be given to the lender. The new wrap loan is simply placed on the property, and the seller continues making payments on the existing first.

What If the Seller Wants to Wrap a Nonassumable?

Sometimes a seller will want to wrap around a nonassumable first mortgage in spite of the problems. You, the buyer, may be told that to avoid accelerating the mortgage because of the due-on-sale clause, the title won't actually be transferred to you. Rather, it will be held in escrow or will be in some other form until you can pay off the equivalent of the second-mortgage portion of the wrap. Then the seller will transfer, and you can get a new first mortgage.

Remember, the problem here is caused by the fact that the existing mortgage cannot be assumed. The wrap in this case is a ploy to get around the nonassumption problem.

Beware of this kind of a deal, as it may end up costing you a lot of money as well as the house. In real estate, your interest in the property is evidenced by title, which means a recorded deed in your name. If you don't have recorded title, you don't effectively own the property. Without your knowledge, the seller, conceivably, could refinance it or even sell it to someone else! Without title, you aren't properly protected.

In a nonrecorded wrap, the best you are likely to have is a contract with the seller. However, no matter how ironclad the contract may appear to be, your only recourse in the event the seller fails to live up to the terms may be to take the seller to court—a long, arduous, and costly process with unpredictable results.

What to Include When You Ask for Seller Financing

It's important to understand that everything in real estate is negotiable. That includes the second mortgage (or wrap) that you seek from the seller. What this means for you is that you can plan the terms and conditions of the loan so that they give you, the borrower, the greatest advantage. This is not to say that the seller will accept your terms. However, unless you have terms you want, how will you know? Following are some terms to look for.

Lower Interest Rate

Of course, one of the most important items to consider is the interest rate. As with most things, this is a trade-off. The higher the interest rate, the more likely the seller is to accept this kind of financing. The lower the interest rate, the less likely. In other words, the more interest you are willing to pay the seller on this note, the more desirable it is.

TIP

The trade-off is usually between purchase price and interest rate. If you are offering a good purchase price (close to market or to what the seller is asking), you are more likely to get a low interest rate. On the other hand, if you are lowballing the seller and demanding a low price, you are better off offering a higher and more appealing interest rate on the second.

TRAP

Be aware of usury laws. Some states still have laws that limit the amount of interest that a seller can charge on a second mortgage. Any amount over that rate is considered usurious and unlawful. (These same laws may not apply to first mortgages offered by institutions.) The seller may insist on an interest rate that is above the usury rate for your state. You can then inform the seller of the problem and in this way get a lower interest rate on your mortgage than you might otherwise secure.

Note: Some states specifically exempt seller financing from usury laws. Here, as a seller, you can charge any amount of interest you want.

Longer Payoff Period

Another negotiable item is the length of the mortgage. A second or wrap can be for any length of time. It can be for 3 months, 3 years, or 30 years. It's all up to what you and the seller agree upon.

In most cases the longer the term, the better for you, the borrower. Most sellers want second mortgages for a relatively short time, say, 18 months to 5 years. Usually during that time you pay interest only, which means at the end, you still owe the full amount that you borrowed. (Balloon payments are discussed in Chap. 13.)

As a result, you must usually refinance or sell the home before the term of the seller's financing runs out. Naturally, the longer the second, therefore, the better it is for you.

On the other hand, sellers usually, but not always, want their money out quickly. Thus, the shorter the term, the more appealing the second is likely to be. Again, if you ask for a longer second, be prepared to give someplace else, such as offering a higher interest rate or perhaps a higher price. On the other hand, if you're willing to settle for a short-term second, say a year, you may be able to negotiate for a lower interest rate (or no interest) and a lower purchase price.

TIP

Most sellers want their money as soon as possible so that they can put it into another home. But sometimes a seller has different ideas. Sellers who are retiring or who have other assets often want a long-term mortgage at a good rate so that they can collect interest, which is usually better than they can get at the bank. Find out your seller's motivation. If, indeed, the seller is looking for interest income, a long-term second may be to both parties' advantage.

TRAP

Beware of short-term seconds. You can never know what the market will be like 3 or 2 years or even 6 months in the future. You may say to yourself, "Sure, it'll be a cinch to refinance when the short-term second comes due." But by then, interest rates may take a jump up, and you won't be able to refinance. Or you could be laid off and not have the income to qualify for a new mortgage. Or the market may head into a tailspin, and you may not be able to sell. Always allow yourself as much of an escape route as possible. In terms of seconds, this means get enough time for you to ride out most adversities. To my mind, any second for less than 5 years is risky.

Many institutional lenders today are giving long-term (15- to 30-year) seconds at competitive interest rates. If there is a problem with seller financing, see if a lending institution can help out.

Better Conditions

Finally, there are the conditions of the second. Keep in mind that whatever conditions are imposed in the second are strictly a matter of negotiation between you and the seller. Unlike a first mortgage from an institutional lender where the conditions will be dictated to you, in a creative second almost everything is negotiable.

In most cases buyer and seller will simply fill out a "standard" second mortgage agreement that a title insurance, escrow company, or broker will provide. However, you can easily deviate from the printed text. Be sure you have a good real estate attorney working with you.

Late Payment Penalty.   One matter you will want to consider is late payment. In almost all first mortgages, there is a provision that if your payment is more than 2 weeks late, you will be fined a penalty usually equal to 5 percent of the mortgage payment ($50 on a $1000 payment).

This clause does not have to be inserted into the second. Unless the seller insists upon it, it would be to your advantage, in fact, to have it left out.

TIP

Some states have a limit on the amount of a late payment penalty. Also, the penalty may or may not be applicable to a balloon payment in your state. Check with a local attorney for help negotiating better terms.

The penalty for late payment can be a negotiating point. If the seller intends to sell the second (see Chap. 15 on yields) to an investor, it is vital to have the penalty. Most investors will either not buy or pay less for a second without a penalty clause. Therefore, if the seller insists on a penalty clause in the second, you may agree, for a better term or interest rate.

Subordination Clause. This is a clause that you may very well want to have in the second, but that the seller, if he or she is bright at all, will usually frown upon. It is difficult to get sellers to agree to subordinate, but if you can, it can be a real plus to you.

A subordination clause means that the second mortgage remains in place even if you refinance the first. While this may seem obvious, it is not. To understand why, it is necessary to remember how mortgages are placed on real estate. They flow chronologically in the order in which they were recorded. What makes a first a first is not so much anything that is stated in the paperwork, but the fact that it was recorded first, before any other mortgages. A second was recorded second, a third recorded third, and so on.

Let's say you have a first and a second, and you want to refinance the first. In order to do this, you have to pay off the existing first and get a new mortgage. However, as soon as you pay off the existing first, the existing second moves up and becomes "first" in chronological order. Therefore, you could not refinance the old first mortgage with a new first mortgage until you also paid off the second.

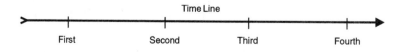

The solution is the subordination clause. When put into a second it requires that mortgage to hold its place. The second remains a second regardless of what happens to the first. If you pay off the first, you can then refinance and get a brand-new first and *the second holds its position.*

The importance to you is that you can usually get a first mortgage for a lower interest rate, longer term, and higher amount than a second. Also, by keeping the second in its position, you can refinance, get more money out and not have to pay off the second. This latter benefit, of course, is why sellers don't like it. A subordination clause weakens a second.

TIP

A seller might be induced into taking a subordination clause if you limit it. For example, you could insert a clause saying that you will get a first of no more than a certain amount. Limiting the amount of the first protects the seller's second.

Automatic Refinance Clause.   This is a tricky little clause that some shrewd borrowers have been inserting into second mortgages of late. If it gets past the seller, it could be worth its weight in gold.

The refinance clause simply states that when the second comes due, the seller agrees to refinance it. In other words, your second may be for 3 years. At the end of the 3 years, at *your* (the borrower's) option, it can automatically be refinanced for an additional 3 years.

Why would the seller accept such a condition? Usually the clause states that the refinance will be at or slightly above the then-current mortgage market rate for first mortgages. In other words, if at the end of 3 years (in this case) the market rate for conventional first mortgages is 8 percent, the second will be refinanced at, say, 9 percent. If the seller doesn't need the cash, this is an excellent way to lock in money for an additional period of time.

If you get a refinance clause inserted into your second, be sure that it is tied to a standard index, which can be provided by any lender (see Chap. 14).

TIP

If you're daring, you may agree to a very high interest rate on the refinance, say 5 percent above going mortgage market rates. The seller may think that he or she is getting a real bonus here, which you can use as a negotiating tool elsewhere in the deal. In reality, of course, the seller is getting nothing, since the refinance is at your option. You can choose not to exercise it and instead to refinance elsewhere or sell the property.

Size of Second Relative to Down.   While it's true that everything is negotiable, some things are harder to negotiate. For example, it may be to your advantage to offer a 5 percent down payment and a 15 percent second. However, if the seller wants to dispose of that second, he or she will find it almost impossible to do so if you only put 5 percent down. In order for a second to be marketable to an investor, the buyer must typically put at least 10 percent down.

Will a Seller Give Me a First Mortgage?

Thus far we've been discussing sellers who are willing to give part of the equity to you in the form of a second mortgage. But there's another, though much smaller, class of sellers who are willing to make first mortgages.

These sellers are typically older people who have been in the property for 20 to 30 years and have either paid off or almost paid off their existing mortgage(s). These people may not have any use for a large amount of cash, as they would receive in an all-cash sale. But instead they may be interested in a kind of annuity. They want so much each month on which to live. A first mortgage is an ideal answer for them...and for you as well.

The reason is that if the seller carries the first, you may get the mortgage for slightly below market interest rates. However, you probably won't have to pay points or other loan fees. And you may not have to qualify as strictly as you would for an institutional lender. A seller may accept a borrower with slightly blemished credit, with a lower down payment, even with less income (less ability to repay) than an institutional lender would, simply to get the house sold.

TIP

To my mind it is worth paying more for a property where the seller will carry the first. The benefits in quicker and easier qualifying as well as lower costs more than justify a higher price.

How Do I Negotiate with the Seller?

We've discussed a variety of options that you may want to consider when having the seller help with the financing. One last matter needs to be discussed: the actual negotiation process. How do you negotiate with the seller to get what you want?

There's a three step process that I use that may be helpful to you:

Step One. Identify what you want.

Step Two. Give in order to get.

Step Three. Try to be flexible.

The bottom line is remembering that everything in real estate is negotiable, including terms. Many sellers simply can't or won't consider helping with the financing. But it usually won't hurt to ask in terms of an offer. (It can hurt if you make an offer asking for favorable terms and lose out to another buyer who comes in with all cash.)

The real trick is getting the right balance between terms, price, and mortgage amount.

21

Should I Consider an FHA or a VA Mortgage?

During the 1950s and part of the 1960s, the most popular mortgages in real estate were those offered under the Federal Housing Authority (FHA) and the Veterans Administration (VA) programs. In those days, it seemed that when a buyer bought a home, he or she first tried to get one of these mortgages. Only after this proved impossible would the buyer settle for a "conventional," or nongovernment, mortgage.

During the 1970s, however, particularly when housing prices skyrocketed, the allure of these mortgages diminished. Private mortgage insurance (PMI) was available to provide low-down-payment conventional financing. Additionally, the bureaucratic red tape made FHA-VAs less desirable choices. By the end of the 1970s, fewer than 10 percent of all mortgages were from these government programs.

Then in the 1980s the FHAs and VAs came roaring back. Assumability became important, and these loans were all assumable. Recently, FHA loans have again fallen into disfavor, largely because of relatively low maximum mortgage amounts. However, new legislation raising the maximum may be enacted by the time you read this.

FHA Mortgages

The FHA does not usually lend money to borrowers. Under the most commonly used programs, the FHA isn't even in the mortgage lending business. Instead, it insures mortgages. The borrower gets a loan from a lender, for instance, an S&L. If it's an FHA loan, the government insures payment of the mortgage to the lender. If the borrower doesn't make the payments, the FHA steps in and pays off the lender. With an FHA loan, the lender can't lose.

There are a number of FHA programs. They have included the following:

Title II

203(b)	Financing of one- to four-family dwellings
203(b)	Special financing for veterans
207	Financing rental housing and mobile home parks
221(d)	Financing low-cost one- to four-family dwellings for displaced or moderate-income families
222	Financing one-family homes for service personnel
234(f)	Financing condominium units
234(d)	Financing condo projects and condo conversion projects
235	Assistance to low-income families to make home purchase by subsidizing mortgage interest payments

Title I

(b)	Financing purchase of a mobile home unit

Many of these programs have been cut or at least severely pruned as federal budget cutting has proceeded in Washington. But the basic program, 203(b), still helps finance home mortgages.

Advantages of FHA Loans

1. *They may be assumable.*   At one time, all FHA loans were fully assumable by any buyer. That meant that any time you wanted to sell your property, all you had to do was turn your existing (often low-interest) FHA loan over to the buyer. After 1987,

however, the FHA imposed stricter rules. Now buyers must qualify, including credit reports and income verifications. When the buyer does qualify, however, he or she still can take over the existing interest rate mortgage.

Additionally, the seller may continue to be liable under certain circumstances. For mortgages issued after December of 1986, liability may extend for 5 years. For those issued after December of 1989, liability may extend for 10 years or more.

2. *There are no prepayment penalties.*   An FHA mortgage may be paid off in full at any time without penalty.

3. *Not only does the buyer have to qualify for the FHA mortgage, but the property has to qualify as well.*   This means something more than the house simply being appraised for enough money to warrant the mortgage. It means that the house has to qualify structurally. Sometimes on FHA mortgages, the seller will be required to bring any substandard construction up to current building codes. Any damage, such as that done by wind, water, termites, fungus, erosion, and so forth, might also have to be corrected. When a buyer purchases a home under an FHA program, he or she has virtually a government stamp of approval on it.

Disadvantages of the FHA Loan

There are some disadvantages (not many) to the FHA mortgage. These include the following:

1. *Maximum loan amount is relatively low.*   That's all right for some parts of the country, but for the West Coast, East Coast, and areas in between where residential property prices are high, it's frequently just too low for the FHA to be a useful source of financing.

2. *The borrower must occupy the property to get the low down payment.* If you want to pay 3 percent down, then you must be an owner–occupant. You can still get the FHA financing as a nonoccupant investor, *but* you're required to put 15 percent down.

3. *The borrower must pay a mortgage insurance premium.*   The premium is a substantial amount.

Mortgage Premium

The mortgage insurance premium (MIP) for residential property must be paid up front at the time the loan is made. (In the past it would have been paid monthly as a slight increase in payment.) The percentage used for the mortgage premium has frequently changed.

Down Payment

As noted, the down payment is 5 percent or less for owner-occupied property or 15 percent for investor-purchased. In the past, this down payment had to be in cash. Recently, however, the FHA has allowed it to be handled through secondary financing.

It works like this: If you want to buy a piece of property using an FHA mortgage, you can either put 15 percent cash down *or* you can put up a second mortgage *on a different piece of property.* Note that the second mortgage *cannot be on the property being financed.* Rather, it has to be on some other property. For example, you may own a lot or another house. You can give the seller of the property you are currently buying a second mortgage on your other house. It may be a bit complicated, but it does work.

The FHA is part of HUD (the Department of Housing and Urban Development), with offices in all major cities and main offices in Washington, D.C.

VA Mortgages

The VA program is similar to the FHA program in that it is administered by the government. However, that's where the similarities tend to end. For new VA mortgages, the borrower has to have one vital ingredient. He or she has to be a veteran and have qualifying duty.

The biggest advantage the VA loan program has over the FHA is that in many cases there is *no down payment*. The borrower doesn't have to put up anything to make the purchase (with, of course, the exception of closing costs).

Literally millions of veterans have used the VA program. Some have gone back and used it many times. (Soon we'll see how.)

How the VA Program Works

Like an FHA mortgage, the VA loan is obtained from a lender such as a bank or an S&L. However, while the FHA insures the lender against loss, the VA "guarantees" a portion of the loan (actually the first money likely to be lost by the lender). If the veteran defaults, the VA will pay the first 25 percent of the debt.

Since that usually represents any loss a lender is likely to sustain, it virtually removes the lender from any risk. In actual practice, when a borrower defaults, the VA, like the FHA, buys the entire mortgage back from the lender and then tries to resell the property. (These are called VA, or FHA, "repos.") Unlike the FHA, however, the VA, if it sustains any loss on the resale of the property, can come after the borrower, a veteran, to try to recoup its loss.

Down Payment

The maximum VA mortgage is currently $204,000. The down payment is negotiated between the lender and the veteran. The VA charges a funding fee to the veteran depending on the amount put down. The fee schedule is as follows:

Less than 5% down	2.0 (% of loan balance)
5% to 10% down	1.5
Over 10% down	1.25

The funding fee is paid by the veteran to the VA. Points are paid by the seller.

Entitlement

The portion that the VA guarantees is called the veteran's "entitlement." When the program was first started, the entitlement was only $2000. However, housing prices have gone up, and so has the entitlement. Recently it was a maximum of $50,750.

Reusing Entitlement

The veteran's entitlement usually remains with the vet for life. This means that if the veteran sells the property *and the VA loan is paid off,* he or she may reapply for and receive back the entitlement; he or she would then be able to get another VA loan.

Using Remaining Entitlement

Because the entitlement amount has risen, there are many veterans who bought homes years ago when the entitlement was lower and who still are eligible for a portion of their entitlement. For example, if a vet bought a home in the 1950s, when the entitlement was $5000, he or she may today be able to claim the difference between the entitlement used ($5000) and the current maximum.

Qualifying for a VA Loan

Unlike the FHA or even conventional lenders, the VA does not have a hard-and-fast formula that it uses to qualify a veteran. Rather, it has criteria. The criteria are as follows:

1. A history of good credit
2. Sufficient income to make the payments and support the veteran's family
3. An eligible veteran with available entitlement

The VA has been extremely flexible in the past regarding mortgages to vets. I have seen cases where a vet who was turned down went directly to the VA and won a reversal on the strength of a promise to make payments. A large part of the VA program has been aimed at helping veterans get a home and get started.

Eligibility Requirements

The eligibility requirements for VA loans seem to be always changing. To determine what the current requirements are, you should check with your nearest VA office.

VA Appraisals

When a veteran applies for a mortgage, the VA appraises the property and then issues a Certificate of Reasonable Value (CRV). Sales contracts that specify that the borrower is obtaining a VA loan must also specify that if the property does not appraise for the sale price (the CRV doesn't equal the sale price), the veteran may withdraw from the sale, *or*, the veteran may opt to pay more than the CRV. However, the loan amount will still be based on the CRV, not the final sale price.

Automatics

Because of the long delays that have occurred in the past in funding VA loans, the VA has designated certain lenders to handle automatic funding. What this means is that the lender qualifies the veteran, makes the loan, and closes the deal. Then the lender secures the loan guarantee from the VA. Most large S&Ls, banks, and mortgage bankers are approved for automatics.

Owner-Occupancy Requirement

The VA has long required that the veteran plan to occupy the property. If the property is larger than a home (a duplex for example), the vet must plan to occupy one unit on the property. There are no age requirements for either VA or FHA loans.

Impound Accounts

Both VA and FHA mortgages require that the borrower establish an impound account (also called a trust fund account). This simply means that the borrower must pay for the taxes and insurance on the property on a monthly basis (i.e., must pay one-twelfth of the yearly total each month). The monthly payment goes into a lender's special impound account, and the lender pays the fees at the appropriate times each year.

22
When Should I Refinance?

When you own property, there is always the temptation to refinance. The question is, should you? There are many reasons to refinance. If you have a lot of equity, you most certainly will keep thinking to yourself of all the ways you could use that money—if you could just get it out of the property. If interest rates have dropped, you'll wonder if maybe now is the time to roll over that old higher-rate mortgage. If you have a lot of bills to pay, you may be wondering if you could cut down on your overall monthly payments as well as interest costs by refinancing.

In this chapter we'll look at three of the refinance temptations and try to come up with a method of determining whether it's a good or bad idea for you. We'll cover the following:

- Falling interest rates
- Home improvement loans
- Debt consolidation mortgages

What If Interest Rates Are Falling?

During the latter half of the 1990s, interest rates fell to historic lows. Many people who had purchased homes earlier realized their current mortgage interest rate was higher than the rates for new loans. The question for them became, when does it pay to refinance?

In the old days (read: about 10 years ago), there was a rule of thumb that said that interest rates had to fall about 2 percent before refinancing made sense. That's because the costs of the refinance (title insurance, escrow, mortgage points, and other fees) were so high. Thus, if you had a mortgage currently at 9 percent, you should wait until rates dropped to 7 percent before refinancing.

Today that rule of thumb makes little sense at all. Instead, every case is judged on its own merits. Here's a way to determine what you should do based on monthly payments:

1. *Determine How Long You Will Own the Property.* The first thing you should consider is how long do you realistically anticipate owning the property. This is the single most critical factor in answering the refinance question, and you should consider it very carefully. Ask yourself the following questions:

    1. Is a job change likely within a year or two?   Yes [ ] No [ ]

    2. Is your family outgrowing the home?   Yes [ ] No [ ]

    3. Are your kids grown up and leaving, making the
       the home too big?   Yes [ ] No [ ]

    4. Are you likely to suffer a financial reversal (job
       loss, alimony reduction, or other income loss),
       making upkeep of the home difficult?   Yes [ ] No [ ]

    5. If you answered "yes" to question four, when is it
       likely to occur?_____

    6. Is the property old and becoming obsolete so that
       you'd like to move to something newer?   Yes [ ] No [ ]

    7. Is the neighborhood declining, meaning
       you'll want to move soon?   Yes [ ] No [ ]

    8. If the answer to number 7 is "yes," how soon? _____

    9. Are there any other factors (health, marriage,
       and so on) that would force you to change your
       plans and move sooner?   Yes [ ] No [ ]

    10. In an ideal world, how long will you realistically
        continue to live in the property? _____

The entire purpose of the quiz is to help you focus on the real possibility of wanting to sell the property and, more important, *when*. A lot of "yes" answers suggest your stay in the property is likely to be short-lived. If that's the case, try to come up with a date for selling that property. Hopefully that date will be exact, such as August 2003 or January 2010.

Once you have the date, calculate how many months there are between the date you want to sell and today's month. Are there 21 months or 210 months?

2. *Find Out Your New Monthly Payment.* Now go out there and find the best mortgage you can get with the same term. (Don't compare a 15-year mortgage with a 30.) Go for a fixed rate because it's easier to determine monthly payments, over time. Determine the actual mortgage payment you'll need to pay.

3. *Add In Costs of Refinancing.* If you get a 0-points and/or 0-cost mortgage, you needn't go any further. Skip down to the next section. If, however, it's going to cost you points and fees to get the mortgage, find out the total amount of these and divide them by the months before you sell. For example, if you anticipate selling within 36 months and your refinance fees are $3600, that comes to $100 a month. Now add this amount to your new mortgage payment.

4. *Compare Old with New Payments.* Finally, compare your new payment to your old one. If the new payment (after you've added in the prorated costs) is lower than your old payment, it usually pays to refinance. If it's the same or higher, it usually doesn't.

Here are the steps to follow:

Making the Refinance Calculation

1. *Determine how long you'll keep the place in months.* We'll assume 36 months.

2. *Determine your new mortgage payment.* We'll assume $900.

3. *Add in the prorated costs of getting the mortgage.* We'll assume $100.

4. *Compare this to your existing monthly mortgage amount.*

Mortgage payment	$ 900	
Prorated costs	100	
Total new monthly	$1000	
Total old monthly	1100	**Higher**—Refinance
Total old monthly	900	**Lower**—Don't refinance

TRAP

There's something important we haven't considered and that's equity return. As you pay off your mortgage, your equity in the property increases. If you have a new mortgage, the return is minimal. However, if you have an old established mortgage, the return is significant. That means that even if you end up saving money monthly as shown above, you could lose by replacing an old mortgage with a new one. You could reduce your equity return too much. When considering refinancing an old mortgage with a new one, consider how much equity return will be reduced. Beware of too easily getting rid of an old mortgage.

TIP

I have seen people, using the above calculation, refinance in order to save just $20 a month! That's cutting it too fine. Remember, when you determine how long you're going to keep the property, it's an estimate. You could be way off. Generally speaking, make sure that the monthly decrease in payments is big enough to offset a miscalculation in time.

Are There Any Problems Associated with Refinancing?

Perhaps the biggest difficulty can be getting equity out. Lenders don't like to see you take your equity out of their loan. In a typical refinance you'll have no trouble getting enough money to pay off the existing mortgage plus all of your costs of refinancing. But try to get a few dollars more and the lender may balk.

If you're an owner–occupant you may find that many lenders will ease the above restriction, particularly if you have a lot of equity. However, if you're an investor, you'll find it very difficult to find lenders who will lend you equity-out money. You'll have to spend more time checking around.

What Type of Mortgage Should I Get When I Refinance?

Generally speaking, if you replace an existing ARM (adjustable-rate mortgage) with a lower-interest fixed-rate mortgage, you are improving your position. Go the other way and you are weakening it. When interest rates are low, try very hard to lock them in with a fixed-rate mortgage. You'll be thankful for this as soon as interest rates climb back up.

If you anticipate only holding the property a short time, an ARM with a very low teaser rate (see Chap. 14) may be your best bet. You'll get the benefit of low interest/low monthly payments while you own the property, and hopefully, just as the rate/payments rise, you'll sell.

As to the almost infinite varieties that exist between these types, see Chaps. 6 and 7 for general advice.

Should I Get a "Debt Consolidation" Mortgage?

Here the motivation is to reduce the interest rate you're paying, typically on credit card and personal loan (such as car) debt and thus reduce the payments. A debt consolidation mortgage simply expresses the purpose of getting the financing—it's still the same old kind of mortgage in every other way.

Usually, but not always, the mortgage obtained is not a "first" but rather a "second." This means that it's an additional mortgage placed on the property so you end up with two. The second almost certainly will have an interest rate higher than the first.

How much higher depends on market conditions, how big the second mortgage is, and your credit standing.

Again, the way to determine if it makes sense to get a new mortgage for the purpose of consolidating debt is to find out how much you need (by adding up all your debt), what your old combined credit payments are, and how big your new mortgage payment will be.

TIP

If you have a lot of credit card debt, chances are that the new single mortgage payment will be significantly lower than the old numerous payments. When you add in car payments, however, this could change because many times car loans are subsidized by manufacturers as an incentive to make the purchase. Your interest rate on a car loan just might be lower than the interest rate on the new consolidation loan. Be careful when you add in all the figures—you could be surprised!

TRAP

Be very careful to compare the length of existing debt with the term of the new mortgage. For example, if the new much lower payment mortgage is for 10 years, but your current debt only has 2 years to run, it may be a terrible deal. You'll be much better to pay off the debt in 2 years than 10. Use the calculation procedure shown earlier in the chapter.

What about Savings on Taxes?

Interest on consumer debt is generally not tax-deductible. Interest on homes loans, up to certain maximums, is. Thus, by consolidating your debt and taking out a home equity loan, you may save additionally by being able to deduct the interest. Check with your accountant to see if you can take such deductions.

What about Home Equity Loans?

A home equity loan is usually just another name for a second mortgage, with a twist. The twist is that it's a revolving loan. You have a maximum amount you can borrow. If you pay down the amount borrowed, you can borrow it again. Typically such revolving loans have a time limit, usually around 10 years, after which they switch to an ARM to be paid back over 20 years.

Home equity loans are a great source of quick credit. Once set up, they're in place whenever you need them. Instead of having to borrow cash at very high interest rates (often 20 percent or more) on credit cards, you can borrow it on the home equity loan, typically for half that amount.

The only drawback to this type of financing is that you must have considerable equity in your property. Generally speaking, your combined mortgages cannot exceed 80 percent of the property value. Thus, if you already have a first mortgage currently at 70 percent of value, the maximum home equity loan you could get would be for 10 percent. Here's a typical home equity loan:

Property value	$200,000	
Existing mortgage	70,000	= 35 percent of market
Maximum home equity	90,000	= 45 percent of market
	160,000	= 80 percent of market

Generally speaking, you can use a home equity loan for any legal purpose. This includes college education, fixing up the property, or taking a cruise.

23

Should I Pay Off My Mortgage Early?

If you're a high-income earner, the last thing you may want to do is to pay off your mortgage. You have plenty of income coming in, and the income tax deduction you get for mortgage interest provides you with what might possibly be your only tax shelter. Paying it off might make no sense at all.

On the other hand, if you're retired and have a very small income but have a fair amount of cash in the bank, paying off that mortgage and eliminating a burdensome payment could make perfectly good sense. In this chapter we're going to consider some of the ramifications of paying off your mortgage. And then at the end, we'll look into a strange plan for getting even more income from a property that's been paid off, a reverse mortgage.

Can You Pay It Off?

If you're in a position to pay off your mortgage early, you are indeed unusual. Typically you've had the mortgage on the property for a fairly long time, and it's close to maturity. Perhaps it

187

has 5 or 10 years to go out of 30. Now you're wondering if it makes sense to pay it off early. What are the advantages and disadvantages?

Note: The decision to pay off an existing mortgage should not be taken lightly, particularly if you are retired and living on a fixed income. Don't simply rely on the information in this chapter. Consult with a trusted advisor who can analyze your particular situation. You don't want to make a mistake and put your future in jeopardy.

Should I Consider Equity Return?

I've mentioned it before, but it's particularly applicable here. The return of equity from a mortgage is much greater in its later years than in its earlier ones. When your mortgage gets to its final years, most of each monthly payment goes to principle, less and less to interest. Thus, what you are doing in those last years is rapidly paying off the mortgage and rapidly adding to your equity in the property.

Many people feel that this period of rapid equity return is the golden period of the mortgage. It's that rare time when you get the benefits instead of the mortgage company. Nevertheless, the question must be asked, could you make better use of that money that you are paying out each month? For example, let's say your monthly payments on the mortgage are $750 a month of which $500 is going to equity and $250 is going to interest. For practical purposes you can think of the $500 as "money in the bank." It's going toward your equity or your savings in the home.

But can you afford to save $500 a month? Perhaps you are struggling to make other payments. Or perhaps you are on a fixed income. Might it not be better to pay off that mortgage and avoid having to pay out $750 a month?

Oftentimes people who find themselves in the position described above have some savings in the bank. They ask themselves, wouldn't it be better to take out those savings and pay off the mortgage, thus avoiding that big monthly payment?

How Do I Make the Payoff Decision?

Your decision depends on at least two factors. One is the interest rate. If the interest rate on the mortgage is *higher* than the interest rate on the money in savings, it definitely makes economic sense.

Consider this: Let's say the outstanding balance on the mortgage is $30,000 and the interest rate is 8 percent. That means that in the current year you are spending roughly $2400 in interest on that mortgage.

On the other hand, let's say that you have $30,000 in the bank earning 5 percent interest. Your money that year earns $1500:

Mortgage interest paid out	$2400
Savings interest earned	+ $1500
Net loss	900

The result of keeping $30,000 in the bank at 5 percent and paying out 8 percent on a mortgage with a $30,000 balance is a loss of $900 a year. In short, simply by paying off the mortgage, you can pick up an additional $900 a year otherwise lost in interest payments.

Of course, the amount to be gained will vary according to the amount of the mortgage and the difference in interest rates. However, I think the point should be clear. Economically speaking, without any other considerations, it makes sense here to pay off the mortgage.

There are, however, other considerations. The first is taxes.

What about Taxes?

Generally speaking, you'll pay taxes on interest you receive from a savings account. (If you have the money invested in certain tax-free mutual bonds or funds, that may not be the case.) On the other hand, generally speaking, you'll be able to deduct the interest you pay on your home mortgage.

Thus, if you take the money out of savings, you'll reduce the interest you receive and pay taxes on. At the same time, however, you'll also pay off the mortgage and eliminate the interest deduction there. Thus, the situation tends to be a bit of a wash. It probably won't come out even, but the tax consequences could come close to offsetting each other.

TIP

Many people in lower income brackets don't itemize on their returns. If you don't itemize, then you can't claim the interest deduction on your mortgage, so it's worth nothing to you. You must still, however, pay taxes on the income received from savings. In this case the economics suggest it may make more sense to pay off the mortgage.

What's the Value of Cash?

There's another consideration that's well worth making, particularly for those on limited incomes. How important is it to you to have cash in the bank? If you need a cash reserve to pay for medical or other unforeseen expenses, then you may be placing yourself in jeopardy by paying off your mortgage early. You may, in fact, be jumping from the frying pan into the fire.

The reason is that it's easy to get hold of cash in a savings account. Just go to the bank and withdraw it. It's hard to get cash out from equity in your home. You have to refinance or sell, and if you don't have a strong income and good credit or if the market's soft, both offer problems.

What's the Value of a Paid-Off Home?

On the other hand, there's a great deal to be said for the value of a paid-off property. I can't think of anything else in our modern world that can give one such a sense of security. You know that no matter what happens you have a place to go that a lender can't take away from you (for failing to make payments). You have to balance the need for cash with the comfort of a paid-off mortgage.

What If I Go Ahead and Pay Off the Property and Later Discover I Need Cash?

As noted earlier, that could be tricky. You'd have to refinance or sell—*Unless* you're retired and opt for a reverse equity mortgage, or REM (also sometimes called a reverse annuity mortgage, or RAM). The reverse equity mortgage takes money out of your home and gives it back to you on a monthly basis. It was designed to help older citizens get their equity out and still have a home to live in.

This mortgage has had a spotted past. It was first conceived on the East Coast, but only a couple of lenders tried it, with mixed results. Then a few lenders in the South tried it with better results, but the savings and loan debacle of the late 1980s made it impractical to use. More recently it is seeing a comeback in different parts of the country, sponsored by the FHA as the home equity conversion mortgage (HECM). (Mortgages really are an alphabet soup of letters!)

How Does a Reverse Equity Mortgage Work?

The way a basic REM works is relatively simple. It assumes that a borrower owns a house free and clear, or close to it. The lender sends out an appraiser who determines current value. Then the lender agrees to a loan to value ratio, typically 80 percent.

The owner/borrower can now receive 80 percent of the value. However, he or she only receives it in the form of a monthly payment, typically about as much as would be paid if the owner had borrowed the whole amount.

As shown in Figure 23-1; as each monthly payment is made, the principal and interest on it is subtracted from the equity in the house. Thus, the mortgage amount increases.

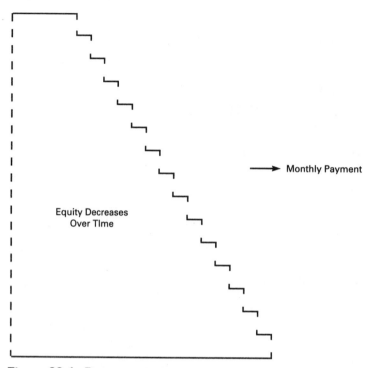

Figure 23-1. Reverse equity mortgage.

What Happens If You Outlive the Equity in the Property?

In the past, that meant that you could be thrown out of the property! With newer plans, particularly those from the FHA, there is a provision that you get to stay in the property for your lifetime. Further, in some cases the payments continue regardless of how long you live.

For this reason, lenders are very hesitant to move forward with reverse equity mortgages. However, those who have done it successfully have consulted with actuaries who come up with fairly accurate longevity tables.

TIP

The reverse equity mortgage can be a lifesaver if you have a paid-off house (or almost paid off), have little to no income, and are elderly. It can provide a steady income for your later years.

TRAP

You won't be able to give your children your home and its equity when you die if you opt for a REM. Rather, it will all go to the lender.

To learn more about the FHA plan, contact an FHA office. They are located in most major cities, with headquarters in Washington, D.C. An FHA office can tell you if any lenders participate in the program in your area (http://www.hud.gov).

24

How Do I Cancel Private Mortgage Insurance?

Any time you get a mortgage for more than 80 percent of the value of the property, you are likely to be faced with mortgage insurance. Mortgage insurance guarantees a portion of the mortgage to the lender in the event that you default.

There are two types of mortgage insurance: government and private. Government mortgage insurance is required on all FHA mortgages. (These days you typically pay the premium for it all up front at the time you get the mortgage.)

Private mortgage insurance (PMI) is available on most other loans provided both you and the property are of sufficiently high quality (creditwise and locationwise) to qualify. It is usually required on all mortgages with higher than 80 percent loan to value ratio. In this chapter we'll consider only PMI.

There is no problem per se with mortgage insurance. It is the lubricant that allows lenders to make bigger loans. For you, the borrower, it often allows you to get into a property that you could not otherwise afford. The problems occur later on down the road.

How Much Does It Cost?

For the privilege of insuring your mortgage, the lender charges you a premium, typically between one-fourth to one-half percent of the loan amount tacked onto the loan. *Note:* The private mortgage insurance does not insure you. It insures the lender against loss.

Why, you may ask, should you then be charged for it? The answer is simple. Without the insurance, most lenders won't make higher than 80 percent loans. If you want a high LTV loan, you have to pay for the insurance.

Must You Pay for the Life of the Mortgage?

A little-known (to most borrowers) aspect of PMI is that it is only required for as long as the loan to value remains above 80 percent. For example, if your original loan was for 90 percent and you've been paying for 10 years, you've probably paid down enough to lower the original loan amount below 80 percent. At that point, there's no further need of the private mortgage insurance.

Removing the PMI can give you an immediate benefit. If you're paying one-half of 1 percent on a $100,000 loan, that's $500 a year—a substantial savings. The trouble is that lenders, at least in the past, have frequently not told borrowers they could have the PMI removed. Indeed, in a few extreme cases, lenders themselves removed the PMI, then continued to receive the extra PMI payment from borrowers, pocketing the extra cash!

How Do I Get the PMI Removed?

There's the rub. You can't. Only the lender can have it removed. What you must do is essentially "petition" the lender for removal. You must be able to demonstrate that your current equity is 20 percent or greater (the mortgage is currently 80 percent or less of the home's market value). Then it's up to the discretion of the lender to have the PMI removed and your payments reduced.

In most cases lenders will comply. But they may require that you get a new appraisal, and you will have to pay for it. However, an appraisal is only a few hundred dollars, and you may save that and more the first year in reduced monthly payments.

TIP

Don't expect lenders to initiate removal of the PMI no matter how much your house appreciates or how much of the mortgage you pay down. They have no incentive to do so, and at best, it just means extra accounting for them. That means that you must get the ball rolling.

TRAP

Some mortgage agreements are written in such a way that the PMI could not be canceled, ever. Be sure you check your mortgage papers for the terms of the PMI on your property. Of course, the best time to check is before you sign.

Many of the problems with PMI arise out of the fact that, as of this writing, lenders are not required to tell borrowers that they need not pay the PMI after their loan balance drops below the original 80 percent loan to value ratio. Rather, the lenders simply keep collecting the money as long as the borrower pays it and doesn't complain.

Is There Any Government Help Here?

Increasingly, borrowers are becoming aware of the difficulty in getting PMI removed. Many have called lenders demanding that the PMI be removed only to be stonewalled. In cases where the mortgage is written in such a way that the lender has the *option* but not the obligation of removing the PMI, sometimes the lender simply refuses to act. If you demand it, they will stall, ignore you, or simply say no. They just don't want the bother.

As a result, legislation is being introduced in many states that would *require* lenders to cancel the PMI premium charged to borrowers on mortgages as soon as the mortgage dropped down to appropriate levels. Check with a lender to see what the status of legislation is in your state. You may find the lender is required to eliminate your PMI and reduce your mortgage payment.

Further, Federal legislation that would require removal of PMI once the mortgage LTV dropped below 80 percent has been introduced, but not passed, at this writing. (Perhaps this legislation has passed by the time you read this.) One problem with the federal legislation, however, is that it may not apply to existing mortgages, only to mortgages put on property *after* the legislation passed.

TIP

In all fairness to lenders and private mortgage insurers, it must be pointed out that a falling market, as was the case in the early 1990s, meant that it was hazardous to remove the PMI. While the mortgage value could indeed be 80 percent or below, if the price of the property fell, it could rise to more than 80 percent. Keeping PMI on in that kind of market made good sense from the lender's perspective.

In up markets leaving PMI on a property any longer than necessary makes no sense at all to the borrower. If your LTV is at 80 percent or lower and you have PMI, you should certainly investigate the possibility of having it removed. Check with your lender.

25

What Should I Do When Facing Foreclosure?

It's a terrible time if and when you ever face foreclosure, or even come close. You're behind on your payments, and after perhaps only a few weeks, you begin getting urgent letters from the lender. Then, if you can't make up the payments, the letters get even more urgent and become threatening. Soon you may get a "notice of default" telling you that if you don't correct the problem within a set period of days, the lender will foreclose.

If you can't make up the back payments, plus penalties, the lender may begin judicial foreclosure (in some eastern and southern states) and foreclosure by advertisement in the West and most other areas. You could soon lose your home.

TIP

Check with a good real estate attorney in your area about the exact procedure followed in your state. There are very specific deadlines that a lender (and you) must follow. If the lender misses a deadline, it could slow down or even cause the entire procedure to go back to the beginning. Miss your deadlines and you could lose your property.

What Can I Do about It?

It's beyond the scope of this book to go into the legal strategies that you can use to slow down or even stop foreclosure. Suffice to say that they run the gamut from the most obvious, making up the back payments and penalties, to the most serious, going into bankruptcy or filing suit against the lender for any possible infractions when the mortgage was made or in the procedure used to carry out the foreclosure. You'll definitely want to consult with a good attorney here.

However, there are a number of investment strategies that are worth noting. Keep in mind that all of these assume that you meet the various deadlines observed by the foreclosure procedure in your state so that you still have the ability to control the destiny of your property.

TRAP

Don't walk away when faced by foreclosure. Although it may seem like the easiest way out at the time, it will come back to haunt you for years. The lender may secure a default judgment against you, meaning that you could still owe the money even after you lose the property. And most certainly the lender will let credit reporting agencies know what happened. This could adversely affect your credit and preclude you from getting a new mortgage for many years to come.

What If I'm Upside Down?

This, of course, is the worst situation. It happens when there's a downward turn in the market. The value of your home falls until the mortgage is bigger than the property's market value. That's called being upside down.

You have no equity, and consequently, if you list the property with an agent, you'll have to pay the commission (plus the closing costs) out of your pocket. In addition, you could have to pay the lender the difference between the loan amount and the sales price. In short, it could cost you a lot of money (money that you probably don't have) to sell. What can you do?

The answer is to try for a "short sale."

What's a Short Sale?

In a short sale you sell the property for less than the mortgage value, and you get the lender to accept a "short payoff." In other words, the lender doesn't insist on the full repayment of the mortgage but instead accepts partial repayment.

For example, say you owe $150,000, but the property is sold for only $140,000. The lender accepts the $140,000 as payment in full for the mortgage.

TRAP

The IRS may consider the money forgiven in a short sale as taxable income. Check with your attorney. Also see Chap. 27.

What about Closing Costs in a Short Sale?

You have to be creative here. Sometimes agents will accept a second mortgage (paper) on the property in lieu of cash. Sometimes the buyer will agree to pay the closing costs, since he or she is getting such a bargain. Other times you end up cutting costs selling the property FSBO (for sale by owner). When you don't have equity, you have to come up with other ways of handling cash problems. Answers can usually be found by people who are determined and creative.

How Do I Get the Lender to Accept a Short Payoff?

That, of course, is the trick. If you can't make the payments and the market is bad, it's usually to the lender's advantage to accept a short payoff. Nationwide, most lenders figure it will cost around $30,000 or more for a full-blown foreclosure of a home, including lost interest, legal fees, cleaning up the property after you're dispossessed, and reselling it. If they can get out with something less in just a short time by accepting a short payoff, it only makes sense to do so.

TRAP

Be aware that some lenders would rather cut off an arm than accept a short payoff. They'll fight the whole way and never will accept what makes better financial sense. If you discover your lender is one of these types, then perhaps you should try one of the alternatives coming up in this chapter.

Usually you must first convince a lender that you can't make the payments. If you're always caught up in your payments, that's a hard thing to do. The lender may assume you're the sort who would rather die than have a late payment and may simply stick it out, counting on your ethics to keep the loan up no matter what.

Therefore, not making the payments is often a first step. This, of course, must be accompanied by constant communication with the lender. You need to explain your predicament, your inability to make payments, the bad market, and your upside down condition.

Most lenders, even given months of seeing what's happening to you, won't agree to a short payoff in advance. The most they'll agree is to "consider it." If that's the case, you should proceed with a contingent sale. Put the house on the market and find a buyer who's willing to purchase, subject to the lender accepting a short payoff.

It's going to be hard for the lender to reject a buyer in hand, even with a short payoff, when the alternative is a long foreclosure.

TIP

It's not going to be an easy or painless process. You have to convince the lender to accept something that, while it may be in the lender's best interests to accept, goes against the grain. Expect frustration, delays, and rejection. Just keep in mind, however, that most lenders are first and foremost business-people, and they can see the writing on the wall. Most will accept the better of two bad alternatives.

If the lender won't accept a short payoff, your alternatives are limited. Either keep the house and make the payments, as difficult as that may be, or sell it by putting in more money of your own. I wouldn't consider walking away even a bad alternative—it's simply not something that makes sense to do.

What about Leasing Out the Property?

Even though you may not be able to make the payments, someone else may be able to make them for you, namely a tenant. Consider renting short term, leasing long term, or doing a lease–option where the tenant has the option of buying. Any good real estate agent can put these together for you.

If you get a good tenant, you may receive enough rent money to pay the mortgage and other costs, thus keeping you out of foreclosure. Of course, there's the matter of where you will live. Some creative borrowers move in with relatives or rent a much less expensive house. Remember, when times are tough you may have to be uncomfortable for awhile to make everything work out.

What about Refinancing?

If you have a high interest rate mortgage, you may be able to dramatically reduce your payments by going for a lower interest rate mortgage or an ARM. While you may not be able to make the current high payments, you might be able to cut them down far enough to be able to keep up.

See also Chap. 22 on refinancing and the benefits that may come from debt consolidation. Even if you can't get your mortgage payments down, by cutting your other monthly payments, you may still be able to keep up.

TRAP

Refinancing is very tough once you're in foreclosure. Lenders don't want to take on another lender's problem. They might still do it, but you'll need a strong credit report and income. Of course, if you had that, why would you be facing foreclosure? Therefore, as soon as you see things are getting tough, consider refinancing. Get the new loan while you're still current on the payment on your old loan.

The bottom line is that if things go bad and you're faced with not being able to keep up the payments on your property, jump right in and start taking action. Talk to brokers, your lender, a CPA, an attorney—anyone who might be able to help out. The last thing you want to do is to become passive and let foreclosure roll over you. It'll flatten you and your credit for years to come. Take steps to avoid it now.

26

How Do I Prepare for the Loan Closing?

Once you are successful in obtaining a mortgage, a time will come when the lender will want you to sign papers. Typically you'll go down to an escrow office (or to the real estate attorney's office who's handling the escrow), and there you'll be given a stack of papers to sign. If it's a refinance, they will just be loan documents. On the other hand, if the mortgage is part of a purchase, there may be other documents involved in the purchase to sign as well.

Should you bring anything with you to the closing? Should you just sign everything on faith? What should you dispute, if anything? These are the questions that most people ask at a closing, and we will take a brief look at some of them.

Who Should I Take to the Closing?

Unless you're well versed in real estate and finance, it's a good idea to bring someone who is. This could be a real estate agent, an attorney, a financial counselor—someone who knows the ropes and who will put your interests first.

TRAP

Often at closings the borrower has many questions about the documents. However, the escrow officer handling the closing may not know the correct answers or may be unwilling to advise you for fear of later being the subject of legal action if things don't go as planned. This is also often the case for real estate agents who, these days, avoid closings like the plague for the same reason. If that's the case, your best bet may be a knowledgeable friend or attorney.

TIP

With a refinance, you'll almost certainly be meeting with a representative of the lender. Feel free to ask this person any and all questions. If you aren't sure the verbal answer corresponds with what's written on the documents, get the representative to write down what he or she is saying and sign it. That will usually help separate the wheat from the chaff.

If there's anything that you don't understand or that you disagree with, don't sign until you get a clear explanation and legal advice. While it may be possible to change an error after you sign, it's much easier to take care of it before you sign.

What Should I Bring to the Closing?

The lender will let you know what to bring. You may need your checkbook if you want to write a personal check to cover some items, such as points. Even though these may be covered by the mortgage, having a check to show that you personally paid for them might be of some help if certain tax problems occur.

In addition, if you're getting a mortgage online, the lender may want to see promised documentation such as W-2 forms, bank statements, paycheck stubs, and so forth. Whatever you're asked to bring, be sure you bring it with you. Otherwise, the whole process may be delayed days until you have everything ready to go.

What Should I Challenge?

Carefully read the fees and charges. You should have been made aware of these early on in a good faith estimate when you applied for the mortgage. If you're not sure what statement you should have gotten or what to challenge, reread Chap. 12 on mortgage costs. These are things best handled long before the closing, but if you find something out of line even now, it may be worthwhile to bring it to the closing officer's attention.

TIP

Double-check the math. In the old days (read: before computers) closing agents were constantly making errors. Today that's much rarer. However, it does still happen. Be sure all the columns add up. Perhaps just as important, be sure that the credits and debits are properly given. If the seller agreed to pay one of your loan points and instead you're shown as paying them all, point out the error and have it corrected on the spot. It will only take a few minutes for a computer to spit out new and correct documents.

If you're self-employed, you may want to pay special attention to IRS form 4506, which the lender may ask you to sign. This form allows the lender to check with the IRS to confirm that the copies of tax returns you submitted with your application are the same as those you filed with the IRS.

The lender's concern is understandable. However, I have heard of cases where the lenders have not properly filled out form 4506. Namely, they have left out the date as well as the name of the party to whom the information is to be released. If you sign the form with these two areas blank, you are virtually signing away your privacy. Anyone's name could go into the blank, and the form could be dated well into the future.

I suspect the reason the lender wants these two areas blank is that the lender is going to sell the mortgage on the secondary market. At the time you sign, the lender may not know the future buyer, hence the name is left blank. Additionally, since the lender doesn't know how long it will be before the sale is completed, and since the form is only good for 60 days after the date, the lender wants that blank as well.

What can you do? This is one of those situations that you will find hard to anticipate. This form undoubtedly won't be shown to you until you're ready to sign. By then, it's going to be tough to stop everything and get another lender. Besides, who's to say another lender won't want the same form signed?

TIP

If you're self-employed, talk to your mortgage broker or loan representative. Bring up form 4506 and express your concern **at the time you apply for the mortgage.** Explain that you are willing to sign, which should allay the lender's concern about your having fudged some documents. But also explain the privacy issue and say you won't sign a form that's not fully filled out. By preparing for it in advance, you may be able to get the lender to agree to filling out the form. Or if the lender won't, you should then have time to find another lender.

TRAP

Would you sign a blank check? If the answer is no (as it should be), then why should you be forced to sign a blank IRS document? Either way, it could lead to all kinds of unforeseen problems.

What Will I Need to Sign?

You'll be expected to sign the loan agreement. That can mean signing several documents including:

- Deed of trust
- Mortgage
- Loan agreement
- Ancillary documents

You should expect that everything will be explained to you. You may find that some of the documents are several pages long and filled with tiny print.

TIP

I encourage you to read everything, no matter how small the typeface or apparently insignificant the material. You may find some onerous terms that you would never agree to. Or you may find the lender has slipped in some clause that you and the lender had previously agreed would not be there. You may have to have the clause deleted and initialed. (Although it's much more likely that the lender will want to have the documents redrawn from scratch.)

Don't be concerned about how long it takes to read what you are expected to sign. You're center stage, and nothing happens until you sign. Once you sign, however, your role diminishes greatly. Although they may complain, everyone will wait while you read it or will make arrangements so you have time and an area to read.

Remember, you hold the leverage...until you sign. Then, you're the borrower with the lender's mortgage around your neck.

27
Are Mortgage Payments Deductible?

There are at least three important tax considerations with regard to mortgages:

- The deductability of points
- The deductability of interest
- How a mortgage affects gain or loss on sale

In this chapter we'll look into each of these and consider a few others besides. But before proceeding, it's important to first understand the nature of tax laws.

The tax laws are always evolving. What is true as I write this, for example, may be different by the time you read it depending on court interpretations, IRS rulings, and new laws passed by the government. Therefore, while a serious effort has been made to see that the following material is as up-to-date and accurate as possible, you should not rely on it. When making any decisions involving taxation, you should first check with a competent professional, such as a tax attorney or accountant.

Are Points Deductible?

Points, as you'll recall, are a form of prepaid interest that you may be required to pay to the lender in order to secure a mortgage. These are paid up front when you get the loan. The question inevitably arises, are these points deductible from your income taxes?

The answer is yes, generally speaking, but not usually all at once. Let's clarify. If the points represent prepaid interest, then you may deduct them. However, you must deduct them over the life of the mortgage. If the mortgage is for 30 years, then the deduction for points must be spread out over that period of time. For example, 2 points on a $120,000 mortgage for 30 years are deductible at $80 a year.

Most borrowers, however, would not find this particularly useful, since we all want deductions in the year we have the expense. How sweet it would be to be able to deduct the $5,000 we pay in points (or however much) in the year we pay it.

Can I Deduct Points in the Year I Pay Them?

There is an exception to the above rule that allows you to deduct points in the year you pay them providing you meet certain criteria. These criteria include the following:

1. *You pay the points out of your own funds.* The points are not paid out of the money loaned by the lender.

TIP

Many borrowers have taken to writing a separate check to the lender to cover the cost of the points. In this way they have a paper record of having paid for them separate from funds advanced by the lender.

2. *The mortgage must be for your principal residence.* It must be used for buying or improving that residence.

TRAP

You cannot deduct points in the year paid on a mortgage for a second residence, even though interest on that mortgage may be deductible. You may be able to deduct the points over the life of the mortgage.

3. *The amount of points charged must be customary for the area.*

TRAP

If you "buy down" a mortgage, as described in Chap. 13, by paying additional points up front, the government may determine that the points you paid were in excess of what is customary for your area and disallow the deduction in the year paid.

4. *The points must represent interest.* They cannot be the fees paid for appraisals, credit reports, or the origination fees charged for FHA loans or special fees charged for VA loans.

TIP

Note that the preceding rules apply to property that is your principle residence. If you are purchasing or refinancing a rental property, different rules apply. There, you may deduct the points only over the life of the mortgage; however, you may also be able to deduct your other costs and fees as a business expense. Check with your accountant.

TRAP

Your principle residence is generally the place where you spend most of your time. Although the rules here are foggy, the government has become increasingly strict in determining what constitutes a principle residence. Unless you spend more than 50 percent of your time there, it might be hard to prove that a house was your principle residence.

5. *The deductions are applicable only if the points do not exceed the maximum interest deduction allowable on a residence.* See the discussion that follows.

Deducting points paid on a home mortgage is one of the biggest areas of confusion when it comes to paying taxes for home owners. The good news is that if you handle it correctly, you probably can deduct some of the points. The bad news is that you probably do need a tax consultant to look at your particular situation to determine what may be deductible and what may not be.

Can I Deduct Interest Paid on a Mortgage?

At one time, all the interest paid on any mortgage was fully deductible. (In fact, you could prepay interest years in advance and then deduct it in the year paid!) All that has changed, however, under the guise of tax reform. Tax reform has severely limited the amount of interest on a home mortgage that you may deduct from your taxes.

Today, the amount of interest you can deduct on a home that you own is limited by the following rules. (*Note:* These rules do not apply to rental/investment property. Totally different rules apply in that situation.)

1. The deduction applies only to your principle residence and to a second home. If it's a second home, you must use it part of the year.

2. The maximum mortgage amount deducted can be $1 million, provided that the mortgage was used to purchase, build, or improve your home.

TIP

Any mortgage debt taken out prior to October 13, 1987 is grandfathered in. For example, if you took out a mortgage for $3 million prior to that date, the interest on all of it is deductible. However, if you took out a mortgage after October 13, 1987, the maximum mortgage amount on which interest is deductible is $1 million including any mortgages grandfathered in.

3. If you take out a mortgage (refinance) on your home for purposes other than to improve, build, or add-on, you are limited to $100,000 of debt on which interest may be deducted.

It's important to understand how this rule works. For example, you may purchase a home with a mortgage of $150,000. Under the rule all of the interest on this mortgage is presumably deductible. After you buy the property, you decide to add to the house and secure a mortgage for $250,000 more. If the money is used to build or improve the property, all the interest on the second mortgage is likewise deductible.

However, if you took out a second mortgage on the same property for $250,000 and used the money to start a business of your own, only the interest on the first $100,000 of the debt would be deductible.

TRAP

If you take out a mortgage against your home and then buy bonds that are tax-free or otherwise receive tax-free income, the interest on the mortgage may not be deductible.

TIP

There may be a special exception available if you use the money for education. Check with your accountant.

As can be seen from the preceding examples and explanations, while home interest is generally deductible, it isn't necessarily so. That being the case, you should consult with an accountant on the tax ramifications before taking out any mortgage.

What about the Tax Considerations When I Refinance?

Generally speaking, there aren't any. For tax purposes, the amount of financing on a home is irrelevant. In other words, it doesn't matter if you paid cash or had a 100 percent mortgage. (However, it could matter if you had a 125 percent mortgage.)

Let's try an example. Say that you purchased a home for $100,000 10 years ago. You obtained an $80,000 mortgage as part of the purchase price.

Since that time the value of your home went up to $250,000. You decide to refinance, and you take out an additional $100,000 in another mortgage. Do you have any taxes to pay at the time of the refinance?

The answer is no. When you refinance, you do not increase your tax liability. But you are reducing your equity in the property and that could come back to haunt you later on. For this reason, often people will choose to refinance instead of sell, particularly with investment properties.

What about Tax Consequences When I Sell?

Selling, however, is a different matter. If you have a gain on the sale, you owe taxes on that gain. (Although you may exclude up to $250,000—up to $500,000 for a married couple filing jointly— if it's a principle residence and you otherwise qualify.)

Gain is calculated as the difference between your adjusted basis and your net selling price. The actual calculation can be difficult and is beyond the scope of this book. Consult with a tax specialist in this case.

TRAP

If you refinanced earlier, you reduced your equity. However, when you sell, the tax is calculated on gain, not equity. Hence, you may be shocked to discover that you owe a significant tax bill, even though your remaining equity in the property is small. That's the hidden tax consequence of refinancing.

How Does Mortgage Interest Compare to Personal Interest?

It is worthwhile noting that today all personal interest is nondeductible. That means that interest on your car loan, credit cards, department stores charges, and so forth are not deductible.

On the other hand, mortgage interest, up to the limits noted earlier, is deductible. Essentially that means that if you borrow $20,000 in personal debt, there is no tax deduction for the interest. However, if you borrow $20,000 on a home equity loan, even if the money is over and above your cost of acquiring the property (up to the $100,000 limit discussed earlier), the money may be tax-deductible.

For this reason, many people today are opting for the home equity loan over other types of personal finance for their personal financing needs.

TRAP

In a 125% "mortgage," that portion which uses the property as collateral may have the interest deducted; that portion which is a personal loan may not. Beware the IRS doesn't construe the entire debt as personal and refuse to allow any interest deduction.

TIP

Be careful of home equity mortgages that are sold on the basis of their tax deductability. Oftentimes the "friendly" lender really doesn't closely examine your personal finances to discover whether such a mortgage would benefit you taxwise. It could turn out that the interest on the loan isn't tax-deductible when you thought it was. That could be a rather annoying discovery.

What about Mortgages That Are Forgiven?

Generally speaking, mortgage debt that is forgiven is considered taxable income by the IRS. This has caused some real shock and dismay for many borrowers.

TRAP

If you're upside down (you owe more than the property is worth) and get a short payoff from the lender, it means that the lender is, in essence, forgiving a portion of your mortgage. That portion may be considered income to you by the IRS. Check with a good tax attorney before accepting any short payoffs.

What about Late Payments on a Mortgage?

These generally may be deductible, if they constitute interest. On the other hand, if they are for a specific service that the lender performs, such as sending out late payment notices, they probably are not deductible.

What about Interest on a Mortgage That Is over and above the Value of the Property?

This happens when there is negative amortization or when you get a 125 percent mortgage. Generally speaking, you can't deduct interest unless you pay it. By converting it to principal, as in negative amortization, it stops being interest. You may, however, be able to deduct the extra interest incurred because of the additional principal.

On the matter of interest paid on a mortgage over and above the value of the property, if the mortgage is actually part of a personal loan, the interest probably is not deductible. Remember, you can only deduct *mortgage* interest, not interest on a personal loan. This is one of the great traps with 125 percent mortgages.

The subject of taxes and mortgages is enormous and treacherous. What appears to make good sense on the surface may have nothing at all to do with the way the laws are interpreted or applied. Therefore, as noted in the beginning, you are urged to consult your tax professional before you make any move involving real estate, including refinancing or purchasing with a mortgage. It may very well be that by just structuring the deal slightly differently, you can save yourself an enormous amount of taxes later on.

28

First-Time Home Buyer and Other Special Loan Programs

You may be eligible for special mortgage terms if you are a first-time home buyer, are a low-income family, are in a "disaster area," or have some other characteristic that singles you out for special treatment. Will this help you get a house and a mortgage? Maybe.

Today there are a raft of new mortgages specially designed for people who have special problems. Sometimes these mortgages offer below-market interest rates or reduced costs and points. If you qualify, you would be foolish not to look for and attempt to get one of them. Just don't hold out too much hope. Sometimes the effort isn't worth the result.

What If I'm a First-Time Home Buyer?

What's a "first-time" home buyer? If you answer it's a person who's never bought a home before, you'd be technically incorrect. According to most government housing programs, a first-time home buyer is someone who has not owned a principle residence within the previous 3 years.

You're thinking, *What? If I previously owned three houses but have rented for 3 years I qualify as a first-time home buyer?* The answer is, probably.

There are city, county, state, and federal mortgages available for first-time home buyers. Typically, in order to qualify, you must meet household size/maximum income requirements. For example, the city of Los Angeles offers a mortgage credit certificate (MCC) to certain qualifying people. While the figures change and the program is subject to change or discontinuance, as of this writing it generally offers the following:

Household size	Maximum income
1	$28,750
2	32,850
3	36,950
-	—
8	54,150

You are also limited to purchasing a new house up to a maximum of $230,564 or an existing house to $196,198. (Unfortunately, in high-priced areas, that tends to rule out most homes.)

The MCC gives the borrower a federal income tax credit of up to 20 percent of the mortgage interest. The borrower, of course, must live in the home and keep the same mortgage. The credit reduces the taxes you pay and thus helps in qualifying for the mortgage as well as in making the payments

Other cities have similar programs, and there are a host of different types of programs that may be suited to other situations. For example, FEMA (Federal Emergency Management Agency) coordinates low interest rate loans to victims of natural disasters. The key, however, is that the area where your home is located must be a federally declared disaster area. Most states have similar programs.

In addition, HUD (Department of Housing and Urban

Development) also offers a host of loans, some directly funded to help with financing. Through the FHA (Federal Housing Administration) there are programs designed for those with little money to put down (see Chap. 21 on government loans), for farmers, and for others.

In addition, there are literally hundreds of other organizations that offer special financing for those in special circumstances.

How Do I Find Out about the Various Mortgage Programs?

You'll have to do the legwork. Most of the programs are government-sponsored and that means calling, writing, and sometimes going down to government offices. Generally, you'll want to see the housing office director, but the title of the person may vary significantly.

TIP

If you're going to apply for these programs, it's a good idea to do it before contacting a lender direct. In some cases you will only be considered after you get a mortgage. In others, however, you can only be considered before you apply. Find out first and avoid being disappointed.

For FEMA, information on mortgage programs is usually widely disseminated at and around disaster sites such as earthquakes, fires, floods, and so on. You can also contact FEMA direct:

FEMA
500 C St., SW
Washington, DC 20472
www.fema.gov

For HUD and FHA programs, contact the administration directly in Washington, D.C., or a state office.

HUD/FHA
451 7th St., SW
Washington, DC 20410
www.hud.gov
www.hud.gov/fha/fhahome.html

Also check with Fannie Mae and Freddie Mac for any programs they may be administering:

Fannie Mae   Freddie Mac
3900 Wisconsin Ave, NW   8200 Jones Beach Drive
Washington, DC 202-752-7000   McLean, Virginia 22101 703-903-
www.fanniemae.com   2000
                                      www.freddiemac.com

Finally, ask your local mortgage broker. He or she may know of programs available in your area that will be ideal for you.

For city and county programs, your best bet is to first contact the general information number and then ask for "housing." You'll have to work your way through to the person who handles special programs in your area.

Appendix **A**

Amortization Table

Use the table on the following page to determine the monthly mortgage payment (principal and interest) when you already know the loan amount. Just multiply the loan amount by the factor, and you'll be given the monthly payment.

Interest	Years					
	3	5	7	10	15	30
7.00	.030877	.019801	.015092	.011610	.008988	.006653
7.25	.030991	.019919	.015215	.011740	.009129	.006822
7.50	.031106	.020037	.015338	.011870	.009270	.006992
7.75	.031221	.020157	.015462	.012001	.009413	.007164
8.00	.031336	.020276	.015586	.012133	.009557	.007338
8.25	.031341	.020396	.015711	.012265	.009701	.007513
8.50	.031567	.020516	.015836	.012399	.009847	.007689
8.75	.041683	.020637	.015962	.012533	.009995	.007867
9.00	.031799	.020758	.016089	.012668	.010143	.008046
9.25	.031916	.020879	.016216	.012802	.010292	.008227
9.50	.032032	.021001	.016344	.012940	.010442	.008409
9.75	.032149	.021124	.016472	.013077	.010594	.008592
10.00	.032267	.021247	.016601	.013215	.010746	.008776
10.25	.032385	.021370	.016730	.013354	.010896	.008961
10.50	.032502	.021494	.016861	.013494	.011054	.009147
10.75	.032621	.021618	.016991	.013634	.011210	.009335
11.00	.032739	.021742	.017122	.013775	.011366	.009523
11.25	.032857	.021867	.017254	.013917	.011523	.009713
11.50	.032976	.021993	.017387	.014060	.011682	.009903
11.75	.033095	.022118	.017520	.014203	.011841	.010094
12.00	.033214	.022244	.017653	.014347	.012002	.010286
12.25	.033334	.022371	.017787	.014492	.012163	.010479
12.50	.033454	.022498	.017921	.014638	.012325	.010673
12.75	.033574	.022625	.018056	.014784	.012488	.010867
13.00	.033694	.022753	.018192	.014931	.012652	.011062
13.25	.033815	.022881	.018328	.015079	.012817	.011258
13.50	.033935	.023010	.018465	.015227	.012983	.011454
13.75	.034056	.023139	.018602	.015377	.013150	.011651
14.00	.034178	.023268	.018740	.015527	.013317	.011849

Appendix **B**

Mortgage Finder

How to Use the Mortgage Finder

The tables in this appendix are probably unlike any you've seen before. They can be used to find the following information.*

1. *To find maximum price you can pay given the maximum monthly payment you can afford.* Read down "Montly Payment" to the maximum you can afford, then right to "Maximum Price,"

2. *To find your monthly payment for a specific purchase price.* Read down "Maximum Price" column to your purchase price, then left to "Monthly Payment" column to see the monthly payment, including principal, interest, taxes, and insurance.

3. *To find the approximate income needed to qualify for a particular mortgage.* Read down "Maximum Amount" to your mortgage amount, then right to "Income to Qualify" column.

Special Note: The following tables can be used to give you a quick estimate of a variety of different mortgage amounts from your maximum price to your principal and interest amount. These tables assume a fixed rate mortgage for 30 years with a 20 percent downpayment and that taxes and insurance will be roughly 2 percent of the purchase price annually. The tables apply several formulas commonly used by lenders, but they do not take into account lenders' profiles (see Chap. 6), your credit, reserves, and other factors, which will significantly affect the loan amount, the payment, and other features of the loan. Therefore, it's important to understand that these tables can only be taken as rough approximations. No guarantee can be given as to their accuracy in any specific case.

4. *To find approximate maximum price you can afford given your income.* Read "Income To Qualify" until you find your income, then read left to "Maximum Price."

5. *To find the maximum mortgage amount given the purchase price.* Read down the column marked "Maximum Price" to your price, then over to the left to "Maximum Amount."

6. *To find the approximate maximum mortgage you can get given your income.* Read down the column marked "Income To Qualify" to your income, then over to the left to "Maximum Amount."

7. *To find the maximum purchase price given a specific mortgage amount.* Read down "Maximum Amount" column, then right to "Maximum Price" column.

8. *To find the pricinpal and interest only monthly payment for a mortgage amount.* Read down "Maximum Amount" column, then right to "Mortgage P&I" column.

7% Interest, 30-Year Term, 20% Down

(2% of purchase price assumed for taxes and insurance; 33% of gross monthly income allowed for mortgage payment)

Monthly payment	Maximum mortgage Amount	P & I	Maximum price	Income to qualify Monthly	Annual
$349	$40,000	$266	$50,000	$1,048	$12,581
$363	$41,600	$277	$52,000	$1,090	$13,084
$377	$43,200	$287	$54,000	$1,132	$13,587
$391	$44,800	$298	$56,000	$1,174	$14,091
$405	$46,400	$309	$58,000	$1,216	$14,594
$419	$48,000	$319	$60,000	$1,258	$15,097
$433	$49,600	$330	$62,000	$1,300	$15,600
$447	$51,200	$341	$64,000	$1,342	$16,104
$461	$52,800	$351	$66,000	$1,384	$16,607
$475	$54,400	$362	$68,000	$1,426	$17,110
$489	$56,000	$373	$70,000	$1,468	$17,613
$503	$57,600	$383	$72,000	$1,510	$18,116
$517	$59,200	$394	$74,000	$1,552	$18,620
$531	$60,800	$405	$76,000	$1,594	$19,123
$545	$62,400	$415	$78,000	$1,636	$19,626
$559	$64,000	$426	$80,000	$1,677	$20,129
$573	$65,600	$436	$82,000	$1,719	$20,633
$587	$67,200	$447	$84,000	$1,761	$21,136
$601	$68,800	$458	$86,000	$1,803	$21,639
$615	$70,400	$468	$88,000	$1,845	$22,142
$629	$72,000	$479	$90,000	$1,887	$22,646
$643	$73,600	$490	$92,000	$1,929	$23,149
$657	$75,200	$500	$94,000	$1,971	$23,652
$671	$76,800	$511	$96,000	$2,013	$24,155
$685	$78,400	$522	$98,000	$2,055	$24,659
$699	$80,000	$532	$100,000	$2,097	$25,162
$713	$81,600	$543	$102,000	$2,139	$25,665
$727	$83,200	$554	$104,000	$2,181	$26,168
$741	$84,800	$564	$106,000	$2,223	$26,671
$755	$86,400	$575	$108,000	$2,265	$27,175
$769	$88,000	$585	$110,000	$2,306	$27,678
$783	$89,600	$596	$112,000	$2,348	$28,181
$797	$91,200	$607	$114,000	$2,390	$28,684
$811	$92,800	$617	$116,000	$2,432	$29,188
$825	$94,400	$628	$118,000	$2,474	$29,691
$839	$96,000	$639	$120,000	$2,516	$30,194
$853	$97,600	$649	$122,000	$2,558	$30,697
$867	$99,200	$660	$124,000	$2,600	$31,201
$881	$100,800	$671	$126,000	$2,642	$31,704
$895	$102,400	$681	$128,000	$2,684	$32,207
$909	$104,000	$692	$130,000	$2,726	$32,710
$923	$105,600	$703	$132,000	$2,768	$33,214
$937	$107,200	$713	$134,000	$2,810	$33,717

Monthly payment	Maximum mortgage		Maximum price	Income to qualify	
	Amount	P & I		Monthly	Annual
$951	$108,800	$724	$136,000	$2,852	$34,220
$965	$110,400	$735	$138,000	$2,894	$34,723
$979	$112,000	$745	$140,000	$2,936	$35,227
$992	$113,600	$756	$142,000	$2,977	$35,730
$1,006	$115,200	$766	$144,000	$3,019	$36,233
$1,020	$116,800	$777	$146,000	$3,061	$36,736
$1,034	$118,400	$788	$148,000	$3,103	$37,239
$1,048	$120,000	$798	$150,000	$3,145	$37,743
$1,062	$121,600	$809	$152,000	$3,187	$38,246
$1,076	$123,200	$820	$154,000	$3,229	$38,749
$1,090	$124,800	$830	$156,000	$3,271	$39,252
$1,104	$126,400	$841	$158,000	$3,313	$39,756
$1,118	$128,000	$852	$160,000	$3,355	$40,259
$1,132	$129,600	$862	$162,000	$3,397	$40,762
$1,146	$131,200	$873	$164,000	$3,439	$41,265
$1,160	$132,800	$884	$166,000	$3,481	$41,769
$1,174	$134,400	$894	$168,000	$3,523	$42,272
$1,188	$136,000	$905	$170,000	$3,565	$42,775
$1,202	$137,600	$916	$172,000	$3,607	$43,278
$1,216	$139,200	$926	$174,000	$3,648	$43,782
$1,230	$140,800	$937	$176,000	$3,690	$44,285
$1,244	$142,400	$947	$178,000	$3,732	$44,788
$1,258	$144,000	$958	$180,000	$3,774	$45,291
$1,272	$145,600	$969	$182,000	$3,816	$45,794
$1,286	$147,200	$979	$184,000	$3,858	$46,298
$1,300	$148,800	$990	$186,000	$3,900	$46,801
$1,314	$150,400	$1,001	$188,000	$3,942	$47,304
$1,328	$152,000	$1,011	$190,000	$3,984	$47,807
$1,342	$153,600	$1,022	$192,000	$4,026	$48,311
$1,356	$155,200	$1,033	$194,000	$4,068	$48,814
$1,370	$156,800	$1,043	$196,000	$4,110	$49,317
$1,384	$158,400	$1,054	$198,000	$4,152	$49,820
$1,398	$160,000	$1,065	$200,000	$4,194	$50,324

7½% Interest, 30-Year Term, 20% Down

(2% of purchase price assumed for taxes and insurance; 33% of gross monthly income allowed for mortgage payment)

Monthly payment	Maximum mortgage		Maximum price	Income to qualify	
	Amount	P & I		Monthly	Annual
$363	$40,000	$280	$50,000	$1,089	$13,069
$378	$41,600	$291	$52,000	$1,133	$13,592
$392	$43,200	$302	$54,000	$1,176	$14,115
$407	$44,800	$313	$56,000	$1,220	$14,638
$421	$46,400	$324	$58,000	$1,263	$15,160
$436	$48,000	$336	$60,000	$1,307	$15,683
$450	$49,600	$347	$62,000	$1,350	$16,206
$465	$51,200	$358	$64,000	$1,394	$16,729
$479	$52,800	$369	$66,000	$1,438	$17,251
$494	$54,400	$380	$68,000	$1,481	$17,774
$508	$56,000	$392	$70,000	$1,525	$18,297
$523	$57,600	$403	$72,000	$1,568	$18,820
$537	$59,200	$414	$74,000	$1,612	$19,342
$552	$60,800	$425	$76,000	$1,655	$19,865
$566	$62,400	$436	$78,000	$1,699	$20,388
$581	$64,000	$448	$80,000	$1,743	$20,911
$595	$65,600	$459	$82,000	$1,786	$21,433
$610	$67,200	$470	$84,000	$1,830	$21,956
$624	$68,800	$481	$86,000	$1,873	$22,479
$639	$70,400	$492	$88,000	$1,917	$23,002
$653	$72,000	$503	$90,000	$1,960	$23,525
$668	$73,600	$515	$92,000	$2,004	$24,047
$683	$75,200	$526	$94,000	$2,048	$24,570
$697	$76,800	$537	$96,000	$2,091	$25,093
$712	$78,400	$548	$98,000	$2,135	$25,616
$726	$80,000	$559	$100,000	$2,178	$26,138
$741	$81,600	$571	$102,000	$2,222	$26,661
$755	$83,200	$582	$104,000	$2,265	$27,184
$770	$84,800	$593	$106,000	$2,309	$27,707
$784	$86,400	$604	$108,000	$2,352	$28,229
$799	$88,000	$615	$110,000	$2,396	$28,752
$813	$89,600	$627	$112,000	$2,440	$29,275
$828	$91,200	$638	$114,000	$2,483	$29,798
$842	$92,800	$649	$116,000	$2,527	$30,321
$857	$94,400	$660	$118,000	$2,570	$30,843
$871	$96,000	$671	$120,000	$2,614	$31,366
$886	$97,600	$682	$122,000	$2,657	$31,889
$900	$99,200	$694	$124,000	$2,701	$32,412
$915	$100,800	$705	$126,000	$2,745	$32,934
$929	$102,400	$716	$128,000	$2,788	$33,457
$944	$104,000	$727	$130,000	$2,832	$33,980
$958	$105,600	$738	$132,000	$2,875	$34,503
$973	$107,200	$750	$134,000	$2,919	$35,025

Monthly payment	Maximum mortgage		Maximum price	Income to qualify	
	Amount	P & I		Monthly	Annual
$987	$108,800	$761	$136,000	$2,962	$35,548
$1,002	$110,400	$772	$138,000	$3,006	$36,071
$1,016	$112,000	$783	$140,000	$3,049	$36,594
$1,031	$113,600	$794	$142,000	$3,093	$37,117
$1,046	$115,200	$806	$144,000	$3,137	$37,639
$1,060	$116,800	$817	$146,000	$3,180	$38,162
$1,075	$118,400	$828	$148,000	$3,224	$38,685
$1,089	$120,000	$839	$150,000	$3,267	$39,208
$1,104	$121,600	$850	$152,000	$3,311	$39,730
$1,118	$123,200	$861	$154,000	$3,354	$40,253
$1,133	$124,800	$873	$156,000	$3,398	$40,776
$1,147	$126,400	$884	$158,000	$3,442	$41,299
$1,162	$128,000	$895	$160,000	$3,485	$41,821
$1,176	$129,600	$906	$162,000	$3,529	$42,344
$1,191	$131,200	$917	$164,000	$3,572	$42,867
$1,205	$132,800	$929	$166,000	$3,616	$43,390
$1,220	$134,400	$940	$168,000	$3,659	$43,913
$1,234	$136,000	$951	$170,000	$3,703	$44,435
$1,249	$137,600	$962	$172,000	$3,747	$44,958
$1,263	$139,200	$973	$174,000	$3,790	$45,481
$1,278	$140,800	$985	$176,000	$3,834	$46,004
$1,292	$142,400	$996	$178,000	$3,877	$46,526
$1,307	$144,000	$1,007	$180,000	$3,921	$47,049
$1,321	$145,600	$1,018	$182,000	$3,964	$47,572
$1,336	$147,200	$1,029	$184,000	$4,008	$48,095
$1,350	$148,800	$1,040	$186,000	$4,051	$48,617
$1,365	$150,400	$1,052	$188,000	$4,095	$49,140
$1,380	$152,000	$1,063	$190,000	$4,139	$49,663
$1,394	$153,600	$1,074	$192,000	$4,182	$50,186
$1,409	$155,200	$1,085	$194,000	$4,226	$50,708
$1,423	$156,800	$1,096	$196,000	$4,269	$51,231
$1,438	$158,400	$1,108	$198,000	$4,313	$51,754
$1,452	$160,000	$1,119	$200,000	$4,356	$52,277

8% Interest, 30-Year Term, 20% Down

(2% of purchase price assumed for taxes and insurance; 33% of gross monthly
income allowed for mortgage payment)

Monthly payment	Maximum mortgage		Maximum price	Income to qualify	
	Amount	P & I		Monthly	Annual
$377	$40,000	$294	$50,000	$1,131	$13,567
$392	$41,600	$305	$52,000	$1,176	$14,109
$407	$43,200	$317	$54,000	$1,221	$14,652
$422	$44,800	$329	$56,000	$1,266	$15,195
$437	$46,400	$340	$58,000	$1,311	$15,737
$452	$48,000	$352	$60,000	$1,357	$16,280
$467	$49,600	$364	$62,000	$1,402	$16,823
$482	$51,200	$376	$64,000	$1,447	$17,365
$497	$52,800	$387	$66,000	$1,492	$17,908
$513	$54,400	$399	$68,000	$1,538	$18,451
$528	$56,000	$411	$70,000	$1,583	$18,993
$543	$57,600	$423	$72,000	$1,628	$19,536
$558	$59,200	$434	$74,000	$1,673	$20,079
$573	$60,800	$446	$76,000	$1,718	$20,621
$588	$62,400	$458	$78,000	$1,764	$21,164
$603	$64,000	$470	$80,000	$1,809	$21,707
$618	$65,600	$481	$82,000	$1,854	$22,249
$633	$67,200	$493	$84,000	$1,899	$22,792
$648	$68,800	$505	$86,000	$1,945	$23,335
$663	$70,400	$517	$88,000	$1,990	$23,877
$678	$72,000	$528	$90,000	$2,035	$24,420
$693	$73,600	$540	$92,000	$2,080	$24,962
$708	$75,200	$552	$94,000	$2,125	$25,505
$724	$76,800	$564	$96,000	$2,171	$26,048
$739	$78,400	$575	$98,000	$2,216	$26,590
$754	$80,000	$587	$100,000	$2,261	$27,133
$769	$81,600	$599	$102,000	$2,306	$27,676
$784	$83,200	$611	$104,000	$2,352	$28,218
$799	$84,800	$622	$106,000	$2,397	$28,761
$814	$86,400	$634	$108,000	$2,442	$29,304
$829	$88,000	$646	$110,000	$2,487	$29,846
$844	$89,600	$657	$112,000	$2,532	$30,389
$859	$91,200	$669	$114,000	$2,578	$30,932
$874	$92,800	$681	$116,000	$2,623	$31,474
$889	$94,400	$693	$118,000	$2,668	$32,017
$904	$96,000	$704	$120,000	$2,713	$32,560
$920	$97,600	$716	$122,000	$2,759	$33,102
$935	$99,200	$728	$124,000	$2,804	$33,645
$950	$100,800	$740	$126,000	$2,849	$34,188
$965	$102,400	$751	$128,000	$2,894	$34,730
$980	$104,000	$763	$130,000	$2,939	$35,273
$995	$105,600	$775	$132,000	$2,985	$35,816
$1,010	$107,200	$787	$134,000	$3,030	$36,358

Monthly payment	Maximum mortgage		Maximum price	Income to qualify	
	Amount	P & I		Monthly	Annual
$1,025	$108,800	$798	$136,000	$3,075	$36,901
$1,040	$110,400	$810	$138,000	$3,120	$37,444
$1,055	$112,000	$822	$140,000	$3,166	$37,986
$1,070	$113,600	$834	$142,000	$3,211	$38,529
$1,085	$115,200	$845	$144,000	$3,256	$39,072
$1,100	$116,800	$857	$146,000	$3,301	$39,614
$1,115	$118,400	$869	$148,000	$3,346	$40,157
$1,131	$120,000	$881	$150,000	$3,392	$40,700
$1,146	$121,600	$892	$152,000	$3,437	$41,242
$1,161	$123,200	$904	$154,000	$3,482	$41,785
$1,176	$124,800	$916	$156,000	$3,527	$42,328
$1,191	$126,400	$928	$158,000	$3,573	$42,870
$1,206	$128,000	$939	$160,000	$3,618	$43,413
$1,221	$129,600	$951	$162,000	$3,663	$43,956
$1,236	$131,200	$963	$164,000	$3,708	$44,498
$1,251	$132,800	$974	$166,000	$3,753	$45,041
$1,266	$134,400	$986	$168,000	$3,799	$45,584
$1,281	$136,000	$998	$170,000	$3,844	$46,126
$1,296	$137,600	$1,010	$172,000	$3,889	$46,669
$1,311	$139,200	$1,021	$174,000	$3,934	$47,212
$1,327	$140,800	$1,033	$176,000	$3,980	$47,754
$1,342	$142,400	$1,045	$178,000	$4,025	$48,297
$1,357	$144,000	$1,057	$180,000	$4,070	$48,840
$1,372	$145,600	$1,068	$182,000	$4,115	$49,382
$1,387	$147,200	$1,080	$184,000	$4,160	$49,925
$1,402	$148,800	$1,092	$186,000	$4,206	$50,468
$1,417	$150,400	$1,104	$188,000	$4,251	$51,010
$1,432	$152,000	$1,115	$190,000	$4,296	$51,553
$1,447	$153,600	$1,127	$192,000	$4,341	$52,096
$1,462	$155,200	$1,139	$194,000	$4,387	$52,638
$1,477	$156,800	$1,151	$196,000	$4,432	$53,181
$1,492	$158,400	$1,162	$198,000	$4,477	$53,724
$1,507	$160,000	$1,174	$200,000	$4,522	$54,266

8½% Interest, 30-Year Term, 20% Down

(2% of purchase price assumed for taxes and insurance; 33% of gross monthly income allowed for mortgage payment)

Monthly payment	Maximum mortgage Amount	Maximum mortgage P & I	Maximum price	Income to qualify Monthly	Income to qualify Annual
$391	$40,000	$308	$50,000	$1,173	$14,073
$407	$41,600	$320	$52,000	$1,220	$14,636
$422	$43,200	$332	$54,000	$1,267	$15,199
$438	$44,800	$344	$56,000	$1,313	$15,761
$453	$46,400	$357	$58,000	$1,360	$16,324
$469	$48,000	$369	$60,000	$1,407	$16,887
$485	$49,600	$381	$62,000	$1,454	$17,450
$500	$51,200	$394	$64,000	$1,501	$18,013
$516	$52,800	$406	$66,000	$1,548	$18,576
$532	$54,400	$418	$68,000	$1,595	$19,139
$547	$56,000	$431	$70,000	$1,642	$19,702
$563	$57,600	$443	$72,000	$1,689	$20,265
$579	$59,200	$455	$74,000	$1,736	$20,828
$594	$60,800	$468	$76,000	$1,783	$21,391
$610	$62,400	$480	$78,000	$1,829	$21,953
$625	$64,000	$492	$80,000	$1,876	$22,516
$641	$65,600	$504	$82,000	$1,923	$23,079
$657	$67,200	$517	$84,000	$1,970	$23,642
$672	$68,800	$529	$86,000	$2,017	$24,205
$688	$70,400	$541	$88,000	$2,064	$24,768
$704	$72,000	$554	$90,000	$2,111	$25,331
$719	$73,600	$566	$92,000	$2,158	$25,894
$735	$75,200	$578	$94,000	$2,205	$26,457
$751	$76,800	$591	$96,000	$2,252	$27,020
$766	$78,400	$603	$98,000	$2,299	$27,583
$782	$80,000	$615	$100,000	$2,345	$28,145
$797	$81,600	$627	$102,000	$2,392	$28,708
$813	$83,200	$640	$104,000	$2,439	$29,271
$829	$84,800	$652	$106,000	$2,486	$29,834
$844	$86,400	$664	$108,000	$2,533	$30,397
$860	$88,000	$677	$110,000	$2,580	$30,960
$876	$89,600	$689	$112,000	$2,627	$31,523
$891	$91,200	$701	$114,000	$2,674	$32,086
$907	$92,800	$714	$116,000	$2,721	$32,649
$923	$94,400	$726	$118,000	$2,768	$33,212
$938	$96,000	$738	$120,000	$2,815	$33,775
$954	$97,600	$750	$122,000	$2,861	$34,337
$969	$99,200	$763	$124,000	$2,908	$34,900
$985	$100,800	$775	$126,000	$2,955	$35,463
$1,001	$102,400	$787	$128,000	$3,002	$36,026
$1,016	$104,000	$800	$130,000	$3,049	$36,589
$1,032	$105,600	$812	$132,000	$3,096	$37,152
$1,048	$107,200	$824	$134,000	$3,143	$37,715

Monthly payment	Maximum mortgage		Maximum price	Income to qualify	
	Amount	P & I		Monthly	Annual
$1,063	$108,800	$837	$136,000	$3,190	$38,278
$1,079	$110,400	$849	$138,000	$3,237	$38,841
$1,095	$112,000	$861	$140,000	$3,284	$39,404
$1,110	$113,600	$874	$142,000	$3,331	$39,967
$1,126	$115,200	$886	$144,000	$3,377	$40,529
$1,141	$116,800	$898	$146,000	$3,424	$41,092
$1,157	$118,400	$910	$148,000	$3,471	$41,655
$1,173	$120,000	$923	$150,000	$3,518	$42,218
$1,188	$121,600	$935	$152,000	$3,565	$42,781
$1,204	$123,200	$947	$154,000	$3,612	$43,344
$1,220	$124,800	$960	$156,000	$3,659	$43,907
$1,235	$126,400	$972	$158,000	$3,706	$44,470
$1,251	$128,000	$984	$160,000	$3,753	$45,033
$1,267	$129,600	$997	$162,000	$3,800	$45,596
$1,282	$131,200	$1,009	$164,000	$3,847	$46,159
$1,298	$132,800	$1,021	$166,000	$3,893	$46,721
$1,313	$134,400	$1,033	$168,000	$3,940	$47,284
$1,329	$136,000	$1,046	$170,000	$3,987	$47,847
$1,345	$137,600	$1,058	$172,000	$4,034	$48,410
$1,360	$139,200	$1,070	$174,000	$4,081	$48,973
$1,376	$140,800	$1,083	$176,000	$4,128	$49,536
$1,392	$142,400	$1,095	$178,000	$4,175	$50,099
$1,407	$144,000	$1,107	$180,000	$4,222	$50,662
$1,423	$145,600	$1,120	$182,000	$4,269	$51,225
$1,439	$147,200	$1,132	$184,000	$4,316	$51,788
$1,454	$148,800	$1,144	$186,000	$4,363	$52,351
$1,470	$150,400	$1,156	$188,000	$4,409	$52,913
$1,485	$152,000	$1,169	$190,000	$4,456	$53,476
$1,501	$153,600	$1,181	$192,000	$4,503	$54,039
$1,517	$155,200	$1,193	$194,000	$4,550	$54,602
$1,532	$156,800	$1,206	$196,000	$4,597	$55,165
$1,548	$158,400	$1,218	$198,000	$4,644	$55,728
$1,564	$160,000	$1,230	$200,000	$4,691	$56,291

9% Interest, 30-Year Term, 20% Down

(2% of purchase price assumed for taxes and insurance; 33% of gross monthly income allowed for mortgage payment)

Monthly payment	Maximum mortgage Amount	Maximum mortgage P & I	Maximum price	Income to qualify Monthly	Income to qualify Annual
$405	$40,000	$322	$50,000	$1,216	$14,587
$421	$41,600	$335	$52,000	$1,264	$15,170
$438	$43,200	$348	$54,000	$1,313	$15,754
$454	$44,800	$360	$56,000	$1,361	$16,337
$470	$46,400	$373	$58,000	$1,410	$16,921
$486	$48,000	$386	$60,000	$1,459	$17,504
$502	$49,600	$399	$62,000	$1,507	$18,088
$519	$51,200	$412	$64,000	$1,556	$18,671
$535	$52,800	$425	$66,000	$1,605	$19,255
$551	$54,400	$438	$68,000	$1,653	$19,838
$567	$56,000	$451	$70,000	$1,702	$20,422
$583	$57,600	$463	$72,000	$1,750	$21,005
$600	$59,200	$476	$74,000	$1,799	$21,588
$616	$60,800	$489	$76,000	$1,848	$22,172
$632	$62,400	$502	$78,000	$1,896	$22,755
$648	$64,000	$515	$80,000	$1,945	$23,339
$665	$65,600	$528	$82,000	$1,994	$23,922
$681	$67,200	$541	$84,000	$2,042	$24,506
$697	$68,800	$554	$86,000	$2,091	$25,089
$713	$70,400	$566	$88,000	$2,139	$25,673
$729	$72,000	$579	$90,000	$2,188	$26,256
$746	$73,600	$592	$92,000	$2,237	$26,840
$762	$75,200	$605	$94,000	$2,285	$27,423
$778	$76,800	$618	$96,000	$2,334	$28,007
$794	$78,400	$631	$98,000	$2,383	$28,590
$810	$80,000	$644	$100,000	$2,431	$29,174
$827	$81,600	$657	$102,000	$2,480	$29,757
$843	$83,200	$669	$104,000	$2,528	$30,341
$859	$84,800	$682	$106,000	$2,577	$30,924
$875	$86,400	$695	$108,000	$2,626	$31,508
$891	$88,000	$708	$110,000	$2,674	$32,091
$908	$89,600	$721	$112,000	$2,723	$32,674
$924	$91,200	$734	$114,000	$2,771	$33,258
$940	$92,800	$747	$116,000	$2,820	$33,841
$956	$94,400	$760	$118,000	$2,869	$34,425
$972	$96,000	$772	$120,000	$2,917	$35,008
$989	$97,600	$785	$122,000	$2,966	$35,592
$1,005	$99,200	$798	$124,000	$3,015	$36,175
$1,021	$100,800	$811	$126,000	$3,063	$36,759
$1,037	$102,400	$824	$128,000	$3,112	$37,342
$1,053	$104,000	$837	$130,000	$3,160	$37,926
$1,070	$105,600	$850	$132,000	$3,209	$38,509
$1,086	$107,200	$863	$134,000	$3,258	$39,093

Monthly payment	Maximum mortgage		Maximum price	Income to qualify	
	Amount	P & I		Monthly	Annual
$1,102	$108,800	$875	$136,000	$3,306	$39,676
$1,118	$110,400	$888	$138,000	$3,355	$40,260
$1,135	$112,000	$901	$140,000	$3,404	$40,843
$1,151	$113,600	$914	$142,000	$3,452	$41,427
$1,167	$115,200	$927	$144,000	$3,501	$42,010
$1,183	$116,800	$940	$146,000	$3,549	$42,594
$1,199	$118,400	$953	$148,000	$3,598	$43,177
$1,216	$120,000	$966	$150,000	$3,647	$43,760
$1,232	$121,600	$978	$152,000	$3,695	$44,344
$1,248	$123,200	$991	$154,000	$3,744	$44,927
$1,264	$124,800	$1,004	$156,000	$3,793	$45,511
$1,280	$126,400	$1,017	$158,000	$3,841	$46,094
$1,297	$128,000	$1,030	$160,000	$3,890	$46,678
$1,313	$129,600	$1,043	$162,000	$3,938	$47,261
$1,329	$131,200	$1,056	$164,000	$3,987	$47,845
$1,345	$132,800	$1,069	$166,000	$4,036	$48,428
$1,361	$134,400	$1,081	$168,000	$4,084	$49,012
$1,378	$136,000	$1,094	$170,000	$4,133	$49,595
$1,394	$137,600	$1,107	$172,000	$4,182	$50,179
$1,410	$139,200	$1,120	$174,000	$4,230	$50,762
$1,426	$140,800	$1,133	$176,000	$4,279	$51,346
$1,442	$142,400	$1,146	$178,000	$4,327	$51,929
$1,459	$144,000	$1,159	$180,000	$4,376	$52,513
$1,475	$145,600	$1,172	$182,000	$4,425	$53,096
$1,491	$147,200	$1,184	$184,000	$4,473	$53,679
$1,507	$148,800	$1,197	$186,000	$4,522	$54,263
$1,524	$150,400	$1,210	$188,000	$4,571	$54,846
$1,540	$152,000	$1,223	$190,000	$4,619	$55,430
$1,556	$153,600	$1,236	$192,000	$4,668	$56,013
$1,572	$155,200	$1,249	$194,000	$4,716	$56,597
$1,588	$156,800	$1,262	$196,000	$4,765	$57,180
$1,605	$158,400	$1,275	$198,000	$4,814	$57,764
$1,621	$160,000	$1,287	$200,000	$4,862	$58,347

9½% Interest, 30-Year Term, 20% Down

(2% of purchase price assumed for taxes and insurance; 33% of gross monthly income allowed for mortgage payment)

Monthly payment	Maximum mortgage		Maximum price	Income to qualify	
	Amount	P & I		Monthly	Annual
$420	$40,000	$336	$50,000	$1,259	$15,109
$436	$41,600	$350	$52,000	$1,309	$15,713
$453	$43,200	$363	$54,000	$1,360	$16,317
$470	$44,800	$377	$56,000	$1,410	$16,922
$487	$46,400	$390	$58,000	$1,460	$17,526
$504	$48,000	$404	$60,000	$1,511	$18,130
$520	$49,600	$417	$62,000	$1,561	$18,735
$537	$51,200	$431	$64,000	$1,612	$19,339
$554	$52,800	$444	$66,000	$1,662	$19,943
$571	$54,400	$457	$68,000	$1,712	$20,548
$588	$56,000	$471	$70,000	$1,763	$21,152
$604	$57,600	$484	$72,000	$1,813	$21,756
$621	$59,200	$498	$74,000	$1,863	$22,361
$638	$60,800	$511	$76,000	$1,914	$22,965
$655	$62,400	$525	$78,000	$1,964	$23,569
$671	$64,000	$538	$80,000	$2,014	$24,174
$688	$65,600	$552	$82,000	$2,065	$24,778
$705	$67,200	$565	$84,000	$2,115	$25,382
$722	$68,800	$579	$86,000	$2,166	$25,987
$739	$70,400	$592	$88,000	$2,216	$26,591
$755	$72,000	$605	$90,000	$2,266	$27,195
$772	$73,600	$619	$92,000	$2,317	$27,800
$789	$75,200	$632	$94,000	$2,367	$28,404
$806	$76,800	$646	$96,000	$2,417	$29,008
$823	$78,400	$659	$98,000	$2,468	$29,613
$839	$80,000	$673	$100,000	$2,518	$30,217
$856	$81,600	$686	$102,000	$2,568	$30,821
$873	$83,200	$700	$104,000	$2,619	$31,426
$890	$84,800	$713	$106,000	$2,669	$32,030
$907	$86,400	$727	$108,000	$2,720	$32,634
$923	$88,000	$740	$110,000	$2,770	$33,239
$940	$89,600	$753	$112,000	$2,820	$33,843
$957	$91,200	$767	$114,000	$2,871	$34,447
$974	$92,800	$780	$116,000	$2,921	$35,052
$990	$94,400	$794	$118,000	$2,971	$35,656
$1,007	$96,000	$807	$120,000	$3,022	$36,260
$1,024	$97,600	$821	$122,000	$3,072	$36,865
$1,041	$99,200	$834	$124,000	$3,122	$37,469
$1,058	$100,800	$848	$126,000	$3,173	$38,073
$1,074	$102,400	$861	$128,000	$3,223	$38,678
$1,091	$104,000	$875	$130,000	$3,274	$39,282
$1,108	$105,600	$888	$132,000	$3,324	$39,887
$1,125	$107,200	$901	$134,000	$3,374	$40,491

Monthly payment	Maximum mortgage		Maximum price	Income to qualify	
	Amount	P & I		Monthly	Annual
$1,142	$108,800	$915	$136,000	$3,425	$41,095
$1,158	$110,400	$928	$138,000	$3,475	$41,700
$1,175	$112,000	$942	$140,000	$3,525	$42,304
$1,192	$113,600	$955	$142,000	$3,576	$42,908
$1,209	$115,200	$969	$144,000	$3,626	$43,513
$1,225	$116,800	$982	$146,000	$3,676	$44,117
$1,242	$118,400	$996	$148,000	$3,727	$44,721
$1,259	$120,000	$1,009	$150,000	$3,777	$45,326
$1,276	$121,600	$1,022	$152,000	$3,827	$45,930
$1,293	$123,200	$1,036	$154,000	$3,878	$46,534
$1,309	$124,800	$1,049	$156,000	$3,928	$47,139
$1,326	$126,400	$1,063	$158,000	$3,979	$47,743
$1,343	$128,000	$1,076	$160,000	$4,029	$48,347
$1,360	$129,600	$1,090	$162,000	$4,079	$48,952
$1,377	$131,200	$1,103	$164,000	$4,130	$49,556
$1,393	$132,800	$1,117	$166,000	$4,180	$50,160
$1,410	$134,400	$1,130	$168,000	$4,230	$50,765
$1,427	$136,000	$1,144	$170,000	$4,281	$51,369
$1,444	$137,600	$1,157	$172,000	$4,331	$51,973
$1,460	$139,200	$1,170	$174,000	$4,381	$52,578
$1,477	$140,800	$1,184	$176,000	$4,432	$53,182
$1,494	$142,400	$1,197	$178,000	$4,482	$53,786
$1,511	$144,000	$1,211	$180,000	$4,533	$54,391
$1,528	$145,600	$1,224	$182,000	$4,583	$54,995
$1,544	$147,200	$1,238	$184,000	$4,633	$55,599
$1,561	$148,800	$1,251	$186,000	$4,684	$56,204
$1,578	$150,400	$1,265	$188,000	$4,734	$56,808
$1,595	$152,000	$1,278	$190,000	$4,784	$57,412
$1,612	$153,600	$1,292	$192,000	$4,835	$58,017
$1,628	$155,200	$1,305	$194,000	$4,885	$58,621
$1,645	$156,800	$1,318	$196,000	$4,935	$59,225
$1,662	$158,400	$1,332	$198,000	$4,986	$59,830
$1,679	$160,000	$1,345	$200,000	$5,036	$60,434

10% Interest, 30-Year Term, 20% Down

(2% of purchase price assumed for taxes and insurance; 33% of gross monthly income allowed for mortgage payment)

Monthly payment	Maximum mortgage		Maximum price	Income to qualify	
	Amount	P & I		Monthly	Annual
$434	$40,000	$351	$50,000	$1,303	$15,637
$452	$41,600	$365	$52,000	$1,355	$16,263
$469	$43,200	$379	$54,000	$1,407	$16,888
$486	$44,800	$393	$56,000	$1,459	$17,514
$504	$46,400	$407	$58,000	$1,512	$18,139
$521	$48,000	$421	$60,000	$1,564	$18,765
$539	$49,600	$435	$62,000	$1,616	$19,390
$556	$51,200	$449	$64,000	$1,668	$20,016
$573	$52,800	$463	$66,000	$1,720	$20,641
$591	$54,400	$477	$68,000	$1,772	$21,267
$608	$56,000	$491	$70,000	$1,824	$21,892
$625	$57,600	$505	$72,000	$1,876	$22,517
$643	$59,200	$520	$74,000	$1,929	$23,143
$660	$60,800	$534	$76,000	$1,981	$23,768
$678	$62,400	$548	$78,000	$2,033	$24,394
$695	$64,000	$562	$80,000	$2,085	$25,019
$712	$65,600	$576	$82,000	$2,137	$25,645
$730	$67,200	$590	$84,000	$2,189	$26,270
$747	$68,800	$604	$86,000	$2,241	$26,896
$764	$70,400	$618	$88,000	$2,293	$27,521
$782	$72,000	$632	$90,000	$2,346	$28,147
$799	$73,600	$646	$92,000	$2,398	$28,772
$817	$75,200	$660	$94,000	$2,450	$29,398
$834	$76,800	$674	$96,000	$2,502	$30,023
$851	$78,400	$688	$98,000	$2,554	$30,649
$869	$80,000	$702	$100,000	$2,606	$31,274
$886	$81,600	$716	$102,000	$2,658	$31,900
$903	$83,200	$730	$104,000	$2,710	$32,525
$921	$84,800	$744	$106,000	$2,763	$33,151
$938	$86,400	$758	$108,000	$2,815	$33,776
$956	$88,000	$772	$110,000	$2,867	$34,402
$973	$89,600	$786	$112,000	$2,919	$35,027
$990	$91,200	$800	$114,000	$2,971	$35,653
$1,008	$92,800	$814	$116,000	$3,023	$36,278
$1,025	$94,400	$828	$118,000	$3,075	$36,904
$1,042	$96,000	$842	$120,000	$3,127	$37,529
$1,060	$97,600	$857	$122,000	$3,180	$38,155
$1,077	$99,200	$871	$124,000	$3,232	$38,780
$1,095	$100,800	$885	$126,000	$3,284	$39,406
$1,112	$102,400	$899	$128,000	$3,336	$40,031
$1,129	$104,000	$913	$130,000	$3,388	$40,657
$1,147	$105,600	$927	$132,000	$3,440	$41,282
$1,164	$107,200	$941	$134,000	$3,492	$41,908

Monthly payment	Maximum mortgage		Maximum price	Income to qualify	
	Amount	P & I		Monthly	Annual
$1,181	$108,800	$955	$136,000	$3,544	$42,533
$1,199	$110,400	$969	$138,000	$3,597	$43,159
$1,216	$112,000	$983	$140,000	$3,649	$43,784
$1,234	$113,600	$997	$142,000	$3,701	$44,410
$1,251	$115,200	$1,011	$144,000	$3,753	$45,035
$1,268	$116,800	$1,025	$146,000	$3,805	$45,660
$1,286	$118,400	$1,039	$148,000	$3,857	$46,286
$1,303	$120,000	$1,053	$150,000	$3,909	$46,911
$1,320	$121,600	$1,067	$152,000	$3,961	$47,537
$1,338	$123,200	$1,081	$154,000	$4,014	$48,162
$1,355	$124,800	$1,095	$156,000	$4,066	$48,788
$1,373	$126,400	$1,109	$158,000	$4,118	$49,413
$1,390	$128,000	$1,123	$160,000	$4,170	$50,039
$1,407	$129,600	$1,137	$162,000	$4,222	$50,664
$1,425	$131,200	$1,151	$164,000	$4,274	$51,290
$1,442	$132,800	$1,165	$166,000	$4,326	$51,915
$1,459	$134,400	$1,179	$168,000	$4,378	$52,541
$1,477	$136,000	$1,194	$170,000	$4,431	$53,166
$1,494	$137,600	$1,208	$172,000	$4,483	$53,792
$1,512	$139,200	$1,222	$174,000	$4,535	$54,417
$1,529	$140,800	$1,236	$176,000	$4,587	$55,043
$1,546	$142,400	$1,250	$178,000	$4,639	$55,668
$1,564	$144,000	$1,264	$180,000	$4,691	$56,294
$1,581	$145,600	$1,278	$182,000	$4,743	$56,919
$1,598	$147,200	$1,292	$184,000	$4,795	$57,545
$1,616	$148,800	$1,306	$186,000	$4,848	$58,170
$1,633	$150,400	$1,320	$188,000	$4,900	$58,796
$1,651	$152,000	$1,334	$190,000	$4,952	$59,421
$1,668	$153,600	$1,348	$192,000	$5,004	$60,047
$1,685	$155,200	$1,362	$194,000	$5,056	$60,672
$1,703	$156,800	$1,376	$196,000	$5,108	$61,298
$1,720	$158,400	$1,390	$198,000	$5,160	$61,923
$1,737	$160,000	$1,404	$200,000	$5,212	$62,549

10½% Interest, 30-Year Term, 20% Down

(2% of purchase price assumed for taxes and insurance; 33% of gross monthly income allowed for mortgage payment)

Monthly payment	Maximum mortgage		Maximum price	Income to qualify	
	Amount	P & I		Monthly	Annual
$449	$40,000	$366	$50,000	$1,348	$16,172
$467	$41,600	$381	$52,000	$1,402	$16,819
$485	$43,200	$395	$54,000	$1,456	$17,466
$503	$44,800	$410	$56,000	$1,509	$18,113
$521	$46,400	$424	$58,000	$1,563	$18,760
$539	$48,000	$439	$60,000	$1,617	$19,407
$557	$49,600	$454	$62,000	$1,671	$20,054
$575	$51,200	$468	$64,000	$1,725	$20,701
$593	$52,800	$483	$66,000	$1,779	$21,348
$611	$54,400	$498	$68,000	$1,833	$21,994
$629	$56,000	$512	$70,000	$1,887	$22,641
$647	$57,600	$527	$72,000	$1,941	$23,288
$665	$59,200	$542	$74,000	$1,995	$23,935
$683	$60,800	$556	$76,000	$2,049	$24,582
$701	$62,400	$571	$78,000	$2,102	$25,229
$719	$64,000	$585	$80,000	$2,156	$25,876
$737	$65,600	$600	$82,000	$2,210	$26,523
$755	$67,200	$615	$84,000	$2,264	$27,170
$773	$68,800	$629	$86,000	$2,318	$27,817
$791	$70,400	$644	$88,000	$2,372	$28,463
$809	$72,000	$659	$90,000	$2,426	$29,110
$827	$73,600	$673	$92,000	$2,480	$29,757
$845	$75,200	$688	$94,000	$2,534	$30,404
$863	$76,800	$703	$96,000	$2,588	$31,051
$880	$78,400	$717	$98,000	$2,641	$31,698
$898	$80,000	$732	$100,000	$2,695	$32,345
$916	$81,600	$746	$102,000	$2,749	$32,992
$934	$83,200	$761	$104,000	$2,803	$33,639
$952	$84,800	$776	$106,000	$2,857	$34,285
$970	$86,400	$790	$108,000	$2,911	$34,932
$988	$88,000	$805	$110,000	$2,965	$35,579
$1,006	$89,600	$820	$112,000	$3,019	$36,226
$1,024	$91,200	$834	$114,000	$3,073	$36,873
$1,042	$92,800	$849	$116,000	$3,127	$37,520
$1,060	$94,400	$864	$118,000	$3,181	$38,167
$1,078	$96,000	$878	$120,000	$3,234	$38,814
$1,096	$97,600	$893	$122,000	$3,288	$39,461
$1,114	$99,200	$907	$124,000	$3,342	$40,108
$1,132	$100,800	$922	$126,000	$3,396	$40,754
$1,150	$102,400	$937	$128,000	$3,450	$41,401
$1,168	$104,000	$951	$130,000	$3,504	$42,048
$1,186	$105,600	$966	$132,000	$3,558	$42,695
$1,204	$107,200	$981	$134,000	$3,612	$43,342

Monthly payment	Maximum mortgage		Maximum price	Income to qualify	
	Amount	P & I		Monthly	Annual
$1,222	$108,800	$995	$136,000	$3,666	$43,989
$1,240	$110,400	$1,010	$138,000	$3,720	$44,636
$1,258	$112,000	$1,025	$140,000	$3,774	$45,283
$1,276	$113,600	$1,039	$142,000	$3,827	$45,930
$1,294	$115,200	$1,054	$144,000	$3,881	$46,577
$1,312	$116,800	$1,068	$146,000	$3,935	$47,223
$1,330	$118,400	$1,083	$148,000	$3,989	$47,870
$1,348	$120,000	$1,098	$150,000	$4,043	$48,517
$1,366	$121,600	$1,112	$152,000	$4,097	$49,164
$1,384	$123,200	$1,127	$154,000	$4,151	$49,811
$1,402	$124,800	$1,142	$156,000	$4,205	$50,458
$1,420	$126,400	$1,156	$158,000	$4,259	$51,105
$1,438	$128,000	$1,171	$160,000	$4,313	$51,752
$1,456	$129,600	$1,186	$162,000	$4,367	$52,399
$1,473	$131,200	$1,200	$164,000	$4,420	$53,045
$1,491	$132,800	$1,215	$166,000	$4,474	$53,692
$1,509	$134,400	$1,229	$168,000	$4,528	$54,339
$1,527	$136,000	$1,244	$170,000	$4,582	$54,986
$1,545	$137,600	$1,259	$172,000	$4,636	$55,633
$1,563	$139,200	$1,273	$174,000	$4,690	$56,280
$1,581	$140,800	$1,288	$176,000	$4,744	$56,927
$1,599	$142,400	$1,303	$178,000	$4,798	$57,574
$1,617	$144,000	$1,317	$180,000	$4,852	$58,221
$1,635	$145,600	$1,332	$182,000	$4,906	$58,868
$1,653	$147,200	$1,347	$184,000	$4,960	$59,514
$1,671	$148,800	$1,361	$186,000	$5,013	$60,161
$1,689	$150,400	$1,376	$188,000	$5,067	$60,808
$1,707	$152,000	$1,390	$190,000	$5,121	$61,455
$1,725	$153,600	$1,405	$192,000	$5,175	$62,102
$1,743	$155,200	$1,420	$194,000	$5,229	$62,749
$1,761	$156,800	$1,434	$196,000	$5,283	$63,396
$1,779	$158,400	$1,449	$198,000	$5,337	$64,043
$1,797	$160,000	$1,464	$200,000	$5,391	$64,690

11% Interest, 30-Year Term, 20% Down

(2% of purchase price assumed for taxes and insurance; 33% of gross monthly income allowed for mortgage payment)

Monthly payment	Maximum mortgage		Maximum price	Income to qualify	
	Amount	P & I		Monthly	Annual
$464	$40,000	$381	$50,000	$1,393	$16,714
$483	$41,600	$396	$52,000	$1,449	$17,382
$501	$43,200	$411	$54,000	$1,504	$18,051
$520	$44,800	$427	$56,000	$1,560	$18,719
$539	$46,400	$442	$58,000	$1,616	$19,388
$557	$48,000	$457	$60,000	$1,671	$20,056
$576	$49,600	$472	$62,000	$1,727	$20,725
$594	$51,200	$488	$64,000	$1,783	$21,394
$613	$52,800	$503	$66,000	$1,839	$22,062
$631	$54,400	$518	$68,000	$1,894	$22,731
$650	$56,000	$533	$70,000	$1,950	$23,399
$669	$57,600	$549	$72,000	$2,006	$24,068
$687	$59,200	$564	$74,000	$2,061	$24,736
$706	$60,800	$579	$76,000	$2,117	$25,405
$724	$62,400	$594	$78,000	$2,173	$26,073
$743	$64,000	$609	$80,000	$2,228	$26,742
$761	$65,600	$625	$82,000	$2,284	$27,410
$780	$67,200	$640	$84,000	$2,340	$28,079
$799	$68,800	$655	$86,000	$2,396	$28,748
$817	$70,400	$670	$88,000	$2,451	$29,416
$836	$72,000	$686	$90,000	$2,507	$30,085
$854	$73,600	$701	$92,000	$2,563	$30,753
$873	$75,200	$716	$94,000	$2,618	$31,422
$891	$76,800	$731	$96,000	$2,674	$32,090
$910	$78,400	$747	$98,000	$2,730	$32,759
$929	$80,000	$762	$100,000	$2,786	$33,427
$947	$81,600	$777	$102,000	$2,841	$34,096
$966	$83,200	$792	$104,000	$2,897	$34,764
$984	$84,800	$808	$106,000	$2,953	$35,433
$1,003	$86,400	$823	$108,000	$3,008	$36,102
$1,021	$88,000	$838	$110,000	$3,064	$36,770
$1,040	$89,600	$853	$112,000	$3,120	$37,439
$1,059	$91,200	$869	$114,000	$3,176	$38,107
$1,077	$92,800	$884	$116,000	$3,231	$38,776
$1,096	$94,400	$899	$118,000	$3,287	$39,444
$1,114	$96,000	$914	$120,000	$3,343	$40,113
$1,133	$97,600	$929	$122,000	$3,398	$40,781
$1,151	$99,200	$945	$124,000	$3,454	$41,450
$1,170	$100,800	$960	$126,000	$3,510	$42,119
$1,189	$102,400	$975	$128,000	$3,566	$42,787
$1,207	$104,000	$990	$130,000	$3,621	$43,456
$1,226	$105,600	$1,006	$132,000	$3,677	$44,124
$1,244	$107,200	$1,021	$134,000	$3,733	$44,793

Monthly payment	Maximum mortgage		Maximum price	Income to qualify	
	Amount	P & I		Monthly	Annual
$1,263	$108,800	$1,036	$136,000	$3,788	$45,461
$1,281	$110,400	$1,051	$138,000	$3,844	$46,130
$1,300	$112,000	$1,067	$140,000	$3,900	$46,798
$1,319	$113,600	$1,082	$142,000	$3,956	$47,467
$1,337	$115,200	$1,097	$144,000	$4,011	$48,135
$1,356	$116,800	$1,112	$146,000	$4,067	$48,804
$1,374	$118,400	$1,128	$148,000	$4,123	$49,473
$1,393	$120,000	$1,143	$150,000	$4,178	$50,141
$1,411	$121,600	$1,158	$152,000	$4,234	$50,810
$1,430	$123,200	$1,173	$154,000	$4,290	$51,478
$1,449	$124,800	$1,189	$156,000	$4,346	$52,147
$1,467	$126,400	$1,204	$158,000	$4,401	$52,815
$1,486	$128,000	$1,219	$160,000	$4,457	$53,484
$1,504	$129,600	$1,234	$162,000	$4,513	$54,152
$1,523	$131,200	$1,249	$164,000	$4,568	$54,821
$1,541	$132,800	$1,265	$166,000	$4,624	$55,489
$1,560	$134,400	$1,280	$168,000	$4,680	$56,158
$1,579	$136,000	$1,295	$170,000	$4,736	$56,827
$1,597	$137,600	$1,310	$172,000	$4,791	$57,495
$1,616	$139,200	$1,326	$174,000	$4,847	$58,164
$1,634	$140,800	$1,341	$176,000	$4,903	$58,832
$1,653	$142,400	$1,356	$178,000	$4,958	$59,501
$1,671	$144,000	$1,371	$180,000	$5,014	$60,169
$1,690	$145,600	$1,387	$182,000	$5,070	$60,838
$1,709	$147,200	$1,402	$184,000	$5,126	$61,506
$1,727	$148,800	$1,417	$186,000	$5,181	$62,175
$1,746	$150,400	$1,432	$188,000	$5,237	$62,843
$1,764	$152,000	$1,448	$190,000	$5,293	$63,512
$1,783	$153,600	$1,463	$192,000	$5,348	$64,181
$1,801	$155,200	$1,478	$194,000	$5,404	$64,849
$1,820	$156,800	$1,493	$196,000	$5,460	$65,518
$1,839	$158,400	$1,509	$198,000	$5,516	$66,186
$1,857	$160,000	$1,524	$200,000	$5,571	$66,855

11½% Interest, 30-Year Term, 20% Down

(2% of purchase price assumed for taxes and insurance; 33% of gross monthly income allowed for mortgage payment)

Monthly payment	Maximum mortgage		Maximum price	Income to qualify	
	Amount	P & I		Monthly	Annual
$479	$40,000	$396	$50,000	$1,438	$17,260
$499	$41,600	$412	$52,000	$1,496	$17,951
$518	$43,200	$428	$54,000	$1,553	$18,641
$537	$44,800	$444	$56,000	$1,611	$19,332
$556	$46,400	$459	$58,000	$1,668	$20,022
$575	$48,000	$475	$60,000	$1,726	$20,712
$595	$49,600	$491	$62,000	$1,784	$21,403
$614	$51,200	$507	$64,000	$1,841	$22,093
$633	$52,800	$523	$66,000	$1,899	$22,784
$652	$54,400	$539	$68,000	$1,956	$23,474
$671	$56,000	$555	$70,000	$2,014	$24,164
$690	$57,600	$570	$72,000	$2,071	$24,855
$710	$59,200	$586	$74,000	$2,129	$25,545
$729	$60,800	$602	$76,000	$2,186	$26,236
$748	$62,400	$618	$78,000	$2,244	$26,926
$767	$64,000	$634	$80,000	$2,301	$27,617
$786	$65,600	$650	$82,000	$2,359	$28,307
$805	$67,200	$665	$84,000	$2,416	$28,997
$825	$68,800	$681	$86,000	$2,474	$29,688
$844	$70,400	$697	$88,000	$2,532	$30,378
$863	$72,000	$713	$90,000	$2,589	$31,069
$882	$73,600	$729	$92,000	$2,647	$31,759
$901	$75,200	$745	$94,000	$2,704	$32,449
$921	$76,800	$761	$96,000	$2,762	$33,140
$940	$78,400	$776	$98,000	$2,819	$33,830
$959	$80,000	$792	$100,000	$2,877	$34,521
$978	$81,600	$808	$102,000	$2,934	$35,211
$997	$83,200	$824	$104,000	$2,992	$35,901
$1,016	$84,800	$840	$106,000	$3,049	$36,592
$1,036	$86,400	$856	$108,000	$3,107	$37,282
$1,055	$88,000	$871	$110,000	$3,164	$37,973
$1,074	$89,600	$887	$112,000	$3,222	$38,663
$1,093	$91,200	$903	$114,000	$3,279	$39,354
$1,112	$92,800	$919	$116,000	$3,337	$40,044
$1,132	$94,400	$935	$118,000	$3,395	$40,734
$1,151	$96,000	$951	$120,000	$3,452	$41,425
$1,170	$97,600	$967	$122,000	$3,510	$42,115
$1,189	$99,200	$982	$124,000	$3,567	$42,806
$1,208	$100,800	$998	$126,000	$3,625	$43,496
$1,227	$102,400	$1,014	$128,000	$3,682	$44,186
$1,247	$104,000	$1,030	$130,000	$3,740	$44,877
$1,266	$105,600	$1,046	$132,000	$3,797	$45,567
$1,285	$107,200	$1,062	$134,000	$3,855	$46,258

Monthly payment	Maximum mortgage		Maximum price	Income to qualify	
	Amount	P & I		Monthly	Annual
$1,304	$108,800	$1,077	$136,000	$3,912	$46,948
$1,323	$110,400	$1,093	$138,000	$3,970	$47,638
$1,342	$112,000	$1,109	$140,000	$4,027	$48,329
$1,362	$113,600	$1,125	$142,000	$4,085	$49,019
$1,381	$115,200	$1,141	$144,000	$4,142	$49,710
$1,400	$116,800	$1,157	$146,000	$4,200	$50,400
$1,419	$118,400	$1,173	$148,000	$4,258	$51,091
$1,438	$120,000	$1,188	$150,000	$4,315	$51,781
$1,458	$121,600	$1,204	$152,000	$4,373	$52,471
$1,477	$123,200	$1,220	$154,000	$4,430	$53,162
$1,496	$124,800	$1,236	$156,000	$4,488	$53,852
$1,515	$126,400	$1,252	$158,000	$4,545	$54,543
$1,534	$128,000	$1,268	$160,000	$4,603	$55,233
$1,553	$129,600	$1,283	$162,000	$4,660	$55,923
$1,573	$131,200	$1,299	$164,000	$4,718	$56,614
$1,592	$132,800	$1,315	$166,000	$4,775	$57,304
$1,611	$134,400	$1,331	$168,000	$4,833	$57,995
$1,630	$136,000	$1,347	$170,000	$4,890	$58,685
$1,649	$137,600	$1,363	$172,000	$4,948	$59,376
$1,668	$139,200	$1,378	$174,000	$5,005	$60,066
$1,688	$140,800	$1,394	$176,000	$5,063	$60,756
$1,707	$142,400	$1,410	$178,000	$5,121	$61,447
$1,726	$144,000	$1,426	$180,000	$5,178	$62,137
$1,745	$145,600	$1,442	$182,000	$5,236	$62,828
$1,764	$147,200	$1,458	$184,000	$5,293	$63,518
$1,784	$148,800	$1,474	$186,000	$5,351	$64,208
$1,803	$150,400	$1,489	$188,000	$5,408	$64,899
$1,822	$152,000	$1,505	$190,000	$5,466	$65,589
$1,841	$153,600	$1,521	$192,000	$5,523	$66,280
$1,860	$155,200	$1,537	$194,000	$5,581	$66,970
$1,879	$156,800	$1,553	$196,000	$5,638	$67,660
$1,899	$158,400	$1,569	$198,000	$5,696	$68,351
$1,918	$160,000	$1,584	$200,000	$5,753	$69,041

12% Interest, 30-Year Term, 20% Down

(2% of purchase price assumed for taxes and insurance; 33% of gross monthly income allowed for mortgage payment)

Monthly payment	Maximum mortgage		Maximum price	Income to qualify	
	Amount	P & I		Monthly	Annual
$495	$40,000	$411	$50,000	$1,484	$17,812
$515	$41,600	$428	$52,000	$1,544	$18,525
$534	$43,200	$444	$54,000	$1,603	$19,237
$554	$44,800	$461	$56,000	$1,662	$19,950
$574	$46,400	$477	$58,000	$1,722	$20,662
$594	$48,000	$494	$60,000	$1,781	$21,375
$614	$49,600	$510	$62,000	$1,841	$22,087
$633	$51,200	$527	$64,000	$1,900	$22,800
$653	$52,800	$543	$66,000	$1,959	$23,512
$673	$54,400	$560	$68,000	$2,019	$24,225
$693	$56,000	$576	$70,000	$2,078	$24,937
$712	$57,600	$592	$72,000	$2,137	$25,650
$732	$59,200	$609	$74,000	$2,197	$26,362
$752	$60,800	$625	$76,000	$2,256	$27,075
$772	$62,400	$642	$78,000	$2,316	$27,787
$792	$64,000	$658	$80,000	$2,375	$28,500
$811	$65,600	$675	$82,000	$2,434	$29,212
$831	$67,200	$691	$84,000	$2,494	$29,925
$851	$68,800	$708	$86,000	$2,553	$30,637
$871	$70,400	$724	$88,000	$2,612	$31,350
$891	$72,000	$741	$90,000	$2,672	$32,062
$910	$73,600	$757	$92,000	$2,731	$32,775
$930	$75,200	$774	$94,000	$2,791	$33,487
$950	$76,800	$790	$96,000	$2,850	$34,200
$970	$78,400	$806	$98,000	$2,909	$34,912
$990	$80,000	$823	$100,000	$2,969	$35,625
$1,009	$81,600	$839	$102,000	$3,028	$36,337
$1,029	$83,200	$856	$104,000	$3,087	$37,050
$1,049	$84,800	$872	$106,000	$3,147	$37,762
$1,069	$86,400	$889	$108,000	$3,206	$38,475
$1,089	$88,000	$905	$110,000	$3,266	$39,187
$1,108	$89,600	$922	$112,000	$3,325	$39,899
$1,128	$91,200	$938	$114,000	$3,384	$40,612
$1,148	$92,800	$955	$116,000	$3,444	$41,324
$1,168	$94,400	$971	$118,000	$3,503	$42,037
$1,187	$96,000	$987	$120,000	$3,562	$42,749
$1,207	$97,600	$1,004	$122,000	$3,622	$43,462
$1,227	$99,200	$1,020	$124,000	$3,681	$44,174
$1,247	$100,800	$1,037	$126,000	$3,741	$44,887
$1,267	$102,400	$1,053	$128,000	$3,800	$45,599
$1,286	$104,000	$1,070	$130,000	$3,859	$46,312
$1,306	$105,600	$1,086	$132,000	$3,919	$47,024
$1,326	$107,200	$1,103	$134,000	$3,978	$47,737

Monthly payment	Maximum mortgage		Maximum price	Income to qualify	
	Amount	P & I		Monthly	Annual
$1,346	$108,800	$1,119	$136,000	$4,037	$48,449
$1,366	$110,400	$1,136	$138,000	$4,097	$49,162
$1,385	$112,000	$1,152	$140,000	$4,156	$49,874
$1,405	$113,600	$1,169	$142,000	$4,216	$50,587
$1,425	$115,200	$1,185	$144,000	$4,275	$51,299
$1,445	$116,800	$1,201	$146,000	$4,334	$52,012
$1,465	$118,400	$1,218	$148,000	$4,394	$52,724
$1,484	$120,000	$1,234	$150,000	$4,453	$53,437
$1,504	$121,600	$1,251	$152,000	$4,512	$54,149
$1,524	$123,200	$1,267	$154,000	$4,572	$54,862
$1,544	$124,800	$1,284	$156,000	$4,631	$55,574
$1,564	$126,400	$1,300	$158,000	$4,691	$56,287
$1,583	$128,000	$1,317	$160,000	$4,750	$56,999
$1,603	$129,600	$1,333	$162,000	$4,809	$57,712
$1,623	$131,200	$1,350	$164,000	$4,869	$58,424
$1,643	$132,800	$1,366	$166,000	$4,928	$59,137
$1,662	$134,400	$1,382	$168,000	$4,987	$59,849
$1,682	$136,000	$1,399	$170,000	$5,047	$60,562
$1,702	$137,600	$1,415	$172,000	$5,106	$61,274
$1,722	$139,200	$1,432	$174,000	$5,166	$61,987
$1,742	$140,800	$1,448	$176,000	$5,225	$62,699
$1,761	$142,400	$1,465	$178,000	$5,284	$63,412
$1,781	$144,000	$1,481	$180,000	$5,344	$64,124
$1,801	$145,600	$1,498	$182,000	$5,403	$64,837
$1,821	$147,200	$1,514	$184,000	$5,462	$65,549
$1,841	$148,800	$1,531	$186,000	$5,522	$66,262
$1,860	$150,400	$1,547	$188,000	$5,581	$66,974
$1,880	$152,000	$1,564	$190,000	$5,641	$67,687
$1,900	$153,600	$1,580	$192,000	$5,700	$68,399
$1,920	$155,200	$1,596	$194,000	$5,759	$69,112
$1,940	$156,800	$1,613	$196,000	$5,819	$69,824
$1,959	$158,400	$1,629	$198,000	$5,878	$70,537
$1,979	$160,000	$1,646	$200,000	$5,937	$71,249

12½% Interest, 30-Year Term, 20% Down

(2% of purchase price assumed for taxes and insurance; 33% of gross monthly income allowed for mortgage payment)

Monthly payment	Maximum mortgage		Maximum price	Income to qualify	
	Amount	P & I		Monthly	Annual
$510	$40,000	$427	$50,000	$1,531	$18,369
$531	$41,600	$444	$52,000	$1,592	$19,103
$551	$43,200	$461	$54,000	$1,653	$19,838
$571	$44,800	$478	$56,000	$1,714	$20,573
$592	$46,400	$495	$58,000	$1,776	$21,308
$612	$48,000	$512	$60,000	$1,837	$22,042
$633	$49,600	$529	$62,000	$1,898	$22,777
$653	$51,200	$546	$64,000	$1,959	$23,512
$674	$52,800	$564	$66,000	$2,021	$24,247
$694	$54,400	$581	$68,000	$2,082	$24,981
$714	$56,000	$598	$70,000	$2,143	$25,716
$735	$57,600	$615	$72,000	$2,204	$26,451
$755	$59,200	$632	$74,000	$2,265	$27,186
$776	$60,800	$649	$76,000	$2,327	$27,920
$796	$62,400	$666	$78,000	$2,388	$28,655
$816	$64,000	$683	$80,000	$2,449	$29,390
$837	$65,600	$700	$82,000	$2,510	$30,125
$857	$67,200	$717	$84,000	$2,572	$30,859
$878	$68,800	$734	$86,000	$2,633	$31,594
$898	$70,400	$751	$88,000	$2,694	$32,329
$918	$72,000	$768	$90,000	$2,755	$33,064
$939	$73,600	$786	$92,000	$2,817	$33,798
$959	$75,200	$803	$94,000	$2,878	$34,533
$980	$76,800	$820	$96,000	$2,939	$35,268
$1,000	$78,400	$837	$98,000	$3,000	$36,003
$1,020	$80,000	$854	$100,000	$3,061	$36,737
$1,041	$81,600	$871	$102,000	$3,123	$37,472
$1,061	$83,200	$888	$104,000	$3,184	$38,207
$1,082	$84,800	$905	$106,000	$3,245	$38,942
$1,102	$86,400	$922	$108,000	$3,306	$39,676
$1,123	$88,000	$939	$110,000	$3,368	$40,411
$1,143	$89,600	$956	$112,000	$3,429	$41,146
$1,163	$91,200	$973	$114,000	$3,490	$41,881
$1,184	$92,800	$990	$116,000	$3,551	$42,615
$1,204	$94,400	$1,008	$118,000	$3,613	$43,350
$1,225	$96,000	$1,025	$120,000	$3,674	$44,085
$1,245	$97,600	$1,042	$122,000	$3,735	$44,820
$1,265	$99,200	$1,059	$124,000	$3,796	$45,554
$1,286	$100,800	$1,076	$126,000	$3,857	$46,289
$1,306	$102,400	$1,093	$128,000	$3,919	$47,024
$1,327	$104,000	$1,110	$130,000	$3,980	$47,759
$1,347	$105,600	$1,127	$132,000	$4,041	$48,493
$1,367	$107,200	$1,144	$134,000	$4,102	$49,228

Monthly payment	Maximum mortgage		Maximum price	Income to qualify	
	Amount	P & I		Monthly	Annual
$1,388	$108,800	$1,161	$136,000	$4,164	$49,963
$1,408	$110,400	$1,178	$138,000	$4,225	$50,698
$1,429	$112,000	$1,195	$140,000	$4,286	$51,432
$1,449	$113,600	$1,212	$142,000	$4,347	$52,167
$1,469	$115,200	$1,229	$144,000	$4,408	$52,902
$1,490	$116,800	$1,247	$146,000	$4,470	$53,637
$1,510	$118,400	$1,264	$148,000	$4,531	$54,371
$1,531	$120,000	$1,281	$150,000	$4,592	$55,106
$1,551	$121,600	$1,298	$152,000	$4,653	$55,841
$1,572	$123,200	$1,315	$154,000	$4,715	$56,576
$1,592	$124,800	$1,332	$156,000	$4,776	$57,310
$1,612	$126,400	$1,349	$158,000	$4,837	$58,045
$1,633	$128,000	$1,366	$160,000	$4,898	$58,780
$1,653	$129,600	$1,383	$162,000	$4,960	$59,515
$1,674	$131,200	$1,400	$164,000	$5,021	$60,249
$1,694	$132,800	$1,417	$166,000	$5,082	$60,984
$1,714	$134,400	$1,434	$168,000	$5,143	$61,719
$1,735	$136,000	$1,451	$170,000	$5,204	$62,454
$1,755	$137,600	$1,469	$172,000	$5,266	$63,188
$1,776	$139,200	$1,486	$174,000	$5,327	$63,923
$1,796	$140,800	$1,503	$176,000	$5,388	$64,658
$1,816	$142,400	$1,520	$178,000	$5,449	$65,393
$1,837	$144,000	$1,537	$180,000	$5,511	$66,127
$1,857	$145,600	$1,554	$182,000	$5,572	$66,862
$1,878	$147,200	$1,571	$184,000	$5,633	$67,597
$1,898	$148,800	$1,588	$186,000	$5,694	$68,332
$1,919	$150,400	$1,605	$188,000	$5,756	$69,066
$1,939	$152,000	$1,622	$190,000	$5,817	$69,801
$1,959	$153,600	$1,639	$192,000	$5,878	$70,536
$1,980	$155,200	$1,656	$194,000	$5,939	$71,271
$2,000	$156,800	$1,673	$196,000	$6,000	$72,005
$2,021	$158,400	$1,691	$198,000	$6,062	$72,740
$2,041	$160,000	$1,708	$200,000	$6,123	$73,475

13% Interest, 30-Year Term, 20% Down

(2% of purchase price assumed for taxes and insurance; 33% of gross monthly income allowed for mortgage payment)

Monthly payment	Maximum mortgage		Maximum price	Income to qualify	
	Amount	P & I		Monthly	Annual
$526	$40,000	$442	$50,000	$1,577	$18,929
$547	$41,600	$460	$52,000	$1,641	$19,687
$568	$43,200	$478	$54,000	$1,704	$20,444
$589	$44,800	$496	$56,000	$1,767	$21,201
$610	$46,400	$513	$58,000	$1,830	$21,958
$631	$48,000	$531	$60,000	$1,893	$22,715
$652	$49,600	$549	$62,000	$1,956	$23,472
$673	$51,200	$566	$64,000	$2,019	$24,230
$694	$52,800	$584	$66,000	$2,082	$24,987
$715	$54,400	$602	$68,000	$2,145	$25,744
$736	$56,000	$619	$70,000	$2,208	$26,501
$757	$57,600	$637	$72,000	$2,272	$27,258
$778	$59,200	$655	$74,000	$2,335	$28,016
$799	$60,800	$673	$76,000	$2,398	$28,773
$820	$62,400	$690	$78,000	$2,461	$29,530
$841	$64,000	$708	$80,000	$2,524	$30,287
$862	$65,600	$726	$82,000	$2,587	$31,044
$883	$67,200	$743	$84,000	$2,650	$31,801
$904	$68,800	$761	$86,000	$2,713	$32,559
$925	$70,400	$779	$88,000	$2,776	$33,316
$946	$72,000	$796	$90,000	$2,839	$34,073
$968	$73,600	$814	$92,000	$2,903	$34,830
$989	$75,200	$832	$94,000	$2,966	$35,587
$1,010	$76,800	$850	$96,000	$3,029	$36,344
$1,031	$78,400	$867	$98,000	$3,092	$37,102
$1,052	$80,000	$885	$100,000	$3,155	$37,859
$1,073	$81,600	$903	$102,000	$3,218	$38,616
$1,094	$83,200	$920	$104,000	$3,281	$39,373
$1,115	$84,800	$938	$106,000	$3,344	$40,130
$1,136	$86,400	$956	$108,000	$3,407	$40,888
$1,157	$88,000	$973	$110,000	$3,470	$41,645
$1,178	$89,600	$991	$112,000	$3,533	$42,402
$1,199	$91,200	$1,009	$114,000	$3,597	$43,159
$1,220	$92,800	$1,027	$116,000	$3,660	$43,916
$1,241	$94,400	$1,044	$118,000	$3,723	$44,673
$1,262	$96,000	$1,062	$120,000	$3,786	$45,431
$1,283	$97,600	$1,080	$122,000	$3,849	$46,188
$1,304	$99,200	$1,097	$124,000	$3,912	$46,945
$1,325	$100,800	$1,115	$126,000	$3,975	$47,702
$1,346	$102,400	$1,133	$128,000	$4,038	$48,459
$1,367	$104,000	$1,150	$130,000	$4,101	$49,217
$1,388	$105,600	$1,168	$132,000	$4,164	$49,974
$1,409	$107,200	$1,186	$134,000	$4,228	$50,731

Monthly payment	Maximum mortgage		Maximum price	Income to qualify	
	Amount	P & I		Monthly	Annual
$1,430	$108,800	$1,204	$136,000	$4,291	$51,488
$1,451	$110,400	$1,221	$138,000	$4,354	$52,245
$1,472	$112,000	$1,239	$140,000	$4,417	$53,002
$1,493	$113,600	$1,257	$142,000	$4,480	$53,760
$1,514	$115,200	$1,274	$144,000	$4,543	$54,517
$1,535	$116,800	$1,292	$146,000	$4,606	$55,274
$1,556	$118,400	$1,310	$148,000	$4,669	$56,031
$1,577	$120,000	$1,327	$150,000	$4,732	$56,788
$1,598	$121,600	$1,345	$152,000	$4,795	$57,545
$1,620	$123,200	$1,363	$154,000	$4,859	$58,303
$1,641	$124,800	$1,381	$156,000	$4,922	$59,060
$1,662	$126,400	$1,398	$158,000	$4,985	$59,817
$1,683	$128,000	$1,416	$160,000	$5,048	$60,574
$1,704	$129,600	$1,434	$162,000	$5,111	$61,331
$1,725	$131,200	$1,451	$164,000	$5,174	$62,089
$1,746	$132,800	$1,469	$166,000	$5,237	$62,846
$1,767	$134,400	$1,487	$168,000	$5,300	$63,603
$1,788	$136,000	$1,504	$170,000	$5,363	$64,360
$1,809	$137,600	$1,522	$172,000	$5,426	$65,117
$1,830	$139,200	$1,540	$174,000	$5,490	$65,874
$1,851	$140,800	$1,558	$176,000	$5,553	$66,632
$1,872	$142,400	$1,575	$178,000	$5,616	$67,389
$1,893	$144,000	$1,593	$180,000	$5,679	$68,146
$1,914	$145,600	$1,611	$182,000	$5,742	$68,903
$1,935	$147,200	$1,628	$184,000	$5,805	$69,660
$1,956	$148,800	$1,646	$186,000	$5,868	$70,417
$1,977	$150,400	$1,664	$188,000	$5,931	$71,175
$1,998	$152,000	$1,681	$190,000	$5,994	$71,932
$2,019	$153,600	$1,699	$192,000	$6,057	$72,689
$2,040	$155,200	$1,717	$194,000	$6,121	$73,446
$2,061	$156,800	$1,735	$196,000	$6,184	$74,203
$2,082	$158,400	$1,752	$198,000	$6,247	$74,961
$2,103	$160,000	$1,770	$200,000	$6,310	$75,718

13½% Interest, 30-Year Term, 20% Down

(2% of purchase price assumed for taxes and insurance; 33% of gross monthly income allowed for mortgage payment)

Monthly payment	Maximum mortgage		Maximum price	Income to qualify	
	Amount	P & I		Monthly	Annual
$542	$40,000	$458	$50,000	$1,625	$19,494
$563	$41,600	$476	$52,000	$1,689	$20,274
$585	$43,200	$495	$54,000	$1,754	$21,054
$606	$44,800	$513	$56,000	$1,819	$21,833
$628	$46,400	$531	$58,000	$1,884	$22,613
$650	$48,000	$550	$60,000	$1,949	$23,393
$671	$49,600	$568	$62,000	$2,014	$24,173
$693	$51,200	$586	$64,000	$2,079	$24,952
$715	$52,800	$605	$66,000	$2,144	$25,732
$736	$54,400	$623	$68,000	$2,209	$26,512
$758	$56,000	$641	$70,000	$2,274	$27,292
$780	$57,600	$660	$72,000	$2,339	$28,071
$801	$59,200	$678	$74,000	$2,404	$28,851
$823	$60,800	$696	$76,000	$2,469	$29,631
$845	$62,400	$715	$78,000	$2,534	$30,411
$866	$64,000	$733	$80,000	$2,599	$31,190
$888	$65,600	$751	$82,000	$2,664	$31,970
$910	$67,200	$770	$84,000	$2,729	$32,750
$931	$68,800	$788	$86,000	$2,794	$33,530
$953	$70,400	$806	$88,000	$2,859	$34,310
$975	$72,000	$825	$90,000	$2,924	$35,089
$996	$73,600	$843	$92,000	$2,989	$35,869
$1,018	$75,200	$861	$94,000	$3,054	$36,649
$1,040	$76,800	$880	$96,000	$3,119	$37,429
$1,061	$78,400	$898	$98,000	$3,184	$38,208
$1,083	$80,000	$916	$100,000	$3,249	$38,988
$1,105	$81,600	$935	$102,000	$3,314	$39,768
$1,126	$83,200	$953	$104,000	$3,379	$40,548
$1,148	$84,800	$971	$106,000	$3,444	$41,327
$1,170	$86,400	$990	$108,000	$3,509	$42,107
$1,191	$88,000	$1,008	$110,000	$3,574	$42,887
$1,213	$89,600	$1,026	$112,000	$3,639	$43,667
$1,235	$91,200	$1,045	$114,000	$3,704	$44,446
$1,256	$92,800	$1,063	$116,000	$3,769	$45,226
$1,278	$94,400	$1,081	$118,000	$3,834	$46,006
$1,300	$96,000	$1,100	$120,000	$3,899	$46,786
$1,321	$97,600	$1,118	$122,000	$3,964	$47,565
$1,343	$99,200	$1,136	$124,000	$4,029	$48,345
$1,365	$100,800	$1,155	$126,000	$4,094	$49,125
$1,386	$102,400	$1,173	$128,000	$4,159	$49,905
$1,408	$104,000	$1,191	$130,000	$4,224	$50,685
$1,430	$105,600	$1,210	$132,000	$4,289	$51,464
$1,451	$107,200	$1,228	$134,000	$4,354	$52,244

Monthly payment	Maximum mortgage		Maximum price	Income to qualify	
	Amount	P & I		Monthly	Annual
$1,473	$108,800	$1,246	$136,000	$4,419	$53,024
$1,495	$110,400	$1,265	$138,000	$4,484	$53,804
$1,516	$112,000	$1,283	$140,000	$4,549	$54,583
$1,538	$113,600	$1,301	$142,000	$4,614	$55,363
$1,560	$115,200	$1,320	$144,000	$4,679	$56,143
$1,581	$116,800	$1,338	$146,000	$4,744	$56,923
$1,603	$118,400	$1,356	$148,000	$4,809	$57,702
$1,625	$120,000	$1,375	$150,000	$4,874	$58,482
$1,646	$121,600	$1,393	$152,000	$4,938	$59,262
$1,668	$123,200	$1,411	$154,000	$5,003	$60,042
$1,689	$124,800	$1,429	$156,000	$5,068	$60,821
$1,711	$126,400	$1,448	$158,000	$5,133	$61,601
$1,733	$128,000	$1,466	$160,000	$5,198	$62,381
$1,754	$129,600	$1,484	$162,000	$5,263	$63,161
$1,776	$131,200	$1,503	$164,000	$5,328	$63,940
$1,798	$132,800	$1,521	$166,000	$5,393	$64,720
$1,819	$134,400	$1,539	$168,000	$5,458	$65,500
$1,841	$136,000	$1,558	$170,000	$5,523	$66,280
$1,863	$137,600	$1,576	$172,000	$5,588	$67,060
$1,884	$139,200	$1,594	$174,000	$5,653	$67,839
$1,906	$140,800	$1,613	$176,000	$5,718	$68,619
$1,928	$142,400	$1,631	$178,000	$5,783	$69,399
$1,949	$144,000	$1,649	$180,000	$5,848	$70,179
$1,971	$145,600	$1,668	$182,000	$5,913	$70,958
$1,993	$147,200	$1,686	$184,000	$5,978	$71,738
$2,014	$148,800	$1,704	$186,000	$6,043	$72,518
$2,036	$150,400	$1,723	$188,000	$6,108	$73,298
$2,058	$152,000	$1,741	$190,000	$6,173	$74,077
$2,079	$153,600	$1,759	$192,000	$6,238	$74,857
$2,101	$155,200	$1,778	$194,000	$6,303	$75,637
$2,123	$156,800	$1,796	$196,000	$6,368	$76,417
$2,144	$158,400	$1,814	$198,000	$6,433	$77,196
$2,166	$160,000	$1,833	$200,000	$6,498	$77,976

14% Interest, 30-Year Term, 20% Down

(2% of purchase price assumed for taxes and insurance; 33% of gross monthly income allowed for mortgage payment)

Monthly payment	Maximum mortgage		Maximum price	Income to qualify	
	Amount	P & I		Monthly	Annual
$557	$40,000	$474	$50,000	$1,672	$20,062
$580	$41,600	$493	$52,000	$1,739	$20,865
$602	$43,200	$512	$54,000	$1,806	$21,667
$624	$44,800	$531	$56,000	$1,872	$22,470
$646	$46,400	$550	$58,000	$1,939	$23,272
$669	$48,000	$569	$60,000	$2,006	$24,075
$691	$49,600	$588	$62,000	$2,073	$24,877
$713	$51,200	$607	$64,000	$2,140	$25,680
$736	$52,800	$626	$66,000	$2,207	$26,482
$758	$54,400	$645	$68,000	$2,274	$27,285
$780	$56,000	$664	$70,000	$2,341	$28,087
$802	$57,600	$682	$72,000	$2,407	$28,890
$825	$59,200	$701	$74,000	$2,474	$29,692
$847	$60,800	$720	$76,000	$2,541	$30,495
$869	$62,400	$739	$78,000	$2,608	$31,297
$892	$64,000	$758	$80,000	$2,675	$32,100
$914	$65,600	$777	$82,000	$2,742	$32,902
$936	$67,200	$796	$84,000	$2,809	$33,705
$959	$68,800	$815	$86,000	$2,876	$34,507
$981	$70,400	$834	$88,000	$2,942	$35,310
$1,003	$72,000	$853	$90,000	$3,009	$36,112
$1,025	$73,600	$872	$92,000	$3,076	$36,915
$1,048	$75,200	$891	$94,000	$3,143	$37,717
$1,070	$76,800	$910	$96,000	$3,210	$38,520
$1,092	$78,400	$929	$98,000	$3,277	$39,322
$1,115	$80,000	$948	$100,000	$3,344	$40,125
$1,137	$81,600	$967	$102,000	$3,411	$40,927
$1,159	$83,200	$986	$104,000	$3,477	$41,730
$1,181	$84,800	$1,005	$106,000	$3,544	$42,532
$1,204	$86,400	$1,024	$108,000	$3,611	$43,335
$1,226	$88,000	$1,043	$110,000	$3,678	$44,137
$1,248	$89,600	$1,062	$112,000	$3,745	$44,939
$1,271	$91,200	$1,081	$114,000	$3,812	$45,742
$1,293	$92,800	$1,100	$116,000	$3,879	$46,544
$1,315	$94,400	$1,119	$118,000	$3,946	$47,347
$1,337	$96,000	$1,137	$120,000	$4,012	$48,149
$1,360	$97,600	$1,156	$122,000	$4,079	$48,952
$1,382	$99,200	$1,175	$124,000	$4,146	$49,754
$1,404	$100,800	$1,194	$126,000	$4,213	$50,557
$1,427	$102,400	$1,213	$128,000	$4,280	$51,359
$1,449	$104,000	$1,232	$130,000	$4,347	$52,162
$1,471	$105,600	$1,251	$132,000	$4,414	$52,964
$1,494	$107,200	$1,270	$134,000	$4,481	$53,767

Monthly payment	Maximum mortgage		Maximum price	Income to qualify	
	Amount	P & I		Monthly	Annual
$1,516	$108,800	$1,289	$136,000	$4,547	$54,569
$1,538	$110,400	$1,308	$138,000	$4,614	$55,372
$1,560	$112,000	$1,327	$140,000	$4,681	$56,174
$1,583	$113,600	$1,346	$142,000	$4,748	$56,977
$1,605	$115,200	$1,365	$144,000	$4,815	$57,779
$1,627	$116,800	$1,384	$146,000	$4,882	$58,582
$1,650	$118,400	$1,403	$148,000	$4,949	$59,384
$1,672	$120,000	$1,422	$150,000	$5,016	$60,187
$1,694	$121,600	$1,441	$152,000	$5,082	$60,989
$1,716	$123,200	$1,460	$154,000	$5,149	$61,792
$1,739	$124,800	$1,479	$156,000	$5,216	$62,594
$1,761	$126,400	$1,498	$158,000	$5,283	$63,397
$1,783	$128,000	$1,517	$160,000	$5,350	$64,199
$1,806	$129,600	$1,536	$162,000	$5,417	$65,002
$1,828	$131,200	$1,555	$164,000	$5,484	$65,804
$1,850	$132,800	$1,574	$166,000	$5,551	$66,607
$1,872	$134,400	$1,592	$168,000	$5,617	$67,409
$1,895	$136,000	$1,611	$170,000	$5,684	$68,212
$1,917	$137,600	$1,630	$172,000	$5,751	$69,014
$1,939	$139,200	$1,649	$174,000	$5,818	$69,817
$1,962	$140,800	$1,668	$176,000	$5,885	$70,619
$1,984	$142,400	$1,687	$178,000	$5,952	$71,422
$2,006	$144,000	$1,706	$180,000	$6,019	$72,224
$2,029	$145,600	$1,725	$182,000	$6,086	$73,027
$2,051	$147,200	$1,744	$184,000	$6,152	$73,829
$2,073	$148,800	$1,763	$186,000	$6,219	$74,632
$2,095	$150,400	$1,782	$188,000	$6,286	$75,434
$2,118	$152,000	$1,801	$190,000	$6,353	$76,237
$2,140	$153,600	$1,820	$192,000	$6,420	$77,039
$2,162	$155,200	$1,839	$194,000	$6,487	$77,842
$2,185	$156,800	$1,858	$196,000	$6,554	$78,644
$2,207	$158,400	$1,877	$198,000	$6,621	$79,447
$2,229	$160,000	$1,896	$200,000	$6,687	$80,249

14½% Interest, 30-Year Term, 20% Down

(2% of purchase price assumed for taxes and insurance; 33% of gross monthly income allowed for mortgage payment)

Monthly payment	Maximum mortgage		Maximum price	Income to qualify	
	Amount	P & I		Monthly	Annual
$573	$40,000	$490	$50,000	$1,719	$20,634
$596	$41,600	$509	$52,000	$1,788	$21,459
$619	$43,200	$529	$54,000	$1,857	$22,284
$642	$44,800	$549	$56,000	$1,926	$23,110
$665	$46,400	$568	$58,000	$1,995	$23,935
$688	$48,000	$588	$60,000	$2,063	$24,760
$711	$49,600	$607	$62,000	$2,132	$25,586
$734	$51,200	$627	$64,000	$2,201	$26,411
$757	$52,800	$647	$66,000	$2,270	$27,236
$779	$54,400	$666	$68,000	$2,338	$28,062
$802	$56,000	$686	$70,000	$2,407	$28,887
$825	$57,600	$705	$72,000	$2,476	$29,712
$848	$59,200	$725	$74,000	$2,545	$30,538
$871	$60,800	$745	$76,000	$2,614	$31,363
$894	$62,400	$764	$78,000	$2,682	$32,189
$917	$64,000	$784	$80,000	$2,751	$33,014
$940	$65,600	$803	$82,000	$2,820	$33,839
$963	$67,200	$823	$84,000	$2,889	$34,665
$986	$68,800	$842	$86,000	$2,957	$35,490
$1,009	$70,400	$862	$88,000	$3,026	$36,315
$1,032	$72,000	$882	$90,000	$3,095	$37,141
$1,055	$73,600	$901	$92,000	$3,164	$37,966
$1,078	$75,200	$921	$94,000	$3,233	$38,791
$1,100	$76,800	$940	$96,000	$3,301	$39,617
$1,123	$78,400	$960	$98,000	$3,370	$40,442
$1,146	$80,000	$980	$100,000	$3,439	$41,267
$1,169	$81,600	$999	$102,000	$3,508	$42,093
$1,192	$83,200	$1,019	$104,000	$3,577	$42,918
$1,215	$84,800	$1,038	$106,000	$3,645	$43,743
$1,238	$86,400	$1,058	$108,000	$3,714	$44,569
$1,261	$88,000	$1,078	$110,000	$3,783	$45,394
$1,284	$89,600	$1,097	$112,000	$3,852	$46,219
$1,307	$91,200	$1,117	$114,000	$3,920	$47,045
$1,330	$92,800	$1,136	$116,000	$3,989	$47,870
$1,353	$94,400	$1,156	$118,000	$4,058	$48,695
$1,376	$96,000	$1,176	$120,000	$4,127	$49,521
$1,399	$97,600	$1,195	$122,000	$4,196	$50,346
$1,421	$99,200	$1,215	$124,000	$4,264	$51,171
$1,444	$100,800	$1,234	$126,000	$4,333	$51,997
$1,467	$102,400	$1,254	$128,000	$4,402	$52,822
$1,490	$104,000	$1,274	$130,000	$4,471	$53,648
$1,513	$105,600	$1,293	$132,000	$4,539	$54,473
$1,536	$107,200	$1,313	$134,000	$4,608	$55,298

Monthly payment	Maximum mortgage		Maximum price	Income to qualify	
	Amount	P & I		Monthly	Annual
$1,559	$108,800	$1,332	$136,000	$4,677	$56,124
$1,582	$110,400	$1,352	$138,000	$4,746	$56,949
$1,605	$112,000	$1,372	$140,000	$4,815	$57,774
$1,628	$113,600	$1,391	$142,000	$4,883	$58,600
$1,651	$115,200	$1,411	$144,000	$4,952	$59,425
$1,674	$116,800	$1,430	$146,000	$5,021	$60,250
$1,697	$118,400	$1,450	$148,000	$5,090	$61,076
$1,719	$120,000	$1,469	$150,000	$5,158	$61,901
$1,742	$121,600	$1,489	$152,000	$5,227	$62,726
$1,765	$123,200	$1,509	$154,000	$5,296	$63,552
$1,788	$124,800	$1,528	$156,000	$5,365	$64,377
$1,811	$126,400	$1,548	$158,000	$5,434	$65,202
$1,834	$128,000	$1,567	$160,000	$5,502	$66,028
$1,857	$129,600	$1,587	$162,000	$5,571	$66,853
$1,880	$131,200	$1,607	$164,000	$5,640	$67,678
$1,903	$132,800	$1,626	$166,000	$5,709	$68,504
$1,926	$134,400	$1,646	$168,000	$5,777	$69,329
$1,949	$136,000	$1,665	$170,000	$5,846	$70,154
$1,972	$137,600	$1,685	$172,000	$5,915	$70,980
$1,995	$139,200	$1,705	$174,000	$5,984	$71,805
$2,018	$140,800	$1,724	$176,000	$6,053	$72,630
$2,040	$142,400	$1,744	$178,000	$6,121	$73,456
$2,063	$144,000	$1,763	$180,000	$6,190	$74,281
$2,086	$145,600	$1,783	$182,000	$6,259	$75,107
$2,109	$147,200	$1,803	$184,000	$6,328	$75,932
$2,132	$148,800	$1,822	$186,000	$6,396	$76,757
$2,155	$150,400	$1,842	$188,000	$6,465	$77,583
$2,178	$152,000	$1,861	$190,000	$6,534	$78,408
$2,201	$153,600	$1,881	$192,000	$6,603	$79,233
$2,224	$155,200	$1,901	$194,000	$6,672	$80,059
$2,247	$156,800	$1,920	$196,000	$6,740	$80,884
$2,270	$158,400	$1,940	$198,000	$6,809	$81,709
$2,293	$160,000	$1,959	$200,000	$6,878	$82,535

15% Interest, 30-Year Term, 20% Down

(2% of purchase price assumed for taxes and insurance; 33% of gross monthly income allowed for mortgage payment)

Monthly payment	Maximum mortgage		Maximum price	Income to qualify	
	Amount	P & I		Monthly	Annual
$589	$40,000	$506	$50,000	$1,767	$21,208
$613	$41,600	$526	$52,000	$1,838	$22,056
$636	$43,200	$546	$54,000	$1,909	$22,905
$660	$44,800	$566	$56,000	$1,979	$23,753
$683	$46,400	$587	$58,000	$2,050	$24,601
$707	$48,000	$607	$60,000	$2,121	$25,450
$731	$49,600	$627	$62,000	$2,192	$26,298
$754	$51,200	$647	$64,000	$2,262	$27,146
$778	$52,800	$668	$66,000	$2,333	$27,995
$801	$54,400	$688	$68,000	$2,404	$28,843
$825	$56,000	$708	$70,000	$2,474	$29,691
$848	$57,600	$728	$72,000	$2,545	$30,540
$872	$59,200	$749	$74,000	$2,616	$31,388
$895	$60,800	$769	$76,000	$2,686	$32,236
$919	$62,400	$789	$78,000	$2,757	$33,085
$943	$64,000	$809	$80,000	$2,828	$33,933
$966	$65,600	$829	$82,000	$2,898	$34,781
$990	$67,200	$850	$84,000	$2,969	$35,630
$1,013	$68,800	$870	$86,000	$3,040	$36,478
$1,037	$70,400	$890	$88,000	$3,111	$37,326
$1,060	$72,000	$910	$90,000	$3,181	$38,175
$1,084	$73,600	$931	$92,000	$3,252	$39,023
$1,108	$75,200	$951	$94,000	$3,323	$39,871
$1,131	$76,800	$971	$96,000	$3,393	$40,720
$1,155	$78,400	$991	$98,000	$3,464	$41,568
$1,178	$80,000	$1,012	$100,000	$3,535	$42,416
$1,202	$81,600	$1,032	$102,000	$3,605	$43,264
$1,225	$83,200	$1,052	$104,000	$3,676	$44,113
$1,249	$84,800	$1,072	$106,000	$3,747	$44,961
$1,272	$86,400	$1,092	$108,000	$3,817	$45,809
$1,296	$88,000	$1,113	$110,000	$3,888	$46,658
$1,320	$89,600	$1,133	$112,000	$3,959	$47,506
$1,343	$91,200	$1,153	$114,000	$4,030	$48,354
$1,367	$92,800	$1,173	$116,000	$4,100	$49,203
$1,390	$94,400	$1,194	$118,000	$4,171	$50,051
$1,414	$96,000	$1,214	$120,000	$4,242	$50,899
$1,437	$97,600	$1,234	$122,000	$4,312	$51,748
$1,461	$99,200	$1,254	$124,000	$4,383	$52,596
$1,485	$100,800	$1,275	$126,000	$4,454	$53,444
$1,508	$102,400	$1,295	$128,000	$4,524	$54,293
$1,532	$104,000	$1,315	$130,000	$4,595	$55,141
$1,555	$105,600	$1,335	$132,000	$4,666	$55,989
$1,579	$107,200	$1,355	$134,000	$4,736	$56,838

Monthly payment	Maximum mortgage		Maximum price	Income to qualify	
	Amount	P & I		Monthly	Annual
$1,602	$108,800	$1,376	$136,000	$4,807	$57,686
$1,626	$110,400	$1,396	$138,000	$4,878	$58,534
$1,650	$112,000	$1,416	$140,000	$4,949	$59,383
$1,673	$113,600	$1,436	$142,000	$5,019	$60,231
$1,697	$115,200	$1,457	$144,000	$5,090	$61,079
$1,720	$116,800	$1,477	$146,000	$5,161	$61,928
$1,744	$118,400	$1,497	$148,000	$5,231	$62,776
$1,767	$120,000	$1,517	$150,000	$5,302	$63,624
$1,791	$121,600	$1,538	$152,000	$5,373	$64,473
$1,814	$123,200	$1,558	$154,000	$5,443	$65,321
$1,838	$124,800	$1,578	$156,000	$5,514	$66,169
$1,862	$126,400	$1,598	$158,000	$5,585	$67,018
$1,885	$128,000	$1,618	$160,000	$5,655	$67,866
$1,909	$129,600	$1,639	$162,000	$5,726	$68,714
$1,932	$131,200	$1,659	$164,000	$5,797	$69,563
$1,956	$132,800	$1,679	$166,000	$5,868	$70,411
$1,979	$134,400	$1,699	$168,000	$5,938	$71,259
$2,003	$136,000	$1,720	$170,000	$6,009	$72,107
$2,027	$137,600	$1,740	$172,000	$6,080	$72,956
$2,050	$139,200	$1,760	$174,000	$6,150	$73,804
$2,074	$140,800	$1,780	$176,000	$6,221	$74,652
$2,097	$142,400	$1,801	$178,000	$6,292	$75,501
$2,121	$144,000	$1,821	$180,000	$6,362	$76,349
$2,144	$145,600	$1,841	$182,000	$6,433	$77,197
$2,168	$147,200	$1,861	$184,000	$6,504	$78,046
$2,192	$148,800	$1,882	$186,000	$6,575	$78,894
$2,215	$150,400	$1,902	$188,000	$6,645	$79,742
$2,239	$152,000	$1,922	$190,000	$6,716	$80,591
$2,262	$153,600	$1,942	$192,000	$6,787	$81,439
$2,286	$155,200	$1,962	$194,000	$6,857	$82,287
$2,309	$156,800	$1,983	$196,000	$6,928	$83,136
$2,333	$158,400	$2,003	$198,000	$6,999	$83,984
$2,356	$160,000	$2,023	$200,000	$7,069	$84,832

Appendix C

Mortgage Terms

If borrowing a mortgage is something that's new to you, the first thing you're going to discover is that lenders speak a different language. There are "points" and "origination fees" and "alienation clauses" and dozens of other terms that can make you think they're talking Chinese.

While this should simply be a tiny stumbling block that can be quickly overcome with occasionally humorous results (over terms you don't understand), too often the real consequences are that borrowers don't get the best loan because they don't understand the terminology. If you don't speak "mortage-ese" and you let this hinder you, you could end up paying a great deal more for your home financing than you need to.

To help you overcome the mystery of the hidden language of mortgage, here are some of the most important terms and their definitions. Knowing these essential terms will help you make intelligent decisions in real estate.

Mortgage Versus Trust Deeds

Before actually looking at mortgage terms, let's clear up one important point. In this book the term *mortgage* is used to mean any financing that you get that is secured by real estate.

In the distant past, almost all of this type of financing was called a mortgage, hence the widespread understanding and use of the term today. However, during the latter half of this century, particularly in California, a different type of mortgage instrument came into existence called the *trust deed*. Today, chances are if you secure financing on your property, you will get a trust deed, not a mortgage. Consequently, it's important to take a few moments to understand the differences between the two types of loan instruments.

Mortgage

There are two parties to a mortgage: the borrower, or *mortgagor*, and the lender or *mortgagee*. Skipping to an eventuality that most of us don't like to consider, the big difference between a mortgage and trust deed has to do with foreclosure.

If we don't make our payments on a mortgage, the lender can only foreclose, or take ownership of the property, by going to court. This court action can take a great deal of time, often 6 months or more. Further, even after the lender has taken back the property, we as borrowers may have an "equity of redemption" that allows us to redeem the property sometimes for years after we've lost it, by paying back the mortgage and the lender's costs. The length of time it takes to foreclose, the costs involved, and the equity of redemption make mortgages undesirable to lenders.

Trust Deed

Trust deeds came into use in the early part of this century, primarily in California, by clever and enterprising lenders. If you wanted to borrow money from them, they would say, "Yes, I'll loan you money on your property. But to insure that my money is guaranteed, you sign a deed over to me. I won't record the deed unless you don't pay."

We borrowers, of course, wouldn't stand for that. If we gave the lender the deed to our property, he or she could take ownership at any time. So the lenders compromised. They said, "Okay, make the deed out to an independent third party, a stake holder. That third party will hold the deed and will sign it over to us only if you don't make your payments." That seemed fair, and borrowers went along with it. Over time, the trust deed, as it came to be called, was codified into law.

There are three parties to a trust deed: the borrower, or *trustor*, the independent third party, the stake holder, called the *trustee* (usually a title insurance company); and the lender, called the *beneficiary*, since the lender stands to benefit if the trustee turns the deed over in the event we fail to make our payments.

The advantage of the trust deed over the mortgage is that foreclosure can be accomplished without court action. The beneficiary (lender) simply informs the trustee that we haven't made our payments, and the trustee issues the lender a deed.

Of course, strict procedures must be followed. In California, for example, the lender must allow the borrower 90 days to make the loan current. Then it must advertise the property for 21 days, during which time we can redeem the loan by paying it back. Finally, it must "sell" the property to the highest bidder (usually the lender) on the courthouse steps.

Nevertheless, the process is relatively fast, there are no court costs, and we have no equity of redemption once the trustee sale is made. Once title passes from the trustee to the beneficiary (lender), we lose all interest in the property.

One other point needs to be mentioned. With trust deed foreclosure, there can be no deficiency judgment. In other words, if the property is worth less than the loan, the lender can't come back to us for the difference. In judicial foreclosure, in some instances, the lender can. For this reason, some lenders who hold a trust deed will opt for judicial foreclosure rather than trustee foreclosure. (See also Purchase Money Mortgage later in this appendix.)

Note: In this book the terms trust deeds and mortgages are used synonymously.

Terms Used in Mortgages

Now let's move forward to consider the most important terms used in *securing* mortgages on single-family residential property:

Abstract of Title

This is a written document produced by a title insurance company (in some states an attorney will do it) giving the history of who owned the property from the first owner forward. It also indicates any liens or encumbrances that may affect the title. A lender will not make a loan nor can a sale normally conclude until the title to real estate is clear, as evidenced by the abstract.

Acceleration Clause

This "accelerates" the payments in a mortgage, meaning that the entire amount becomes immediately due and payable. Most mortgages have this clause, which kicks in if, for example, you sell the property. (Also called an "alienation clause.")

Adjustable-Rate Mortgage (ARM)

The interest rate on this mortgage fluctuates up or down according to an index and a margin agreed to in advance by the borrower and the lender. In some cases when there are limits to the amount of change that can be made to the interest, a change may actually be made to the principal. (See Negative Amortization.)

Adjustment Date

This is the day on which an adjustment is made in an adjustable rate mortgage. It may occur monthly, every 6 months, once a year, or as otherwise agreed.

Alienation Clause

This is a clause in a mortgage that usually specifies if you sell or transfer the property to another person, the mortgage becomes immediately due and payable. (Also called an "acceleration clause.")

ALTA

American Land Title Association. This is a more complete and extensive policy of title insurance that most lenders insist upon.

It involves a physical inspection and often guarantees the proper-ty's boundaries. Lenders will often insist on an ALTA policy with themselves named a beneficiary.

Amortization

This refers to paying back the mortgage in equal installments. In other words, if the mortgage is for 30 years, you would have 360 equal installments. (The last payment is often a few dollars more or less.) This is opposed to a balloon payment in which one pay-ment is larger than the rest.

Annual Percentage Rate (APR)

This tells you the actual rate you will pay including interest, loan fees, and points.

Appraisal

Lenders usually require that the property be appraised by a quali-fied appraiser. The amount of the appraisal is the maximum value on which the loan will be based. For example, if the appraisal is $100,000 and the lender will loan 80 percent of value, the maximum mortgage would be $80,000.

ASA

American Society of Appraisers. An appraiser who displays this designation belongs to this professional organization.

Assignment of Mortgage

The lender may sell your mortgage without your permission. For example, you may obtain a mortgage from XYZ savings and loan. It may then sell that mortgage to Bland Bank. You will then get a letter saying the mortgage was assigned, and you make your pay-ments to a new entity. The document used between lenders for the transfer is an "assignment of mortgage." *Note:* Beware of receiving any letter saying you should send your mortgage pay-ment elsewhere. Unscrupulous individuals have sent out such letters to borrowers in the hopes of cheating them out of payments. Verify any such letters with your old lender.

Assumption

This means to take over an existing mortgage. For example, a seller may have an "assumable" mortgage on a property. When you buy the property, you take over that seller's obligation under the loan. Today most fixed-rate mortgages are not assumable. Most adjustable-rate mortgages are, but the borrower must qualify. FHA and VA mortgages may be assumable, but certain conditions may have to be met. When you assume the mortgage, you are liable if there is a foreclosure.

Automatic Guarantee

Some lenders who make VA loans are empowered to guarantee the loans without first checking with the VA. These lenders can often make the loans quicker.

Balloon Payment

One payment, usually the last, on a mortgage is larger than the others. In the case of second mortgages held by sellers, often only interest is paid until the due date—then the entire amount borrowed (the principal) is due.

Biweekly Mortgage

You make your payments every other week instead of monthly. Since there are 52 weeks in the year, you end up making 26 payments, or the equivalent of 1 month's extra payment. The additional payment significantly reduces the amount of interest charged on the mortgage and often reduces the term of the loan.

Blanket Mortgage

Here you have one mortgage that covers several properties instead of a single mortgage for each property. It is used most frequently by developers and builders.

Buy-down Mortgage

You receive a lower-than-market interest rate either for the entire term of the mortgage or for a set period at the beginning, say 2 years. This is made possible by the builder or seller paying an up-front fee to the lender.

Call Provision

A clause in the mortgage allowing the lender to call in the entire unpaid balance of the loan providing certain events have occurred, such as your selling the property. Also called an "acceleration clause" and an "alienation clause."

Caps

These are limits put on an adjustable-rate mortgage. The interest rate, the monthly payment, or both may be capped.

Certificate of Reasonable Value (CRV)

When getting a VA loan, the Veteran's Administration will secure an appraisal of the property and will issue this document establishing what they feel is its maximum value. In some cases, you may not pay more than this amount and still get the VA loan.

Chain of Title

This gives the history of ownership of the property. The title to property forms a chain going back to the first owners, which in the Southwest, for example, may come from original Spanish land grants.

Closing

This occurs when the seller conveys title to the buyer and the buyer makes full payment, including financing, for the property. Closing means the deal is consummated or concluded, all required documents are signed and delivered, and funds are disbursed.

Commitment

When a lender issues a written promise to you as a borrower to offer a mortgage at a set amount, interest rate, and cost. Typically commitments have a time limit on them—for example, they are good for 30 days or 60 days. Some lenders charge for making a commitment if you don't subsequently take out the mortgage (since they have tied up the money for that amount of time). When the lender's offer is in writing, it is sometimes called a "firm commitment."

Construction Loan

A mortgage made for the purpose of constructing a building. The loan is short term, typically under 12 months, and is usually paid in installments directly to the builder as the work is completed. Usually it is interest-only.

Conventional Loan

Any loan that is not government guaranteed or insured.

Convertible Mortgage

This is an adjustable-rate mortgage (ARM) that contains a clause allowing it to be converted to a fixed-rate mortgage at some time in the future. You may have to pay an additional cost to obtain this mortgage.

Cosigner

If you don't have good enough credit to qualify for a mortgage, the lender may be willing to make the loan if you have someone with better credit (usually a close relative) also sign. This cosigner is equally responsible with you for repayment of the loan. (Even if you don't pay it back, the cosigner can be responsible for the *entire* balance.)

Credit Report

This is a report of your credit history usually made by one of the country's three large credit reporting companies. It will typically state if you have any delinquent payments or any failures to pay, as well as any bankruptcies and, sometimes, foreclosures. Lenders use it to determine whether to offer you a mortgage. The fee is usually under $50 and charged to you.

Discount

This has two meanings. When you borrow from a lender, the lender may withhold enough money from the mortgage to cover the points and fees. For example, you may be borrowing $100,000, but your points and fees come to $3000; hence, the lender will only fund $97,000, discounting the $3000.

In the secondary market a discount is the amount less than face value a buyer of a mortgage pays in order to be induced to purchase it. The discount here is calculated on the basis of risk, market rates, interest rate of the note, and other factors.

Due-on-Encumbrance Clause

This is a little-noted and seldom-enforced clause in many recent mortgages that allows the lender to foreclose if you, the borrower, get additional financing. For example, if you secure a second mortgage, the lender of the first mortgage with the clause may have grounds for foreclosing. The reasoning here is that the lender wants you to have a certain level of equity in the property. If you reduce your equity level by taking out additional financing, the lender may be placed in a less secure position.

Due-on-Sale Clause

This is a clause in a mortgage that says the entire remaining unpaid balance becomes due and payable on sale of the property. See also "acceleration clause."

Escrow Company

The escrow is the stake holder—an independent third party that handles funds; carries out the instructions of the lender, buyer, and seller in a transaction; and deals with all the documents. In most states, companies are licensed to handle escrows. In some parts of the country, particularly the Northeast, the function of the escrow company may be handled by an attorney.

FHA Loan

A mortgage insured by the Federal Housing Administration. In most cases FHA advances no money but instead insures the loan to a lender such as a bank. There is a fee to the borrower, usually paid up front, for this insurance.

Graduated Payment Mortgage

Here the payments you make vary over the life of the loan. They start out low, then slowly rise until, usually after a few years, they reach a plateau where they remain for the remainder of the term. This mortgage is particularly useful when you want low initial payments. It is primarily used by first-time buyers. It often is used in combination with a fixed-rate or an adjustable-rate mortgage.

Growing Equity Mortgage

This is a rarely used type of mortgage where the payments increase according to a set schedule. The purpose is to pay additional money into principal and thus pay off the loan earlier and save interest charges.

Index

An index is a measurement of an established interest rate used to establish the periodic rate adjustments for adjustable-rate mortgages. There are a wide variety of indices used including Treasury bill rates, cost of funds to lenders, and others.

Lien

A claim for money against real estate. For example, if you had work done on your property and refused to pay the workperson, he or she might file a "mechanic's lien" against your property. If you didn't pay taxes, the taxing agency might file a "tax lien." These liens "cloud" the title and usually prevent you from selling the property or refinancing it until they are cleared by paying off the debt.

Loan-to-Value Ratio

The percentage of the appraised value of a property that a lender will loan. For example, if your property appraised at $100,000 and the lender was willing to loan $80,000, then the loan to value ratio would be 80 percent.

MAI

American Institute of Real Estate Appraisers. An appraiser who has this designation has passed rigorous training.

Margin

An amount, calculated in points, that a lender adds to an index to determine how much interest you will pay during a period for an adjustable-rate mortgage. For example, the index may be at 7 percent, and the margin, agreed upon at the time you obtained the mortgage, may be 2.7 points. The interest rate for that period, therefore, would be 9.7 percent.

Negative Amortization

Negative amortization occurs when the payment on an adjustable-rate mortgage is not sufficiently large to cover the interest charged. When this happens, the excess interest is added to the principal, thus the amount borrowed actually increases. The amount the principal can increase is usually limited to 125 percent of the original mortgage value. *Anytime you have a cap on the mortgage payment,* you are looking at a mortgage that has the potential to be negatively amortized.

Origination Fee

Today this usually refers to the total costs to you when you obtain a mortgage. In the past it has meant a charge that lenders make for preparing and submitting a mortgage. It originally was used only for FHA and VA loans where the mortgage package had to be submitted to the government for approval. With an FHA loan the maximum origination fee used to be 1 percent.

Personal Property

Any property that does not go with the land. This includes automobiles, clothing, and most furniture. Some items are disputable, such as appliances and floor and wall coverings. See the related discussion under real property.

PITI

This is an acronym for principal, interest, taxes, and insurance, the major components that go into determining your monthly payment on a mortgage. (They leave out other items such as home owner's dues, utilities, and so forth.)

Points

A point is equal to 1 percent of a mortgage amount. For example, if your mortgage was $100,000 and you were required to pay $2\frac{1}{2}$ points to get it, the charge to you would be $2500. Some points that you pay when obtaining a mortgage may be tax-deductible. See Chap. 27.

Lenders use the term "basis points." A basis point is $\frac{1}{100}$ of a point. For example, if you are charged $\frac{1}{2}$ point ($\frac{1}{2}$ percent of the mortgage), the lender will think of it as 50 basis points.

Prepayment Penalty

This is a charge made by the lender to the borrower for paying off a mortgage early. In times past (more than 25 years ago) nearly all mortgages carried prepayment penalties. However, those mortgages were also assumable by others. Today virtually no fixed-rate mortgages (other than FHA or VA) are truly assumable and, hence, almost none carry a prepayment penalty clause.

Private Mortgage Insurance (PMI)

PMI is insurance that protects the lender in the event you default on a mortgage. It is written by an independent third-party insurance company and typically covers only the first 20 percent of the lender's potential loss. PMI is normally required on any mortgage that exceeds 80 percent loan to value ratio.

Purchase Money Mortgage

When you get a mortgage as part of the purchase price of a home (usually from the seller) rather than through refinancing it's called a "purchase money mortgage." In some states, no deficiency judgment can be obtained against a borrower of a purchase money mortgage. (If there is a foreclosure and the property brings less than the amount borrowed, you, as a borrower, cannot be held liable for the shortfall.)

Real Property

Another word for real estate. This includes the land and anything appurtenant to it, including the house. Confusion often exists when differentiating between real and personal property with regard to such items as floor and wall covering. To determine whether an item is real property (goes with the land), certain tests have been devised. For example, if curtains or drapes have been attached in such a way that they cannot be removed without damaging the home, they may be spoken of a real property. On the other hand, if they can easily be removed without damaging the home, they may be personal property. It is a good idea to specify in any contract whether items are real or personal. This avoids confusion later on.

RESPA

An acronym for Real Estate Settlement Procedures Act. This act requires lenders to provide you with specified information as to the cost of securing financing. Basically it means that before you proceed far along the path of getting the mortgage, the lender has to provide you with an estimate of costs. Then, before you actually sign the documents binding you to the mortgage, the lender has to provide you with a breakdown of the actual costs.

Second Mortgage

An inferior mortgage usually placed on the property after a first mortgage. In the event of foreclosure, this mortgage would be paid off with funds from a foreclosure sale only after the first mortgage had been fully paid. Many lenders will not offer second mortgages, insisting instead on firsts only.

SREA

An acronym for Society of Real Estate Appraisers. This is a professional association to which qualified appraisers can belong. Whenever you hire an appraiser you are encouraged to look for the SREA designation.

Subject To

A contingency clause. Also a phrase often used to indicate that a buyer is not assuming the mortgage liability of a seller. For example, if the seller has an assumable loan and you (the buyer) "assumes" the loan, you are taking over liability for payment. On the other hand, if you purchase "subject to" the mortgage, you do not assume liability for payment.

Subordination Clause

A clause that can be inserted into a mortgage document to keep that mortgage secondary to any other mortgages. Mortgages are valued according to the chronological order on which they are put onto a property. The first mortgage on a property is called a "first" in time, the next mortgage is a "second" in time, the next a "third" in time, and so forth. The order is important because in the event of foreclosure, all the money from a foreclosure sale goes to pay off the lender of the first. Only if there is any left over does it then go to pay off the holder of the second. Then any subsequent money left over goes to pay off the lender of the third, and so forth. The earlier the number of the mortgage, the more desirable and the more superior the mortgage is considered.

Normally, when a first mortgage is paid off, the second advances to become the first, the third to the second, and so forth. However, since some lenders only offer first mortgages, having a second advance to the first position could prevent you from refinancing with a new first (unless the second and other inferior mortgages were fully paid off). This you might not want to do.

Hence, a subordination clause can be inserted into the second and other inferior mortgages. It specifies that the mortgage will forever remain in its current position, thus allowing you to pay off the existing first and get a new first.

This is a technique used by developers who give the sellers of land a second mortgage and then get a new first for construction. Today, most institutional lenders either will not allow a subordination clause inserted in any second or inferior mortgage they make; or if they do subordinate, they will limit the amount of the first.

Title

This is evidence that you actually have the right of ownership of real property. It is in the form of a deed (there are many different types of deeds) that specifies the kind of title you have (joint, common, or other).

Title Insurance Policy

This is an insurance policy that covers the title to your home. It may list you or the lender as a beneficiary. The title insurance policy is issued by a title insurance company or through an attorney underwritten by an insurance company. It specifies that if for any covered reason your title is defective, the company will correct the title or pay you up to a specified amount, usually the amount of the purchase price or the mortgage.

Before issuing such a policy, for which either the buyer or the seller or both (as determined by local custom) must pay a fee, the title insurance company investigates the chain of title and notifies all parties of any defects, such as liens. These must then be paid off. Sometimes if it is not desirable to pay them off (as in the case of old bonds), a policy of title insurance with an exception may be issued.

Most states have standard title insurance policies. For example, California has a CLTA, or policy approved by the California Land

Title Association. It may not be a very complete policy and may not give you total coverage. A more complete policy is the ALTA, defined earlier in this appendix.

VA Loan

A mortgage guaranteed by the Veteran's Administration. The VA actually only guarantees a small percentage of the amount loaned, but since it guarantees the first monies loaned, lenders are willing to accept it. In a VA loan the government advances no money; rather, the mortgage is made by a private lender such as a bank.

Wraparound Financing

Here a lender blends two mortgages. If the lender is a seller, then he or she doesn't receive all cash. However, instead of simply giving the buyer–borrower a simple second mortgage, the lender combines the balance due on an existing mortgage (usually an existing first) with an additional loan.

Thus the wrap includes both the second and the first. The borrower makes payments to the lender, who then keeps part of the payment and in turn makes payments on the existing mortgage.

The wrap is used typically by a seller who either doesn't trust the buyer to make payments on a first or who wants to get a higher interest rate.

Index

About the Author

Robert Irwin, noted real estate broker and the author of the best-selling *Tips & Traps* series, has been steering buyers and sellers nationwide through every kind of real estate transaction. He has published more than 30 books including *Tips & Traps When Buying a Home* and *Pocket Guide for Home Buyers*. Look, too, for his upcoming book, *Buying a Home on the Internet*.